ISBN 978-1-330-96300-5
PIBN 10127010

1 MONTH OF
FREE
READING

at

www.ForgottenBooks.com

By purchasing this book you are eligible for one month membership to ForgottenBooks.com, giving you unlimited access to our entire collection of over 700,000 titles via our web site and mobile apps.

To claim your free month visit:

www.forgottenbooks.com/free127010

English
Français
Deutsche
Italiano
Español
Português

www.forgottenbooks.com

Mythology Photography **Fiction**
Fishing Christianity **Art** Cooking
Essays Buddhism Freemasonry
Medicine **Biology** Music **Ancient
Egypt** Evolution Carpentry Physics
Dance Geology **Mathematics** Fitness
Shakespeare **Folklore** Yoga Marketing
Confidence Immortality Biographies
Poetry **Psychology** Witchcraft
Electronics Chemistry History **Law**
Accounting **Philosophy** Anthropology
Alchemy Drama Quantum Mechanics
Atheism Sexual Health **Ancient History**
Entrepreneurship Languages Sport
Paleontology Needlework Islam
Metaphysics Investment Archaeology
Parenting Statistics Criminology
Motivational

BRITISH WAR DOGS

THEIR TRAINING AND PSYCHOLOGY

BY

Lt.-Colonel E. H. RICHARDSON

Late Commandant of the British War Dog School

LONDON: SKEFFINGTON & SON, LTD.

34, SOUTHAMPTON STREET, STRAND, W.C.2

This book is dedicated to the brave Dogs of Britain who helped their country in her hour of need. :: ::

FAITHFUL UNTO DEATH.

"And God made the beast of the earth . . . and God saw that it was good."—*Gen. i. 25.*

CONTENTS

LIST OF ILLUSTRATIONS

LIST OF ILLUSTRATIONS

BRITISH WAR DOGS

CHAPTER I

HISTORICAL

When wise Ulysses . . . .
Arrived at last,
Poor, old, disguised, alone,
To all his friends and even his queen unknown,
The faithful dog alone his master knew.
Him, when he saw, he rose and crawled to meet,
('Twas all he could), and fawned and kissed his feet.
Seized with dumb joy—
Then falling by his side,
Owned his returning lord,
Looked up, and died."

POPE.

THE earliest remains of the dog are found in the Upper Pliocene deposits and at the end of the Tertiary period. There have been five distinct varieties discovered at different times, but the three most important are the *canis familiaris palustris, canis familiaris Anutschin* and the *canis familiaris* of the Bronze Age.

The skull of the first-named represents a smallish dog, and would seem to be the parent of the Chows, Pomeranian and Spitz dogs. The skull of the Bronze Age dog shows a much larger development, and is practically identical with the modern sheep dog. Some dog skulls, which were dug up in Roman remains, closely resemble those of the

Bronze period, and also of our sheep dogs, and form an interesting link between the dog of prehistoric man and our own, and also show how true to type this particular dog seems to have remained, in essential characteristics.

The actual origin of the dog—that is to say, whether it has always been a species by itself, or whether it is a descendant of a wild animal, such as the wolf or jackal, has never been satisfactorily decided. Many naturalists and scientific men have leant to the conclusion, that it has always been a distinct species, and certainly, the more one studies the subject, the greater does the likelihood seem that they are right. Count Buffon, in his book on " Natural History," A.D. 1749, gives an account of an experiment he carried out. He says : " In our climates the wolf and fox make the nearest approach to the dog, particularly the shepherd's dog, which I consider as the original stock of the species ; and as their internal structure is almost entirely the same and their external differences very slight, I wished to try if they would intermix and produce together. . . . With this in view, I reared a she-wolf, taken in the woods at the age of three months, along with an Irish greyhound of the same age. They were shut up together in a pretty large court, to which no other beast could have access, and they were provided with shelter for their retirement. They were kept in this state three years, without the smallest restraint. During the first year they played perpetually, and seemed extremely fond of each other. The second year they began to quarrel about their food, though they were supplied in a plentiful manner. The wolf always began the dispute. The wolf, instead of seizing the meat, instantly drove off the dog, then laid hold of the edge of the plate so dexterously, as to allow nothing to fall, and carried off the whole. I have seen her run in this manner five or six times round the wall, and never set it down, save to take breath, to devour the meat, or to attack the dog when he approached. After the second year these quarrels and combats became more frequent and more serious. In the third year it was hoped to breed from them, but this condition, instead of softening them and making them approach each other, rendered them more intractable and ferocious. Nothing now was heard but dismal howlings and cries of resentment."

Finally this sad story is closed with an account of the destruction of the wolf by the dog.

Buffon also tried experiments in the same way with foxes and dogs, but the result was the same—strong antagonism or indifference. It therefore seems impossible to credit that any races, with such intensely strong natural antipathy to each other, can at any time have been united in a common ancestor. And the fact that, although so like each other in structure and appearance, this great antagonism does exist, seems to emphasize with corresponding significance the curious differences in the appearance of dogs themselves, and yet the entire absence of enmity. For instance, the St. Bernard dog and the Pekinese spaniel are, in appearance, as opposite as possible, and yet they each recognize in each other the same species.

There is no doubt but that scent enters very largely into this question of species. As human beings, we have, to a great extent, lost all understanding of the properties of scent, as understood by the dogs, and animal creation generally. They are far ahead of us in this respect. The greater part of their powers of recognition come from this quality of scent, and they also use it as a means of communication from the one to the other, and, in fact, it assumes the importance of a form of language with them.

I believe it is in this particular, that the great ineradicable separation exists, between the dog, and those animals of kindred appearance. The body scent is completely different, and we human beings are unable to explain the meaning of the difference, because we do not understand the language of scent. Buffon continued many experiments with wolves and wolf cubs, but found that the natural habits and instincts of the latter varied from the dog in so many ways, such as the time of gestation, its manner of selecting its mate, rearing the young, etc., etc. He sums the whole matter up in the following downright sentence " The wolf and the dog have never been regarded as the same animal, but by the nomenclators of Nature History, who, being acquainted with the surface of nature only, never extend their views beyond their own methods, which are always deceitful and often erroneous, even in the most obvious facts."

That the association of the dog with man, is of such an ancient origin, is, in itself, a very remarkable fact. The cause of that association, in the first place, was probably the recognition of a common interest. Thus, just as the starlings associate with sheep, so the dog found that the habits and food of man, accorded with its own desires, and it began to follow the tracks of the hunters in the chase, with the hope of participating in a portion of the remains of the quarry. It would also frequent the camps and dwellings of primitive man, to inspect the offal heaps. Man would soon observe the useful scenting properties of the dog, and also its natural instinct for guarding, and would lay himself out to tame and train such a useful animal. The dog, being naturally sociable, would quickly respond, and would also soon find, that, as so many of the pleasures and comforts of man, were such as it thoroughly appreciated, it was well worth while to adopt man and his surroundings, as its natural master and habitat.

An interesting deduction on this point is made by some writers, who state, that because in some of the most ancient middens, no small bones of wild animals are discovered, but only those of large size, the inference is, that the small-sized bones were eaten by the camp dogs.

In considering this question of the association of dog with man during the earliest times, we seem again to deduce, that the dog must always have been a distinct race, from the fact, that the other animals of similar appearance, had the same opportunities to act in a like manner towards man, but did not do so. The instinct did not seem to be there. To this day, the wolf and the fox, and other allied animals, are practically untameable, and where the dog instinctively licks your hand, the wolf licks the blood.

It seems certainly most probable, therefore, that all dogs are descended from a common ancestor of the same species. Opinion varies as to which is the most ancient breed, but it seems likely that the sheep dog can claim precedence over all others. Many people assume that the greyhound is the most ancient, by the fact that specimens are represented on some of the oldest Egyptian monuments, or, at all events, representations of dogs that most resemble this breed. This might easily be, however, because they were useful to the upper classes of that period for hunting purposes, and, therefore, stood for the canine aristocracy of the age. The same impression might be conveyed to future remote generations of the present age—and quite erroneously—if a number of canvases of the Royal Academy were dug up, in which the fashionable ladies are depicted with Pekinese spaniels, while the honest, homely, working drover's collie, one of our most important breeds from a practical point of view, would not be ce!　ـ ted pictorially. It is, however, an open question, as to whether the ᵔʰ‥ep dog was not quite as ancient as the greyhound, as we have very ancient testimony as to its use by the keepers of the flocks, and for guarding purposes of all kinds. The Tibetan sheep dog of the present day stands for a very ancient race, which was probably of a larger and fiercer description. The Pyrenean dog is also the descendant of the guardians of mountain fastnesses, as is also the same type of dog to be found in the mountainous region of Italy and Middle Europe. There seems to be every reason for believing, that this class of animal in all these countries, is descended from a common ancestor of great size and courage, in some cases shaggy, and in others more of the mastiff appearance, and greatly prized on account of the determined and unflinching fidelity to the property and person of its owners. Referring to such animals, Homer says :

> " Nor last forget thy faithful dogs, but feed
> With fattening whey the mastiff's generous breed
> And Spartan race, who for the fold's relief,
> Will prosecute with cries the nightly thief ;
> Repulse the prowling wolf, and hold at bay
> The mountain robbers rushing to their prey.

In Job is found the following allusion to dogs, in Chapter XXX., verse 1 :

" Whose fathers I would have disdained to have set with the dogs of my flocks."

There are, however, dogs of other breeds depicted on the ancient temples of Assyria, and which have been brought to light during excavations. Some of these show a large-headed dog somewhat like a St. Bernard. A collar of leaves, or of leather, or of metal wrought in design, is round the neck .. The name of the dog is also frequently g· ·.. and generally indicates some form of prowess.

Evliya Effendi, the Turkish traveller of the seventeenth century, when commenting on many things, mentions dogs. He says : " The size of asses, and fierce as lions from Africa, in double or triple chains, covered with rich cloth, and wearing silver collars and neck rings. They perform everything they are told to perform, and if bid to do so, will bring down a fellow from horse-back, however stout a fellow he may be. The shepherds look on these as their companions and brethren, and do not object to eat out of the dish with them."

It must be remembered that although these dogs may be termed sheep dogs, they were really used for war purposes in their daily work. Owing to the savage and warlike state of the tribes of the world for many centuries, the possessor of flocks and herds, or valuable property of any description, was never safe from massed attacks from envious neighbours, and had to be perpetually on his guard. After all, war, as we now understand it, is only a more organized form of this same spirit, and it is difficult to distinguish in any way between the dogs deputed to guard the mountain passes leading to the pastures of their masters, or of those posted on the battlements of the castle, and the modern sentry dog, standing alert with pricked ears, listening for the stealthy tread of the Boche across No Man's Land, or of the guardian of the magazine or canteen. In fact, these sheep dogs of olden times, are almost entirely spoken of in the light of guardians, and it is not until considerably later in history, that there is any mention of them taking part in driving the sheep, or aiding in any way after that peaceful manner. But it is interesting to note, how very ancient, nevertheless, is the association of the sheep dog with sheep, and it is therefore not to be wondered at that the modern animal takes so instinctively to the idea of this useful method of turning its capabilities to account.

Not only were there human marauders to be feared during these early times of which we are speaking, but the persons of both the keepers and their flocks were in constant danger from attack by bands of ferocious wolves. These guardian dogs, watchful and alert through the dark hours, must have been supremely valuable, and terrific and desperate must the conflicts have been at times, when the prowling hordes attempted to break through the guarding cordon.

Later on, as this guerilla mode of warfare ceased, and wolves became extinct, the qualifications of the sheep dogs changed, and it was no longer necessary for them to display such an aggressive disposition. A quaint writer of the sixteenth century—Dr. Cains—describes this change in the duties of the sheep dog :

" Our shepherd's dog is not huge and vast and big, but of indifferent stature and growth, because it has not to deal with the bloodthirsty wolf, since there be none in England, which happy and fortunate benefit is ascribed to Prince Edgar, who, to the intent the whole country might be evacuated and quite cleared from wolves, charged and commanded the Welshmen, (who were pestered with these butcherly beasts above measure), to pay him yearly tribute, which was, (note the wisdom of the King !), three hundred wolves. Some there be which write that Ludwall, Prince of Wales, paid yearly to King Edgar three hundred wolves in the name of an exaction, (as we have said before), and that by means thereof, within the compass and term of four years, none of these noisome and pestilent beasts were left on the coasts of England and Wales. This Edgar wore the crown and bare the sceptre imperial of his kingdom about the year of Our Lord 959. Since which time we read that no wolf has been seen in England, bred within the bounds and borders of this country, although there have been divers brought over from beyond the seas for greediness and gain, and to make money for gazing, gaping, staring and standing to see them, being a strange beast, rare and seldom seen in England.

" But to return to our shepherd's dog. This dog, either at the hearing of his master's voice, or at the wagging of his fist, or at his shrill and hoarse whistling and hissing, bringeth the wandering wether and straying sheep into the self-same place, where his masters will and work to have them, whereby the shepherd reapeth the benefit, namely, that with little labour and no toil of moving his feet, he may rule and guide his flock according to his own desire, either to have them go forward, or to stand still, or to draw back, or to turn this way, or to take that way."

The late Mr. Rawdon Lee, in describing the work of the shepherd's dog, says ·

" The shepherd has but to wave his hand in a certain direction and away gallops his faithful friend to seek what is to be found, and the little flock is quickly gathered and brought right up to their master. One sheep may be missing. The dog goes back to seek it. The last one may be hurt and lame. The dog, by its manner, lets the shepherd know such is the case. ' Bring in the cows,' said a farmer friend of mine to his dog, which lay down at his feet by the kitchen fire. Up jumps the fine old chap, and darting through the door and the farmyard, is out across two or three fields, and barking behind the kye, soon brings them to the shippon. . . . Such is the every-day work of the farm dog, and he is almost always a collie now."

In writing of the change of employment of the dogs working with the sheep, and change also of both disposition and appearance, it is of interest to point out that the War Dogs of the present day are types, to a certain extent, of both those sheep dogs of the early centuries, and of the milder and intelligent assistant of more peaceful times. The guard dogs, which were trained for our Army during the war, in many cases much resembled the indomitable guardians of old. In a later chapter of this book, I describe the method of recruiting the dogs for the Army, and the many splendid animals that were presented by the public. Some of these—mastiffs, St. Bernards, Danes, bull-mastiffs—would have been highly appreciated by Cæsar's legions, for guarding their camps, and in the twentieth century they performed valuable service, by presenting an absolutely incorruptible obstacle to those with felonious intent on all sorts of valuable military property and positions.

The sentry dogs of the trenches, on the other hand, are a link between the large and powerful guardians just described, and the more mild and entirely non-aggressive working sheep dog, which was, however, equally useful in its way, and whose wonderfully intelligent independence of thought, was adapted to, and utilized with, the messenger service of our Army.

The modern sentry dog (as distinguished from the guard dog, which should certainly be of a distinctly aggressive character for certain very responsible guard duties) must be of an alert but not savage disposition. His duty is to give warning more than to attack, and a medium size is all that is necessary.

To return to earlier times once more.

The reason dogs were found useful for the attack during the early ages was on account of the absence at that period of gunpowder. A warrior would be preceded by a slave leading a fierce dog, which would attack at word of command, and while it engaged in close combat with the enemy, the master would dash into the conflict with every chance of success. The Romans trained their dogs to attack men armed with swords. They also had a system of training whereby the dogs were held, while their masters were engaged in mock combat, being attacked by soldiers armed with swords. The dogs were then loosed, with the idea that these should rush in and defend the master against the attacker. This form of training would, of course, make the dogs very savage, and very brave. Strabo says the Chiefs of Gaul had bodyguards of dogs armed with coats of mail.

When opposing armies both possessed dogs of war, the canine conflicts must have been prodigious.

When gunpowder was invented and used, the attacking duties of the dogs were no longer required, and they were then employed for defensive purposes by giving warning of the approach of the enemy.

The intelligence and fidelity of the dog has been recognized as a valuable asset in the protection of person and property from time immemorial, and military commanders have appreciated this during many previous centuries, and have utilized dogs with their armies. Plutarch and Pliny both mention war dogs in their writings. The dogs were employed as a means of defence against enemy attack, and also as actual weapons of attack. They were used thus at the Siege of Mantenea, and King Cambyses also employed large numbers in his campaign in Egypt.

There is a story related that when the King of the Spartans

was besieging Mantenea, he discovered treachery among some of his own forces, and that provisions were being carried into the town by night. He stopped this, by surrounding the town with a cordon of dogs, which no one was able to penetrate, owing to the vigilance of the animals.

When Philip of Macedon made war against the Thracians, the latter took to the forests, and the only satisfactory means he had of tracing them was by using dogs.

It is related that the garrison at Corinth were asleep after a lengthy carouse, and were only saved from a surprise attack from the enemy, by the faithful watch-dogs on duty on the ramparts, who neither slumbered nor slept, but remained, unlike the men, faithful to their trust. They were ever afterwards held in the greatest reverence by the garrison.

In their accounts of their incursions all over the world, we find a constant repetition of the statement, that the Romans took dogs with them, and, in fact, that they recognized in the latter, a necessary and reliable auxiliary in warfare; thus we find them in constant use as guards, and sentries for their camps, and for the ramparts of their towns. They were taken in large groups, when the Roman legions penetrated into the Sahara against the Samarantes.

Marius, a Roman Consul, gives an interesting account of how, at the Battle of Versella, 101 B.C., against the Teutons, the Romans, having overcome the defending forces, found they then had to take into account very seriously, the hordes of dogs, which were organized and furiously urged against them by the " blonde-haired women of Wagenburg."

We also read, that in the war against the natives of Sardinia, in 231 B.C., the latter were scented out of the woods and caves, by means of dogs.

It is also interesting to observe, that, on the column of Marcus Aurelius in Rome, dogs are represented fighting beside the men, clad in mail, and with spiked collars.

Vegetious, the Roman historian, alludes to the dogs used by the Teutonic tribes against the Roman legions, which were perhaps the ancestors of some of the present German war dogs. Large and powerful dogs were at all times greatly prized. Sometimes they were supplied with complete suits of armour, consisting of a body covering and a head-piece. In Madrid Museum there is an interesting specimen of this accoutrement, mounted on a stuffed dog.

Certain of these are described by a writer—Camerarius—in his book, " Living Librarie or Historical Meditations," printed in 1625. He says · " The dogs of Albania bring under all other beasts, throttle bulls, kill lions, stay all that is thrown against them ; and therefore are very famous in histories. We read that Alexander, going to the Indies, received two of them, which the King of Albania presented him with. These dogs grow very high and bark with a stronger voice than the roaring of lions."

Perhaps the dog of Andronicus, the King of Constantinople, was of this race. " This Prince was much hated because of his villainies and mischiefs, and made himself be guarded, not only with companies of strange soldiers, but also with a very great dogge, who made no bones to fight with lions, and could turn a man all armed off his horse. The guard kept watch in the night a prettie way from his chamber, and at his chamber door this dog was tied, who at the least noise that was, made a terrible barking."

Andronicus seems to have trusted dog more than man. Camerarius also narrates a curious instance of guard dogs distinguishing between Christians and Turks. This, however, is quite to be understood by all who have studied the question of scenting powers in dogs. They learn to distinguish the scents of different races very readily, and also between communities of people. It will be observed that differing modes of living and also of food produce varying scents in people, and communities living together have each their distinctive scent. This also applies even to the men of different regiments, and I have found that dogs can quite easily detect a man of a regiment belonging to another than their own.

" The Rhodians held a very strong and well-fortified citie, called the Castle of S. Peter, in a place of the firme land, over against the Isle Coos, being the only retrait for the Christians of Asia, that saved themselves from being slaves to the Turkes. The enemy was master of all without and about this place, in so much as the citisens could not safely fetch wood or other fuell for their use. Some bodie had told the Venetians strange things of the sence and service of the dogs that were within the Citie, to the number of fiftie, all which the Inhabitants put forth every night (as it were) for Sentinels. If during the night, these watchers met with any Christian, they would receive him, and with fawning and joy conduct him into the Citie : contrariwise, if they discovered a Turke, they would first keepe a great barking, and then falling upon him, pull him down and then teare him in pieces. These are the words of Sabellicus. At Renes in Brittaine, at Saint Malo, and at Saint Michaels, they keepe a great many dogs, that watch and ward both night and day, as I have heard reported by many. Plutarch showeth that it is an antient custome ; for he saith, That the enterprise of Aratus, which he undertooke for the freeing of his countrey, had like to have bin mar'd, by the watchfulnesse of a dog. By this it appeareth, what moved Socrates to sweare commonly by the dog, as Plato noteth ; who thereby would point out an unmatchable faithfulnesse, such as is seene in those creatures."

Camerarius also quotes another writer, Pierius, who shows forth the faithful and discerning qualities of guard dogs, by stating that ancient authors had written that :

" Near to Mount Gibell, in Cicilia, there was a temple builded to Vulcan, the groave whereof was guarded by dogs (as M. Marlianus also reporteth, that in old Rome, before Vulcan's chappell, in the Flaminian Cirque, were certain dogs that would never barke but against church-robbers), which would run with great fawning to meet the good and devout Pilgrims ; but if any that were villanous and dishonest came thither, they were miserably torne in pieces by those dogs."

There was a breed of dogs much prized in the Middle Ages which went by the name of Allan, Alaunt or Allande. The place of their origin is obscure, but it seems probably to have been in some parts of Southern Europe. They were probably a cross between a wolf hound and a mastiff, as their characteristics were strength, speed, and a very determined disposition. For this reason, they were frequently used as war dogs, and were brought up to be of as fierce a nature as possible, as a protection to their own people against foreign enemies.

Ulysses Aldrovandus wrote, in 1607, a work on natural history, and in this he describes such dogs as " terrible and frightful to behold, and more fierce and fell than any Arcadian curre. . . . In build he resembles the hound. He ought to be gentle to his own household, savage to those outside it, and not to be taken in by caresses. He should be robust, with a muscular body, and noisy in his deep bark, so that, by his bold baying, he may threaten on all sides, and frighten away prowlers. He should have a fierce light in his eyes, portending the lightning attack on the rash enemy. He should be black in his coat, in order to appear more fearful to the thieves in the daylight, and being of the same shade as night itself, to be able to make his way quite unseen by enemies and thieves."

A writer in the *Spectator* gives an interesting account of the use of this class of dog in the war of the Spanish Conquest in America. He says :

" The dogs of the *conquistadores* were of a race of large mastiffs. One of them, called Bercerrillo, was of enormous size ; he was so much appreciated for his ferocity that he got double rations, and his master received a salary for his services. Another hound named Leoncico, which belonged to Balboa, the discoverer of the South Sea, always fought at the side of his master, who drew an officer's pay for the services of the animal. When Jiménez de Quesada came from Spain to conquer the empire of the Chibchas (to-day Colombia), he brought with him a large dog ; but the most murderous and savage pack of canine *conquistadores* was that brought from Spain by Federmann, one of the Germans who followed Charles V. to the Peninsula. The animals of this last-mentioned lot were of the most savage breed, so much so that, according to a modern Colombian writer, the unfortunate natives feared them more than a regiment of harquebusiers. All these dogs wore armour (a coverlet lined with cotton) to preserve them against the poisoned arms of the natives."

Attila, King of the Huns, one of the great military commanders of the early centuries, always used dogs to guard the approaches to his camp.

Camerarius also refers to two other writers, Coelius

Rhodiginus and Alexander of Alexandria, who write as follows :

" The faithfulnesse of a dog hath been the cause that many have chosen to trust their lives with that beast, and to commit themselves to the good of him rather than of reasonable men. As we read of King Massinissa, who by the barking of dogs freed himself many times from the ambuscadoes that were laid for him, discovered afar off the coming of his enemies, stood upon his guard, and, by the helpe of dogs, sometimes carryed away the victorie. Plinie reporteth to this purpose, that the Colophonians tooke great care to traine their dogs and make them fit for warre, insomuch as they made squadrons of them, which fought in the first rankes with a wonderful boldnesse, and would never give back : above all, they did good service in the night. We read also that the King of the Gara-mantes, driven by sedition out of his realme, was re-establisht againe by the helpe of two hundred hunting dogs. It may bee that Henry the VIII., King of England (accord-ing to the purport of a letter which his Ambassadour sent from Spire to the King of Polonia, An. 1544, by the report of Olaus Magnus) had an eye to this prompt fidelitie of dogs, when in the armie which he sent to the Emperour Charles the Fifth against the French King, there were foure hundred souldiers that had the charge of the like number of dogs, all of them garnished with good yron collers after the fashion of that countrey : no man being able to say, whether they were appointed to be sentinels in the night, or to serve for some stratagem for obtaining the victorie. Strabo saith, that the like was practised in old time, and that the English dogs went to warre with the Gaules : and there is mention of a Procurator or Commissarie that had charge of the dogs of Britanie, in the Emperour's behalfe.

And at this day there be some of them found, which Camden calleth Agase-hounds, and named Agasæi by Oppian. Andrew Thenet, speaking of the King of Cephala, writeth, That when he will give battell to his enemies, he commonly mingleth many troupes of dogs among the squadrons of his souldiers. We will hereafter make mention of a dog so couragious in the warre, that the Indians were more afraid of his teeth, than of any other Spanish weapons, and that the owner received extraordinary pay every moneth for the services that were done by that dog."

In Somer's Tracts, containing " The Actions of the Lowe Countries," written by Sir Roger Williams, it is stated how Julian Romero, under the Duke of Alva, in 1572, made a night attack on the camp of the Prince of Orange :

" Julian seconded with all resolution, in such sort, that hee forced all the guards that he found in his way into the place of armes before the prince's tent. Here he entered divers tents ; amongst the rest his men killed two of the prince's secretaries hard by the prince's tent, and the prince himselfe escaped very narrowly.

" For I heard the prince say often, that he thought, but for a dog he had been taken. The camisado was given with such resolution, that the place of armes tooke no alarme, until their fellowes were running in with the enemies in their tailes ; whereupon this dogge hearing a great noyse, fell to scratching and crying, and withall leapt on the prince's face, awaking him being asleepe, before any of his men. And albeit the prince lay in his armes, with a lackey alwaies holding one of his horses ready bridled, yet at the going out of his tent, with much adoe hee recovered his horse before the enemie arrived. Nevertheless one of his quiries was slain taking horse presently after him, and divers of his servants were forced to escape amongst the guardes of foote, which could not recover their horses ; for troth, ever since, untill the prince's dying day, he kept one of that dog's race ; so did many of his friends and followers. The most or all of these dogs were white little hounds, with crooked noses, called camuses."

Motley, in his " Rise of the Dutch Republic," quotes Hoofd and Strada for this, and says :

" But for the little dog's watchfulness, William of Orange, upon whose shoulders the whole weight of his country's fortunes depended, would have been led within a week to an ignominious death. To his dying day the Prince ever afterwards kept a spaniel of the same race in his bedchamber. In the statues of the Prince a little dog is frequently sculptured at his feet."

As time went on, the scenting powers of dogs were utilized, and it is said that Christopher Columbus took bloodhounds with him on his voyage of discovery, and found them useful for scenting out ambushes prepared by the Indians. Tracking dogs were used by Essex in Ireland, and also against the clansmen in Scotland, while they were frequently employed on the Border after raiders. These raiders assumed a very serious aspect in the life of the inhabitants of the Border country between England and Scotland, and, indeed, of the whole of the southern part of Scotland. These wild outlaws organized themselves into more or less drilled bands, and descended on the unfortunate dwellers of the fertile districts, seizing anything of value they could lay their hands on, and driving flocks and herds before them as they returned to their fastnesses. These strongholds were usually situated in the midst of the bogs and moss-land, of which the Border country was greatly composed. All the secret paths and ways of escape across the bogs were known to these desperate ruffians, who were called Moss Troopers, on account of their place of residence, and also because they wore clothes, the dull-brown colour of the moss-land. This made them very invisible, and made escape easy at all times, and especially so at night. In this adoption of nature-colouring for clothes, we see the first hint of khaki, and, indeed, the Moss Troopers' conduct in no way differs from that of the modern Bolsheviki. This state of affairs became so serious in the sixteenth and seventeenth centuries, that vigorous measures had to be taken by the Crown, to protect the peaceful country people. There was a system of beacon fires arranged, whereby on any warning of a raid, these fires were ignited, and the country people were drawn together to unite against the common foe. It was ordered, that tracking dogs were to be kept in the various districts, to assist the Crown forces in locating the marauders across the treacherous swamps.

Leslie, Bishop of Ross, in a volume printed in 1578, states :

" There is also another kind of scenting dogs (I am not speaking of the common sort which pursues hares and roe-bucks), far different from the other ; it is for the most part red, marked with black spots, or vice versa. These are endowed with so great sagacity and fierceness, that they pursue thieves in a direct course without any deviation ; and this with such ferocity of nature that they tear them to pieces even by chance lying down in company with many others : for from the first scent the dog perceives (with his master following), although other men meet, come behind, or cross him, he is not at all confused, is not in the least diverted, but constantly sticks to the footsteps of his departing prey. Only in passing rivers they are at a loss, because there they lose the scent : which the thieves and cattle-stealers knowing, they, with many circles and mazes, pressing now this, now the opposite bank, drive off their plunder, and, pretending to make their exit both ways beyond the banks, rejoin at the same spot. In the meantime, the dog, filling the heavens with his clamour, does not desist till he has overtaken the steps of the fugitives."

In Nicolson and Burns' " History of the Antiquities of Westmorland and Cumberland," published in 1777, there is a statement as to these dogs :

" *Slough-dogs* were for pursuing offenders through the *sloughs*, mosses and bogs, that were not passable but by those who were acquainted with the various and intricate by-paths and turnings. These offenders were peculiarly styled *moss-troopers :* and the dogs were commonly called blood-hounds ; which were kept in use till within the memory of many of our fathers.

" And all along, the pursuit of *hot trod* (*flagranti delicto*), with *red hand* (as the Scots term it) was by *hound*, and horn, and voice. And the following warrant ascertains by whom and where those dogs were to be kept :

" *September* 29, 1616.—Sir Wilfride Lawson and Sir William Hutton, Knights, two of His Majesty's Commissioners for the government of the middle shires of Great Britain, to John Musgrave, the Provost-Marshall, and the rest of His Majesty's garrison (of Carlisle), send salutations. Whereas upon due consideration of the increase of stealths daily growing both in deed and report among you on the borders, we formally concluded and agreed, that for reformation therefore] watches should be set, and slough-dogs provided and kept, according to the contents of His Majesty's directions to us in that behalf prescribed."

The method of distributing the dogs and the tax for their keep imposed on the inhabitants is here described :

" Imprimis, beyond Eske by the inhabitants there, to be kept above the foot of Sarke .... 1 Dogge.

Item, by the inhabitants the inside of Eske to Richmont's Clugh, to be kept at the moat...................... 1 Dogge.

Item, by the inhabitants of the parish of Arthered, above Richmont's Clugh, with the Bayliffe and Black quarter ; to be kept at the Bayliehead   1 Dogge.

Item, Newcastle parish, besides the Baylie and Black quarters ; to be kept at Tinkerhill .... 1 Dogge.

Item, the parish of Stapylton .... 1 Dogge.

Item, the parish of Irdington .... 1 Dogge.

Item, the parishes of Lanercost and Walton .... 1 Dogge.

Item, Kirklington, Skaleby, Houghton, and Richarby .... 1 Dogge.

Item, Westlinton, Roucliff, Etterby, Stainton, Stanwix, and Cargo ; to be kept at Roucliff .... 1 Dogge.

" The sheriff, officers, bailiffs, and constables, within every circuit and compass wherein the slough-dogs are appointed to be kept, are to take care for taxing the inhabitants towards the charge thereof, and collect the same, and for providing the slough-dogs ; and to inform the commissioners if any refuse to pay their contribution, so as thereby such as refuse may be committed to the gaol till they pay the same "

In his book on the dog, Jesse gives a curious correspondence from James V. of Scotland to the Archdeacon of the East Riding, on the subject of his desire to procure bloodhounds trained to ride on a saddle on a horse behind a man. His mother, Queen Margaret, seemed equally interested in the quest for such dogs, and also writes to the Archdeacon from Edinburgh. It seems uncertain as to what was in their minds, in desiring the dogs to ride in this position, but Jesse suggests that: " These were perhaps to be taken up when the tracks of the marauders pursued were plainly visible in soft ground. Swift pursuit was then made, till hard ground was come to, when the slow hound was dropped again to pick up the trail."

If this was the idea, it was a strange one, as the hounds could easily have kept up with the horsemen by galloping alongside ; and it would be next to impossible to get any sort of saddle capable of holding the dog, or, for that matter, a hound willing to sit on such a contrivance, even though some such device could be invented.

The correspondence is extremely quaint, and the polite Archdeacon, in expressing his willingness to gratify the desire of his Royal correspondents, conveys many fulsome compliments, and while he does not in any way suggest that the request cannot be complied with, seeks to pacify them in the first place, by a gift of ordinary hounds for hunting purposes, procured from his patron, the Duke of Richmond and Somerset, who sent his own huntsman with them for the space of a month, and, furthermore, promises that inquiries will be made as to the possibility of procuring such horseback hounds. I greatly fear he was not successful in his search.

Seeing that tracking was of such great importance at this period of history, when the whole country was in a

1616

3

more or less roadless condition, and the inhabitants in the wilder regions were thus enabled to live securely by lawless means of supply, the soldiery, and, indeed, all the respectable members of society, regarded these tracking hounds as part of the machinery for clearing the land of desperadoes, and every method of following a trail was carefully studied.

Those who were pursued, also took all the " tricks of the trade," so to speak, into account, and, from their point of view, sought out every sort of means to counteract the successful working of the hounds, and made use of every obstacle, which it was known would divert them from the trail.

It is a common belief, that if the fugitive crosses water, that the trail can no longer be followed, and this is so very often, unless those who are working the hounds, have some sort of understanding of the method of assisting them to overcome this obstacle. The only way to proceed, is to take the hounds across the river either by boat, or to swim them, and cast them again and again on the opposite bank, until they pick up the trail again. This has sometimes to be done for a considerable distance down the river, as the fugitive may have allowed himself to drift down-stream with the current, in order to confuse the hounds still further. In the case of a lake, or still water of any sort, the fresh cast will have to be made both up and down the opposite bank. Well-trained, eager hounds will quite understand the desire of their keepers to assist them, and will energetically seek the scent again on the other side. I have even known unusually eager hounds, where the scent has been hot, plunge into the water on their own account, and swim to the other side and commence their fresh search for the broken trail. This is, however, exceptional, as the marauders of old well knew, and hounds usually require assistance in such a dilemma, and during the delay occasioned by crossing and taking up the trail again, the scent is all the time becoming fainter.

Another, and much more serious trick for stopping the pursuit, was for the fugitive to spill blood on the trail. The strong smell of this would completely destroy the fine scenting qualities of the hounds. In some of the punitive expeditions of the northerners, a captive was sacrificed to this end.

Jesse, commenting on the work of bloodhounds in the Middle Ages, mentions that "Henry the Minstrel tells us a romantic story of Wallace founded on this circumstance. The hero's little band had been joined by an Irishman named Fawdon, or Fadzean, a dark, savage and suspicious character. After a sharp skirmish at Black Erneside, Wallace was forced to retreat with only sixteen followers. The English pursued with a border sleuth bratch, or bloodhound. In the retreat, Fawdon, tired, or affecting to be so, would go no further. Wallace having in vain argued with him, in hasty anger struck off his head, and continued the retreat. When the English came up, the hound stayed upon the dead body."

It will be seen that the authorities placed considerable value on the services of these tracking dogs. In the wild, untrodden country of that period and neighbourhood, the hounds would have every chance to follow the trail successfully, and the moist nature of the ground, would also be of great assistance in retaining the scent for a considerable time after the fleeing bands had passed, especially if they were driving herds of animals.

At this early period the War Dog and the Police Dog were one and the same, but later on, as the country became more settled, and the bands of marauders were broken up,

3*

owing to new roads being made, and the country opened up generally, the criminal began to be much more an isolated individual, which made pursuit more difficult, as, naturally, one man was more difficult to pursue than a band, and also the fact of so many high roads, with steadily-growing traffic along them, presented bad surfaces for scent, so different from the soft, moist mosses of the wilder and uncultivated period. Nevertheless, bloodhounds continned their work with the various bodies on whom devolved the duties of preserving order in the country, until fairly modern times, when, however, they fell to a great extent into disuse.

In spite of many difficulties presented by present-day conditions, as mentioned above, however, they have even so done good work. At the present day, one of the obstacles to be encountered, (and overcome as well as may be), by the owner and worker of tracking hounds in this country, is the attitude of mind of the people of our nation towards any new device to which they have not been accustomed. There is generally suspicion and reluctance to make use of it, simply on the ground that it is new. This statement applies to a certain extent to the police, who, when a crime occurs, prefer to unravel the mystery as far as they can without extraneous assistance. When at length the bloodhounds are eventually asked for, as they sometimes are, owing to civilian pressure, or to a sudden conviction that the police themselves do not feel confident of success, it is generally after too long a time has elapsed. When the wuer arrives with the hounds at the scene of the crime, even if his task is made as easy as possible by the Chief Constable of the district, he has frequently to meet covert hostility from the local constables, who resent outside interference, especially as represented by dogs, which aid they seem to regard as an insult to their intelligence. He may thus encounter a sort of passive resistance, and every effort made to prevent him from obtaining clues to assist him in following out the trail. Such was certainly not the attitude of the Border soldiery in days gone by, who must have carefully pieced together every shred of evidence available, and worked the hounds in conjunction with this. The confirmation of the hounds as to a certain line of evidence would be the sign to proceed with increased vigour in that direction. Owing to this childish prejudice on the part of a certain portion of the police, (but not of all, as I have met some very fine, open-minded fellows amongst them), it would be better perhaps, from every point of view, if a certain number of bloodhounds were apportioned to the police of each county. They would in that case be available by motor-car quite quickly, and being accredited members of the force, would not be likely to be held in light esteem.

I give an account from the Press of a case, in which a conviction was obtained by the use of bloodhounds at the present day, in this country. I may add that the work was carried out under very great difficulties, but was nevertheless successful :

" FIRST CONVICTION FROM BLOODHOUND EVIDENCE

" At the Northamptonshire Assizes, the evidence of Major Richardson's bloodhounds was accepted as conclusive. Shaw, one of Lord Lilford's gamekeepers, who will be well remembered by visitors to the trials of the English Setter Club each spring, was shot at by poachers early in the morning of December 22nd. Bloodhounds were telegraphed for, and at half-past nine o'clock the same evening, twenty hours after the affray, they were laid on the trail with definite result.

" At the trial, Mr. Simpson, who prosecuted for the Crown, said : ' With reference to the service of the hounds, this was valuable for the reason, that on the next morning, as soon as it was daylight, a search was made along the line of retreat (which had been run by the hounds during the night), and the barrel of a gun was picked up, opposite a stile in a field, over which the bloodhounds had gone.' The barrel of the gun was identified, and through it, the poachers were arrested, and each got twelve years' penal servitude. This is interesting, as showing that the bloodhounds ran the true line in the dark with a very cold scent, and it is the first conviction obtained from bloodhound evidence."

Mr. Charles Gordon, Superintendent of Police, Saharanpur, United Provinces, India, procured a tracking blood hound from me some years ago, and took it out to India. He later sent me the following report on the work of the dog :

" My bloodhound was of great service in a dacoit gang robbery, which was committed at a village in the Bulanshar Districts, in the autumn of 1910. The dacoits had crossed a line of rails on their way to the village, and had picked up a quantity of stone ballast in use as missiles. The villagers were reinforced, and the dacoits finally bolted, carrying off with them twelve hundred rupees in loot. When bolting, the dacoits threw away the balance of the ballast which they had not thrown, and this gave their line of retreat. The bloodhound was put on the trail next morning, and was instrumental in tracking down three men   As a result of this, twelve more dacoits were arrested, and in the course of the inquiry another dacoit was brought home to this gang, both cases resulting in conviction.

" 2. Autumn of 1911, a dacoity was committed at midnight in Saharanpur District. A bullock cart in which was some police was attacked by dacoits. The dacoits were Sanasias (an aboriginal tribe of criminal propensities). One dacoit was wounded, and the night being dark, the others succeeded in getting away. My dog was put on the trail, ten hours subsequent to the crime. Some indistinct footprints were found on the scene and leading to some fields to the south of the road. One of the dacoits was recognized at the time of the occurrence as being by name Mara (Sansia). He, however, managed to escape. The bloodhound was put on the trail of their footprints, which, however, ceased after twenty yards. The hound ran the trail across country until he came to a canal, which he skirted until he came to a bridge over which he crossed. Then he continued the trail along the bank of a feeder canal ; then leaving this, he struck across four rice-fields, which had been irrigated from the canal.

" The water was about four inches deep and growing rice about five inches above the water. (This was a partiticularly good piece of work.)

" On arriving on the other side of the rice-field, he journeyed across country until he came to a village, through which he passed, and ended up at a house in a Sansia settlement to the far side of the village. Not a single Sansia man was present in the settlement, only women and children. On making inquiry, I ascertained that the house in question was that of Mara. Mara was arrested the following night.

" An amusing episode occurred when Mara and the other dacoits were on trial before the judge. Mara denied that he was present at the dacoity and knew nothing about it. How comes it that the dog tracked you for four and a half miles from the scene of the dacoity up to your house? Mara replied that he did not know, but then volunteered the following statement quite on his own account

"'Agar Kutta aisa patta pagata Koon shars chouri Karskta.' A translation of this being : 'When the dog tracks in this manner, what chance has a fellow of committing thefts ? '"

The present-day hound has in nearly every case lost all savage traits, and concentrates all its ardour on the single fact of running his quarry to earth, and has no desire to injure him in any way when it comes up with him. As a matter of fact, the animal fawns on him usually, or, at all events, merely moves around him in a desultory manner. I have only known two hounds that were dangerous when on the trail. One of these, was very incensed when it came across anyone in the line of trail, and would have attacked them, if it could have done so ; but this was an exceptional case, and must have been a throw-back to ancestors of previous centuries, in whom a relentless and savage spirit was cultivated and appreciated.

There was a certain species into which it must be suspected there had been introduced a strain of mastiff, and which went by the name of Cuban bloodhounds. These dogs undoubtedly had tracking powers, but which were allied to a most determined and aggressive spirit.

To quote Jesse again : " A hundred of these sagacious, but savage dogs, were sent, in 1795, from Havana to Jamaica, to extinguish the Maroon War, which at that time was fiercely raging. They were accompanied by forty Spanish Chasseurs, chiefly people of colour, and their appearance and that of the dogs struck terror into the negroes. The dogs, muzzled and led in leashes, rushed ferociously on every object, dragging the Chasseurs along in spite of all their endeavours. Dallas, in his History of the Maroons, informs us that General Walpole ordered a review of these dogs and the men, that he might see in what manner they would act. He set out for a place called Seven Rivers, accompanied by Colonel Skinner, whom he appointed to conduct the attack.

" Notice of his coming having preceded him, a parade of the Chasseurs was ordered, and they were taken to a distance from the house, in order to be advanced when the General alighted.

" On his arrival, the Commissioner, (who had procured the dogs), having paid his respects, was desired to parade them. The Spaniards soon appeared at the end of a gentle acclivity, drawn out in a line, containing upwards of forty men, with their dogs in front unmuzzled, and held by cotton ropes. On receiving the word ' Fire ! ' they discharged their fusils and advanced as upon a real attack. This was intended to ascertain what effect would be produced on the dogs if engaged under a fire of the Maroons. The volley was no sooner discharged, than the dogs rushed forward with the greatest fury amid the shouts of the Spaniards, who were dragged on by them with irresistible force. Some of the dogs, maddened by the shout of the attack, while held back by ropes, seized on the stocks of the guns in the hands of their keepers and tore them to pieces. Their impetuosity was so great, that they were with difficulty stopped before they reached the General, who found it necessary to get expeditiously into the chaise from which he had alighted ; and if the most strenuous exertions had not been made, they would have seized upon the horses."

This scene must have appeared in a distinctly amusing aspect in some respects to an onlooker. Nevertheless, it is stated that " this terrible exhibition produced the effect intended—the Maroons at once capitulated, and were subsequently sent to Halifax, North America."

Another account of these Cuban bloodhound warrior dogs is given by the writer Bingley, who says ·

" In the Spanish West India Islands there are officers called Chasseurs, kept in continual employment. The business of these men is to traverse the country with their dogs, for the purpose of pursuing and taking up all persons guilty of murder, or other crimes ; and no activity on the part of the criminal will enable them to escape.

" The following is a very remarkable instance which happened not many years ago.

" A fleet from Jamaica, under convoy to Great Britain, passing through the Gulf of Mexico, beat up the north side of Cuba. One of the ships manned by foreigners, (chiefly renegade Spaniards), in standing in with the land at night, was run on shore. The officers, and the few British seamen on board, were murdered, and the vessel was plundered by the renegades. The part of the coast on which the vessel was stranded, being wild and unfrequented, the assassins retired with their booty to the mountains, intending to penetrate through the woods to some remote settlements on the southern side, where they hoped to secure themselves, and elude all pursuit. Early intelligence of the crime had, however, been conveyed to Havana. The assassins were pursued by a detachment of Chasseurs del Rey with their dogs, and in the course of a very few days they were every one apprehended and brought to justice."

Bingley further describes the method of working these hounds :

" The dogs carried out by the Chasseurs del Rey are all perfectly broken in. On coming up with the fugitive, they bark at him till he stops. They then crouch near him, terrifying him with ferocious growling if he attempts to stir. In this position they continue barking to give notice to the Chasseurs, who come up and secure their prisoner.

" Each Chasseur can only hunt with two dogs. These people live with their dogs, and are inseparable from them. At home the animals are kept chained, and when walking out with their masters, they are never unmuzzled, nor let out of ropes, but for attack."

There is no doubt that the Spaniards, in their dealings with any people they considered their foes, or who stood in their light in any way, were extremely cruel ; and one reads with regret of the way they hunted the Indians, who certainly seemed to have hated their foreign masters, and to have used every means of aggression against them that lay within their power. But, after all, the Indians were the original inhabitants, and although " a barbarous people, sensual and brutish, hating all labour and only inclined to killing and making war against their neighbours," it is to be questioned if they were much worse than the Spaniards themselves.

" The Indians, it being their custom to make the woods their chief places of defence, at present made these their chief places of refuge, whenever they fled from the Spaniards. Hereupon, these, the first conquerors of the New World, made use of dogs to range and search the intricate thickets of wood and forests for their implacable and unconquerable enemies ; thus they forced them to leave their old refuge, and to submit to the sword, seeing no milder usage would do it.

" But this severity proved of ill consequence, for instead

of frightening them, and reducing them to civility, they conceived such horror of the Spaniards, that they resolved to detest and fly their sight for ever ; hence the greatest part died in caves and subterranean places of wood and mountains, in which places I have myself often seen great numbers of human bones."

One is indeed glad that the functions of the modern war dog with civilized armies no longer include these ferocious characteristics, but, on the contrary, are all directed to the saving of life instead of destroying it.

It is also interesting to find, that in very much later times, another enemy of the Spaniards might be said to have distinctly " scored off " them by means of dogs. I quote the following remarks from the *Daily Telegraph*, which paper sent a reporter to me to obtain information as to the Spanish campaign against the Riffs in Morocco. I had gone to join the Spaniards in this campaign with one of my own hounds for purposes of experiment, at the request of King Alfonso.

" They (the Riffs) have learned the value of dogs in warfare. For instance, at night, a Riff could creep towards the Spanish outposts with his dog. Having gone part of the way with the animal, he would send it on, and himself retire. The dog, on hearing the Spanish sentry, would bark, and the Riffs from places of safety would concentrate their fire in the direction whence the barking proceeded, giving time for the knowing animal to retreat. Or perhaps the sentry would give himself away by firing at the dog, and so reveal his position.

" Another trick, which they successfully practised, was to put a burnous and turban on a dog, and send him along from point to point in front of the Spanish lines. At a distance, the dog looked very like a man creeping along, and at once the Spaniards were blazing away at the supposed Moor. The Moors were, of course, carefully watching, and took aim at any soldier who revealed himself.

" They had still another trick with their dogs, which was to send them towards a Spanish post or camp during the day. The barking of the dogs generally brought some unwary soldiers out, and many soldiers lost their lives in this way.

" I would remind you that the French, when fighting in Algiers, found that the natives made a similar use of their dogs."

To turn to other countries, we find that the German custom of exploiting our dogs for their own purposes, as is shown in several instances later in this book, seems to be an old one, as we find Frederick the Great ordering one of his Generals to obtain a number of Scotch collies to act as sentries to his army.

He is credited with the following remark · " The more I see of men, the more I like dogs."

Napoleon believed in them, and used a number in his Italian campaign. Some of the dogs, such as " Moustache," became famous. A good account of this faithful dog " Moustache " is written by Colonel J. P. Hamilton, and published in 1860, as follows :

" Moustache was born at Calais, 1799. At the tender age of six months, he was disposed of to an eminent grocer at Caen, who treated him in the kindest manner. But strolling about the town one day, not long after his arrival, Moustache happened to come upon a parade of Grenadiers. They were brilliantly equipped. Their spirits were high, and their drums loud. Moustache, instantly smitten with their fine appearance, cut the grocer for ever, slunk out of the town, and joined the Grenadiers. He was dirty, and tolerably ugly, but there was an intelligence, a sparkle, a brightness about his eye, that could not be overlooked. ' We have not a single dog in the regiment,' said the *petit tambour*, ' and, at any rate, this one looks clever enough to forage for himself.' The drum-major assented, and Moustache attached himself to the band, and was soon found to possess considerable tact and talent. He had already learned to carry admirably, and ere three weeks were over, he could stand with as erect a back as any private in the regiment, act sentinel, and keep time in the march. Soldierlike, he lived from paw to mouth. He endured the fatigues of Mont St. Bernard with as good grace as any veteran in the army. They were soon near the enemy, and Moustache, having become familiar with the sound of musketry as well as of drums, seemed to be inspired with new ardour as he approached the scene of action. The first occasion on which he distinguished himself was this. His regiment, being encamped on the height above Alexandria, from the Vale of Balbo attempted a surprise during the night. The weather was stormy, and the French had no notion that the Austrians were advancing so close. The camp was in danger, but Moustache was on the alert. Walking his rounds as usual, with his nose in the air, he soon detected the Austrians. He gave the alarm, and the Austrians rapidly retreated. Next morning, it was resolved, that Moustache should receive the rations of a grenadier. He was now cropped *à la militaire*, a collar with the name of the regiment was hung round his neck, and the barber was ordered to comb and shave him once a week. (He was a cross-bred poodle.)

" In a skirmish which occurred, Moustache received a bayonet wound in his left shoulder. He was not perfectly recovered from this accident when the great Battle of

Marengo took place. Lame as he was, he could not keep away from so grand a scene. He kept close to the banner, which he had learnt to recognize among a hundred, and never gave over barking until the evening closed upon the combatants. The sun of Austerlitz found him with his chasseurs. In the heat of the action he perceived the ensign, who bore the colours of his regiment, surrounded by a detachment of the enemy. He flew to his rescue, barked with all his might, did all he could, but in vain. The ensign fell covered with wounds, but not before, feeling himself about to fall, he had wrapped his body in the folds of the standard. Five or six Austrians still remained by the ensign, to obtain possession of the colours he had so nobly defended. Moustache, having thrown himself on the colours, was on the point of being pierced by bayonets, when a timely discharge of grapeshot swept the Austrians into oblivion. The moment when Moustache perceived that he was delivered from his assailants, he took the staff of the French banner in his teeth, and strenuously endeavoured to disengage it, but ineffectually. He succeeded in tearing away the silk, and with this glorious trophy returned to the camp, limping and bleeding.

"One day, a chasseur, mistaking the dog, hit him a chance blow with the flat side of his sabre. Moustache, piqued to the heart, deserted from his regiment, attached himself to some dragoons, and followed them into Spain. On the 11th March, 1811, he was killed by a cannon ball, at the taking of Badajos. He was buried on the scene of his last glories, collar, medal and all. A plain stone, with the simple 'Ci git le brave Moustache,' was placed over his grave; but the Spaniards afterwards broke the stone, and the bones of the poor animal were burnt by order of the Inquisition."

The following story is taken from Miss Williams's " Sketches of the French Republic " :

" At the moment when the ranks of the Imperialists were broken at the famous Battle of Castiglione, and the heat of the pursuit was in proportion to the obstinacy of the contest, Buonaparte coming to the spot where the thickest of the combat had taken place, where the French and Austrians lay strewn in horrible profusion, he perceived one living object amid those piles of corpses which was a little Barbet dog. The faithful creature stood with his forefeet fixed on the breast of an Austrian officer. His long ears hung over his eyes, which were riveted on those of his dead master. The tumult seemed neither to distract the attention nor change the attitude of the mourner, absorbed by the object to which he clung. Buonaparte, struck with the spectacle, stopped his horse, called his attendants round him, and pointed out the subject of his speculation.

" ' The dog,' said Buonaparte, ' as if he had known my voice, removed his eyes from his master, and throwing them on me for a moment, resumed his former posture ; but in that momentary look there was a mute eloquence beyond the power of language. It was a reproach, with all the poignancy of bitterness.' Buonaparte felt the appeal ; he construed the upbraiding of the animal into a comprehensive demand for mercy ; the sentiment was irresistible ; it put to flight every harsh and hostile feeling. Buonaparte gave orders to stop the carnage instantly."

Writing to Field-Marshal Marmont, Napoleon said : " Collect all the savage dogs you can, and picket them down outside the ramparts to give warning of attack."

We find the alertness of the dog appreciated in the Crimean War. The Russians constantly had them with their sentries, and in the American War, North and South, they were used as sentries and guards. The French also had a system of sentry dogs in Tunis and Algeria, and also in their colonies of Dahomey, Cochin China and Madagascar.

Towards the end of the last century, and at the commencement of 1900, several Continental nations began the study of dog service for the army. Training was commenced in Germany, Holland, France, Russia and Sweden, and was more or less in all these countries under official recognition. In Germany especially, the work was much thought of, and the Jäger regiments especially had large numbers of dogs trained as sentries and messengers. These proved of great value on the outbreak of war. Besides encouraging these military dogs, the authorities in most of these countries had also recognized the value of dogs to the police, and here again Germany was to the fore, and the large service of police dogs in the Fatherland was transferred to the army during the war. They did excellent service for their army, when unfortunately we had hardly any on our side.

In my book, " War, Police and Watch Dogs," published some years before the war, there is a photograph, depicting a number of English-bred dogs with a German regiment. I mentioned my fears that these dogs might be used against us some day, while we were doing nothing in preparation along the same line. I also stated how I discovered the German agents buying up large quantities of our good Airedales, sheep dogs and collies, for military and police purposes.

At the outbreak of the war, the French had a certain number of dogs with seven or eight infantry regiments, and there was a certain official encouragement extended to various dog clubs, which made trained dogs a speciality ; but there was no properly organized training school in connection with the army until the official establishment was started by the War Office during the war about the same time as the English one.

The Italians had had previous experience with sentry dogs in the Tripoli campaign, and in the Great War used the mountain sheep dogs a good deal with their sentries on the frontier.

In England, before the war, I was the sole person who took any interest in trained dogs for the army and police, and the outflow from my kennels constituted the only source of supply.

Most of the countries I have mentioned had been experimenting with ambulance dogs for searching for the wounded, and I also had given a good deal of attention to this service, but it was found unworkable under modern conditions of trench warfare.

The messenger dog came very much to the front, and has come to stay in modern warfare. Like the Tank, it may be said to be particularly a product of this war. At first there were many sceptics, but as the barrage form of attack became part of the army system, the casualties among runners increased at a terrible rate. Could the dogs take their place ? Would they face the shell-fire ? Could they be depended on ? These questions came to be answered in the affirmative. Yes ! They did their duty nobly, passing rapidly through the danger areas, and often over land surface impossible of traverse by man, and thus saved countless lives—not only the lives of runners, but also those of the individual units whose urgent messages they carried.

CHAPTER II

HOW THE MOVEMENT BEGAN IN THE BRITISH ARMY

" But if you visit the Morinian shores
　And thence across to Britain,
　Set aside the form and colour,
　Which in British dogs are the worst points,
　But when the tug-of-war and inbred courage spur them to their work,
　Then is their mettle seen ! "　　　　　　　　　GRATIUS.

WHEN the war opened, in 1914, there were practically no military dogs of any sort attached to the British Army. The sole exception was an Airedale which I trained as a sentry, and which went to manœuvres with the 2nd Battalion Norfolk Regiment, and on the outbreak of war accompanied it to France, where it was eventually killed by a shell on the Aisne. For many years previously I had been studying this subject, and as the result of my convictions had accumulated a large kennel of dogs with which I made constant experiments. The study was also applied to the use of dogs with the police, and my conviction of the great value of trained dogs to the Army and police became of the most emphatic character. I brought the matter from time to time to the notice of the authorities, and, although the police supported the idea to a certain extent, especially the forces in provincial towns, who used a number of dogs for patrolling suburban areas, I could get no generally concerted action taken. I did not give up hope, however, and continued my private experiments. Many people came to me for advice in obtaining safety for themselves or their property. There are very few parts of the world from which I did not receive either visitors or letters in connection with this subject. Owners of tea and coffee estates, sugar plantations, poultry farms, and animal farms in all parts of the world, penitentiaries in North and South America, rubber estates, large rambling mansions, factories, docks, etc. In fact, all suffering from the same trouble, namely, the difficulty and unreliability of the human being, unaided, to provide the necessary guarantee of security. Each case was treated separately, according to the circumstances, climate, personnel and environ-ment.

As it was necessary to specialize in certain breeds, it was found that for the particular needs of these pre-war years the Airedale, as an all-round, courageous, reliable and hardy individual, could not be beaten, and the extra-ordinary way in which he is able to adapt himself to both northern and tropical climates is exceedingly remarkable and useful. I paid many visits to the Continent to those countries which specialized in trained police or military dogs. In France tentative experiments with army dogs were carried on, largely owing to the energy and initiative of M. Megnin, of Paris, and police dogs were used in suburban areas of large towns. Russia had a definite establishment of military dogs in which the Tsar took a great interest and which were attached to many regiments. I may here incidentally remark that I was in Russia three weeks before the war broke out, acting as judge at the army trials of these military dogs. The two other judges were Germans.

Holland, Sweden and Italy all had canine military

establishments, in a more or less experimental stage, and in the case of Italy the experience gained was put to good use in the Tripoli campaign. I visited Tripoli personally during that war, and gained many valuable hints, and I was allowed to visit the battlefields in Morocco, at the invitation of King Alfonso, in the Riff campaign, taking one of my own dogs with me. These experiences in actual warfare were added to by a visit to the Balkans when war broke out there in 1911. The Albanians used many of their shaggy sheep dogs of ferocious disposition, which rendered excellent service in the mountains as guards to their sentries. The Bulgarians also used sentry dogs. I was able to send out a pair of dogs from my own kennels to the 8th Ghurkas for the Abor campaign in India. These were used by sentries and patrols, and rendered considerable service in the dense scrub by preventing the sentries from being surprised and the battalions rushed. One was an Airedale and the other a cross-bred sheep dog.

It was in Germany that I found much the most organized service of both military and police dogs. Between the years 1900 and 1914 I paid several visits to their training establishments, and had admired many of their methods, but I quickly saw that we had the advantage in this country by the possession of a better choice of dogs for the work, and also I questioned whether the immensely detailed system of training the keepers of the dogs, and also the dogs themselves, was to any useful purpose. It seemed to me that, as in other forms of German organization, not enough attention was directed to the psychology of the subject, and too much to the letter of mechanical instruction. I knew that in the event of dogs being employed at all in war large supplies, and quickly trained, would be needed, and that, therefore, a quicker system of instruction was required, at all events for our country, where no preparations were being made in peace-time in this branch.

When the thunderbolt of war fell in this country, the first shock seemed to bring to the surface, among other things, the fact that we had been harbouring quantities of bitterly hostile, treacherous aliens, about whom only one thing was certain, which was that we could not trust them in any direction whatever. Our whole nation began to be immensely on the alert within a few days, and I saw at once that a properly organized system of sentinels and guard dogs all over the country would be of enormous service in guarding bridgeheads, magazines, factories, and valuable property of all kinds. I judged from my experience of years in the same sort of work for civilians how immensely valuable an adaptation of the same idea would be for the Army. I very urgently represented this, and offered to present my whole kennel of trained dogs that experiments might immediately be made. My ideas were, however, not in any way understood at the time, and I could make no headway.

When my offer of sentry dogs was rejected in the first days of the war, I turned to another branch of work in which I had frequently experimented in previous years—tracing the wounded on the battlefield. These dogs were, of course, used with ambulance sections. At this period a war of movement was the only method conceived, and also we in this country were convinced of the inviolability of the sacred symbol of the Red Cross, whether on man or beast, hospital or ship. Had these conditions obtained in this war, ambulance dogs would have been of great assistance. As it was, however, when the French army hurriedly sent some of their ambulance dogs with their keepers to the front in the earliest feverish days, the first thing that happened was that, although both men and dogs wore the Red Cross, the enemy brutally shot them all down whenever they attempted to carry out their humanitarian work. It was also found that, when the opposing forces settled down into trench warfare, the opportunities on the Western front were closed. The only ambulance dogs that were used with any success were those with the German army when the Russians were retreating on the Eastern front.

I offered my services to the British Red Cross Society with some trained ambulance dogs, and was sent by the society to Belgium early in August, 1914. I made my way as far as Brussels, only to find the enemy entering the city from the east, and the Belgians falling back, while our own army had not come up. I succeeded in getting out of Brussels with the dogs and reached Ostend, but the conditions on the Western front soon became, as I have said, impossible for the successful use of ambulance dogs. The French War Office entirely forbade their use with their army after the first few weeks.

After some months I received a number of requests from officers for dogs for sentry and patrol work. I did my best to supply these, and found Airedales answered the purpose well. I also sent some to the Belgian army. During this time I understand many officers were writing to the War Office, asking that dogs should be supplied officially for several purposes. In the winter of 1916 I received a letter from an officer in the Royal Artillery, in which he expressed a great desire for trained dogs to keep up communications between his outpost and the battery, during heavy bombardment, when telephones are rendered useless, and the risk to runners is enormous. He asked if I would train some dogs to carry messages, and I promised to do so. I made many experiments with a large number of dogs, and at last I got two dogs to carry messages homewards regularly without a hitch for two miles. They were both Airedales, and their names were Wolf and Prince.

They left for France on the last day of 1916, and went direct to Thiépval, under escort of a gunner. The dogs were very intelligently managed in France, for although they had been trained without any of the adjuncts of war, they settled down successfully, and began to carry messages regularly. Colonel Winter, R.A., to whom they went, was very kind in assisting me with suggestions, and I found the hints he gave me very useful later on. The first report on these two dogs was as follows ·

" From : O.C. 56th Brigade, Royal Field Artillery.

" To : R.A. Headquarters, 11th Division.

" In continuation of my letter No. 549, dated on the 7th inst., during the operations against Wytschaete Ridge, two messenger dogs attached to this brigade were sent forward at one a.m. One was attached to the forward liaison officer and one with the group forward observation officer.

" After being led up through communication trenches during darkness, they went forward as soon as the attack was launched, passing through the smoke barrage. . . . One was dispatched at 10.45 a.m. and the other at 12.45 p.m.

" Both dogs reached brigade headquarters, travelling a distance as the crow flies of 4,000 yards over ground they had never seen before and over an exceptionally difficult terrain. The dog dispatched at 12.45 p.m. reached his destination under the hour, bringing in an important message, and this was the first message which was received, all visual communication having failed.

" (Signed) O.C. 56th Brigade, R.F.A."

Two other reports on these dogs are as follows ·

" When the Germans withdrew their line in the spring of 1917, the dogs were taken up the night before to a wood east of Bucquoy. They were then sent up to a forward observation post, 4,000 yards to the east of the wood, and were released with important messages. They found their way back through masses of troops on the march, to the wood, although they had only arrived there the night previously, and the ground was quite unknown to them."

" On the attack on the Vimy Ridge the dogs were employed with an artillery observation post. All the tele phones were broken, and visual signalling was impossible. The dogs were the first to bring through news."

The definite results obtained through these two dogs, and through Colonel Winter's initiative, led the authorities to inquire into the question of establishing some means whereby supplies of these messenger dogs could be provided for the Army. I was ordered to the War Office to discuss the matter. Suffice it to say, I was glad to propose a definite plan for starting an official school of instruction for military dogs, and that my ideas were agreed to. It was decided that the school should be formed at Shoeburyness, for the reason that the constant firing of the big guns would be excellent training for the dogs. Mrs. Richardson accompanied me. She has a great gift for training animals, and much of the success of the military dog service was due to her skill and devotion to duty.

A certain number of men were to be sent to the school each month for instruction in handling the dogs, and these men at the end of the course, which lasted about five weeks, took the dogs overseas. The men were at first recruited in France from battalions whose commanding officers expressed a wish to have dispatch dogs. This system was carried on for several months, but while the utility of the dogs was clearly proved, it was found that there was not enough supervision over their working and management in the field, and the full measure of usefulness was not being brought out in many regiments. In certain battalions, commanding officers with a sympathy for dogs and an eye to the value to be obtained from their service, would make arrangements that full use should be made of them, and, moreover, kept records of their work and sent them to G.H.Q. in France. The inability of our people to recognize that a dog is capable of real work and is worth taking seriously, was a stumbling-block in many cases, and it was soon reported to me that the capabilities of these valuable and highly-trained dogs were being inadequately recognized, and their keepers could not get sufficient attention paid to the working needs of their service. I reported the matter, and as the result an officer was appointed, Major Waley, M.C., R.E., to superintend the organizing of the messenger-dog service in France. It was found that better results could be obtained by withdrawing all the dogs with their keepers from the separate battalions, and forming the whole into a complete unit. A central kennel was formed at Etaples, where the dogs and keepers were collected on being withdrawn from the battalions. From this central kennel the dogs were, with their keepers, posted to sectional kennels behind the front line. Each sectional kennel was in charge of a sergeant, and had about forty-eight dogs and sixteen men allotted to it. From these sectional kennels the dogs were sent, with their keepers, to the proportion of three dogs to one man, to the active sectors. His dogs were then taken away from him by certain men detailed from the infantry battalions in the brigade, and were led up to the front line. The keeper remained at brigade headquarters, watching for the dogs' return, and ready to deliver the messages they brought to the officer commanding. Very careful regulations for the correct management of the messenger dogs and their keepers were drawn up and issued. This method of concentration and supervision soon began to give excellent results.

In the meantime the training work proceeded steadily at the War Dog School at Shoeburyness, and class after class of trained men and dogs were sent overseas, where they were concentrated, in the first place, at the central kennels before being distributed to the sectional kennels. A new branch of activity had besides commenced at Shoeburyness. As the demand for fighting men became increasingly insistent, large numbers who had been doing guard duty all over Britain were withdrawn, and the security of munition factories, magazines, and vulnerable points of all kinds was an anxious one for the Government. I was sent for and questioned as to whether the dogs could be of service at this juncture, to act as guards and replace man-power. I said most emphatically they could. From my experience, however, in pre-war years, as applied to civilian needs, I knew that, in order to be successful, careful management of these guard dogs would be necessary, and therefore I drew up a list of regulations which was issued to each centre where these dogs were employed. Once this branch was fairly started, applications began to pour in from all parts of the country.

At this time, also, a request for sentry dogs for use with the troops at Salonika was referred to me. The desire was particularly for Airedales, and they were to be used in the listening-posts in the front line to give warning of enemy approach. There were thus, at this time, three separate branches of training proceeding at the school. With these increasing demands upon the school, it was found that the supply of suitable dogs so far obtained was becoming inadequate. At first the only supply was from the Home for Lost Dogs at Battersea. Then the Birmingham, Liverpool, Bristol and Manchester Dogs' Homes were invited to help by sending any suitable dogs to the school. Many a homeless, deserted " stray " was saved from the lethal chamber, and transformed into a useful member of His Majesty's Forces. Later, the Home Office ordered the police all over the country to send all stray dogs of certain breeds to the school. Finally, when even these sources were not sufficient, the War Office decided to appeal to the public for gifts. The response was exceedingly generous. The country was, at this time, passing through especially serious times, and many people were only too glad to help by sending their dogs. The food shortage also was much accentuated, and it was felt that the family friend would be certain to receive good food and care in the Army.

Some of the letters received at this time testify to the unselfish spirit in the country. A lady wrote : " I have given my husband and my sons, and now that he too is required, I give my dog." From a little girl : " We have let Daddy go to fight the Kaiser, and now we are sending Jack to do his bit." An " Old Contemptible " said · " I have been through Mons, and have lost a leg and nearly lost my life, and have not much I can give my country, but I gladly give my dog to help." A sporting person sent his lurcher, with the remark · " I am sending you my dog Sam. He has always found his own grub and has plenty of sense so should be of use." Sam did not have to find his own grub any longer when at the school, but he nevertheless earned it.

A splendid collection of dogs was daily assembled. Many of them were fine show specimens, while others of humble ancestry nevertheless came with wise faces and willing hearts. They were one and all welcome, and were made to feel so. The attitude of mind was in most cases that of a schoolboy plunged into a large public school—bewilderment and sometimes homesickness for a short time—but as it was found that reassuring, kindly human voices were all around, and that excellent dinners were going, they soon became quite at home. Added to this, life offered most interesting companionship with other dogs, and also a completely new experience in what seemed to the dog the learning of a new sort of game.

Each recruit was carefully tested for three different duties—messenger, sentry, or guard work. Sometimes they failed in one but succeeded in another, but all had a good chance to show some sort of initiative. In the event of a dog showing no desire for work of any sort it was returned to the source whence it came. The more one has to do with the canine race the clearer it is seen that as regards psychology there is little difference between it and the human race, and I much regret to say that it was my experience to find occasionally the canine " conscientious objector " among the recruits. There was, however, a convenient method of dealing with the offenders which unfortunately is not available for human beings—an excellent lethal chamber at Battersea !

We had many distinguished visitors. Field-Marshal French inspected the school, accompanied by General Lowther. This was before the results of the work that had been done had been fully demonstrated, and the genuine interest Lord French showed in the dogs, and the few words of helpful encouragement he gave me, at a time when very great difficulties were being overcome, will always be remembered with gratitude. A large number of officers belonging to the Allied and neutral countries also visited the school, besides various travelling parties of Allied and Colonial editors. During the summer of 1917 so numerous were the requests from various officials to visit the school, that a special day had to be set aside once a week for this purpose, so that the training should not be hampered.

Everything by this time was going with a swing. A large number of men and dogs were being turned out fully trained, and Major Waley had the system of posting in France on a good basis. The demand for more and yet more dogs, both as messengers and guards, became insistent. The former proved themselves speedy and life-saving in maintaining communication in the field, and the latter as a means of substituting man-power and protecting Government property of every kind. In June, 1918, I made an inspection of the entire messenger dog service in France, accompanied by Major Waley. We also visited the French front, and were greatly interested in the work done in the French Army with dogs. I had a conversation with the famous General Gouraud, whose wonderful defence near Rheims in July, 1918, will be remembered. The general is a great believer in dogs, and in speaking of messenger dogs he said : " If only two out of six dogs come back with their messages I am satisfied."

Previous to this I had already paid two visits to the dogs on the French front. In April, 1915, I visited the French 6th Army at Villers Cotterets, and also in December the same year I visited the 7th French Army in the Vosges, where I was hospitably received by Monsieur Paul Megnin, who has done so much to forward this work in the French Army.

On my return to England a large extension to the work, and a proportionate increase to the establishment of the War Dog School was ordered by the War Office. By this time it was found that the available training-ground at Shoeburyness was becoming too congested. A site was chosen on Matley Ridge, above Lyndhurst. There was a splendid stretch of country here, and the training went on satisfactorily until May, 1919. During that month the school was moved to Bulford, on Salisbury Plain.

In November, 1918, the armistice came, but just before that event the latest instructions for divisional attack were issued. In these it was ordered that infantry battalions in the attack were to be provided with messenger dogs. This seemed to set a seal on the work. The long uphill struggle, the open sneers, the active obstruction, the grudging assistance, all was forgotten, in the knowledge that countless men's lives had been saved and that this fact had now been realized and acknowledged.

Field-Marshal Haig, in his final dispatch on the war, pays a tribute to the work the messenger dogs did in the field.

CHAPTER III

THE MESSENGER DOG : TRAINING AND MANAGEMENT.

> The tither was a plowman's collie,
> A rhyming, ranting, roving billie,
> He was a gash and faithfu' tyke,
> As ever lap a sheugh or dike.
> His honest sonsie, bawsie face,
> Aye gat him friends in ilka place.
> . . . . When up they gat and shook their lugs,
> Rejoiced they were na men but dogs."
>
> BURNS.

THE training of the messenger dog requires a decidedly special gift in the instructor. Without a long, intimate, and practical working experience among dogs on a large scale, no one need attempt to train messenger dogs in wartime. It must be understood that training includes the instruction of the men who are to act as keepers to the dogs, as well as of the dogs themselves.

In organizing the school in the first place, I recommended that gamekeepers, shepherds, and hunt servants should be especially asked for, and this may be said to be a fair working basis on which to start, but my experience goes to show that many of the men who had actually worked among dogs all their lives were not necessarily the best for this particular branch. In order to be a good keeper for a messenger dog in the field, a man must in the first place

Training the messenger dog to go over the top.

[*To face p.* 64.

A sentry dog.

be brave, and he must be fit. He is no use if he is afraid of the front line, or if he is incapacitated. In fact, he should be an A1 man. The men comprising the personnel require to be of an honest, conscientious character, with sympathetic understanding for animals. A keeper, when in the front line, though governed by definite regulations, requires to use his own initiative to a great extent in handling his dogs, and men of intelligence and faithfulness to duty are absolutely essential. It will thus be seen that a really high standard of character is of first importance. This must be accompanied by a fondness for, and a gentleness with, dogs. Complete confidence and affection must exist between dogs and keeper, and the man whose only idea of control is by coercion and fear is quite useless. I have found that many men, who are supposedly dog experts, are not sufficiently sympathetic, and are apt to regard the dog too much as a machine. They do not study the psychology of their charges sufficiently. Another type of man to avoid is one who has trained or bred a few dogs, and thinks in consequence that he knows all there is to know. This unteachable attitude disqualifies a man at the outset. Some of the most successful keepers, that is to say, those who obtained the best results from the dogs in the field, and were also the most helpful when under instruction at the school, were those who, having a natural love of animals, had had no previous experience of a particular nature with dogs.

Now the most important point in the whole messenger service is this question of the keepers. It is more important than that of the dog. The cleverest dog is nonplussed in charge of a stupid or unconscientious keeper. Therefore, in order to obtain the highest efficiency, it is most essential that the personnel at the school should be always kept in a fluid condition. The men, when they are recruited from the commands, should, in the first place, have a distinct understanding that they are in every case liable for the trenches. This precaution excludes the shirker, who jumps at any job that he thinks will keep him at home. Each man must come on probation, and when the classes are evacuated from the school for overseas at stated intervals the choice of individual men must always be left to the Commandant, who judges, not by the length of time a man has been in the school, but by the results of that man's work. Some men reveal themselves much quicker than others, and it is a mistake to have the training period bound by any particular time, as regards the individual man. Some men will show very quickly that they are quite unfitted for the work, and these should be returned to their units at once. Others, again, take pleasure in their duties from the commencement, and display initiative, and when they thoroughly understand their duties they can be transferred to the Royal Engineers and are ready for service in the field. This system of selection should apply to all ranks of the establishment, including officers. It should be understood that most of the work is technical, and the instructors require certain mental qualifications. The training of messenger and guard dogs is so different from every other kind of dog work that practically anything that a man has learned before about dogs has to be forgotten before he is qualified to be trained himself, and to train others. Added to this, the fact of managing several hundred dogs is a new lesson to learn in itself.

All officers should be appointed to the school on probation.

RECRUITING THE DOGS

These are the methods of recruiting the dogs :

1. From the dogs' homes.
2. From the public as gifts through the Press.
3. From the police stations in all parts of the country.

For messenger dogs the following breeds should be asked for : Sheep dogs, collies, drovers' dogs, lurchers (and all crosses of the above), Irish terriers, Welsh terriers, Airedales, and deerhounds.

As each dog arrives, its full description is tabulated in a ledger, with all particulars concerning it, and it is given a collar and a number. It now takes its place among the new recruits and is given a couple of days' rest, after which it may be paraded with the other dogs of its own class for the purpose of testing its capabilities. In analysing the capabilities of the breeds above recommended for message-carrying, experience goes to show that all these have given good results in the field. Fox terriers, besides being too small, are too fond of play, and do not take work seriously. It must be admitted, however, that many of our best dogs were Irish terriers and Welsh terriers. These little fellows were remarkably easily taught, and were tremendously keen on their work. Retrievers, unless they have a strong cross of collie or sheep dog in them, may be ruled out. They were very seldom entirely satisfactory. I put that down to the use of this breed for sport. Under that system of training the dog does his work always more or less under his keeper's control, within sound of his voice, and the habit of independent thinking, which has to be inculcated in the messenger dog, is therefore difficult to instil. The sheep dogs, and by this I mean the shaggy or Highland variety, frequently make good dogs. They are sometimes

5*

rather highly strung, and for that reason their training takes longer and requires great patience, but if one can overcome their tendency to nervousness, they are naturally extremely intelligent and conscientious workers.

The show collie is quite as good as the working type, which one might not expect. Lurchers and lurcher crosses are very wise dogs, and train well. Greyhounds, on the other hand, are of no use. Hounds are also untrainable. I have succeeded in training one or two to carry messages short distances, but when the distance is above a mile the hound seems to lose interest. Poodles are too fond of play, and I found that any poodle cross seemed to diminish a dog's capacity. Another curious fact to be noted is that I have rarely found a dog with a gaily carried tail, which curled over its back or sideways, of any value. This method of carrying the tail seems to indicate a certain levity of character, quite at variance with the serious duties required.

It is this testing process which calls for so much insight, patience, and experience in the instructor. Certain dogs will show what is in them in a very few days, and these can be put aside and accepted for future training. There are others which show no particular aptitude at all, and in some cases refuse all invitations to learn anything. Now the instructor has to judge whether the dog is refusing to work from timidity and bewilderment, or whether it is stupid or lazy. There are cases again where the dog shows considerable aptitude for a few days, and then falls away. In this case, it will be necessary to judge whether it is worth while continuing the dog's education at all, or whether it should be rested for a few days and brought out again. Sometimes the change and excitement may be affecting the dog's health, and a few days' longer rest may improve it. The dogs pass through many phases before they are fully qualified messengers, and without a natural gift for discerning the individual nature of each dog, the instructor may very easily lose patience, and reject a half-trained recruit which later would turn out a first-class worker. At the same time, he must know when he is up against a real shirker, and save unnecessary waste of time in training. Rapidity of output is of the highest importance, and only a long previous experience with dogs, on a large scale, will give the necessary understanding of the methods of rapid training. The dogs should not be under one year, nor older than four years. It is better, if the supply is sufficient, to confine the choice of dogs to those of the male sex.

The heavy bombardments which are a feature of modern warfare render communication with the front line exceedingly difficult to maintain. The object of the use of messenger dogs, therefore, is :

1. To save human life.

2. To accelerate dispatch-carrying. ˙

Telephones soon become useless, and the danger to the human runner is enormous. Added to the difficulties are the shell-holes, the mud, the smoke and gas, and darkness. It is here that the messenger dog is of the greatest assistance. The broken surface of the ground is of small moment to it, as it lightly leaps from point to point. It comes to its duty in the field well broken to shell-fire, and so has no fear. Its sense of direction is as certain at night as in the day, and equally so in mist or fog. Being a smaller and more rapidly-moving object, the danger of its being hit is much less than in the case of a runner, and it is a fact that during the war casualties were extraordinarily low among the messenger dogs, especially when it is taken into consideration that their work was always in the hottest of the fight. There is a most remarkable record of the tenacity and courage with which the dogs did their work in the face of every kind of difficulty. There have been many occasions when a situation, at one moment so full of anxiety and uncertainty, has been completely transformed by the arrival, out of the chaos and darkness, of one of these brave dogs bearing its message of information and appeal.

Now it must here be observed why the training of the messenger differs from that of any other dog. In the first place, the dog has to work entirely on its own initiative, and may be miles away from its keeper. It has to know what it has to do, and to think out how it is to do it. The only training that approaches it is that of the shepherd's dog, where a man may send his dog up the hill-side with directions to gather in the sheep. But the distance is not so great, nor are the difficulties to be encountered to be compared. It is easy to understand, therefore, that the messenger dog has to be trained in such a way that it takes keenest delight and pride in its work. The highest qualities of mind—love and duty—have to be appealed to and cultivated. Coercion is of no avail, for of what use would this be when the dog is two or three miles away from its keeper? In fact, it may be said that the whole training is based on appeal. To this end the dog is gently taught to associate everything pleasant with its working hours. Under no circumstances whatever must it be roughly handled or roughly spoken to. If it makes a mistake, or is slack in its work when being trained, it is never chastised, but is merely shown how to do it over again. If any of the men under instruction are observed to display roughness or lack of sympathy with the dogs, they should be instantly dismissed, as a promising young dog could easily be thrown back in his training, or even spoiled altogether, by sharp handling.

In the early days of the dog's training, it is not asked to travel very long distances, but before it is considered ready for the field it must have been in the regular habit of carrying messages over different sorts of country for three and a half to four miles.   The ground over which the dogs are trained must be varied as much as possible.   They must be taught to travel along high roads, amongst lorry and other traffic, through villages, and past every sort of camp and cook-house temptation.   They must be taught not to be afraid of water, or of any inequalities in the ground. To aid the dogs in overcoming all these difficulties, all sorts of artificial obstacles are introduced into the route of the dog's journey over and above those he would meet in the ordinary way.   Barbed wire entanglements, palings, fences, water dykes, smoke clouds, made by harmless means, etc., should intercept its homeward journey, and it must be induced at all costs, one way or another, to surmount these difficulties by going over, through, or under.   It is left to the dog to choose, but come he must.   Competition with each other is a very strong educator here, and is one of the great aids to training.   When a dog begins to be keen on its work, it takes great pride in everything connected with its training, and is greatly displeased to see another passing it.

It was my custom at the school to divide the messenger dogs into classes according to their progress.   There was a first, second, and third class.   Sometimes one class would be left in while the others were taken out for work.   If the first class, which was the most highly trained, happened to be left in, it was most amusing to watch the indignation and contempt with which the incoming efforts of the lesser-trained dogs were greeted by its members.   They generally elected to watch the proceedings perched on the top of their kennels, and loud choruses of derision were hurled at the raw recruits. When the turn came afterwards for members of the first class to exhibit their prowess, great was the assumption of superiority and determination to show how much better they could do.

In order to accustom them to gunfire, the best method is to encourage the young recruit with a daily practice under rifle fire with blank ammunition. One or two rifles are sufficient at the start, and the number may be increased as the dogs get accustomed to them. Afterwards thunder-flash bombs can be used at varying distances. At Shoeburyness the dogs were also taken daily to the batteries, first of all to the 18-pounders and afterwards to the heavies. Much gentleness and careful treatment is needed here, so that the dog may not be unduly scared at first. The whole process must be gradual. It is a good plan to feed the dog with tit-bits during the firing. It is remarkable how soon most dogs get accustomed to the heaviest firing. I am frequently asked how long it takes to train a messenger dog, and to this no very definite answer can be given, as so much depends on the individual dog's intelligence and stamina. For it must be understood that not only has the mind to be instructed, but the health and muscular activity have to be brought up to a high standard. The great proportion of the dogs sent to the school have been previously living indoors, sometimes in hot kitchens. The change to an outdoor life is quite an experience, and it takes a little time for them to become hardened to weather conditions. Then, again, very few dogs have been accustomed to gallop several miles every day over every sort of surface, and their feet are rarely in good working condition. Another point is that the usual manner of feeding a single house-dog on any odd scraps that may be left over from the household meal is not a good preparation for the steady working diet provided for them when under training. It is quite difficult for them to believe that dog biscuits cooked with horseflesh will really very soon seem to them the most delightful fare that could be provided. It may be stated that no dog should leave the war-dog school under five weeks, and only a few should do so then, the majority requiring six weeks to two months to become thoroughly trained and hardened.

The best method of kennelling the dogs when at the school is for each dog to be chained to a separate kennel. These should be of the box pattern, with a sloping roof which opens upwards, and with a sliding door. Each kennel should have in front of it a movable shelter, with a wooden roof and floor. These shelters are a great comfort to the dog, as they give it protection from both the rain and the sun. Such kennels have proved exceedingly satisfactory, and the health of the dogs has been very good indeed. They are also easily shifted about, so that the ground does not get foul. This system of kennelling was adopted at the Central Kennels in France. The kennels should be periodically and frequently whitewashed inside.

A man should be set aside to attend to the grooming of the dogs. In the case of the old English sheepdogs, it is as well to clip the legs, as all that long fur is uncomfortable for the dog when in hard training, and when it gets wet. In fact, all dogs with extremely shaggy coats should be trimmed, especially about the legs, leaving only a good thick saddle of fur along the back. One good, reliable man should be put on duty as head nurse. He must be kind, gentle, and practical, and not fond of dosing. Sick dogs are far better without any drugs. Rest, warmth, and dieting in an intelligent manner is the quickest and surest way to bring dogs into health again. I may also add that prevention is better than cure, and if the dogs are kept in the manner directed, well fed, well groomed, and exercised, they will be happy, and when dogs are happy they are always healthy. In the case of wounds or bites from other dogs, I am very much against putting on any ointment or medical dressing of any sort, beyond sometimes a mere bandage. I find that the healing takes place much quicker if the wound is kept clean and left alone.

THE LIAISON DOG

Before concluding these remarks on Messenger Dogs I should like to mention the liaison dog—or the messenger dog trained to run backwards and forwards. This system of training was not adopted for the British Army as a whole, for two good reasons. First, when the War Office found that dog-messengers would be a valuable means of life-saving to runners, and also for keeping up communication with the front-line trenches, the order was for unlimited output with the utmost celerity. The liaison training takes double the time of the one direction method. Secondly, the system of one direction running only necessitates one set of keepers. In this case the keeper who has charge of these dogs remains at the battalion headquarters, and his dogs are taken from him up to the front-line trenches by soldiers of the unit. When it is desired to send a message the dogs are slipped, and readily run back to where they last left their keeper.

The liaison system, on the other hand, necessitates two keepers to each set of dogs. The second keeper takes the dogs outwards and slips each dog, himself remaining in the trenches to receive the dog on its return from battalion headquarters, where it will have delivered its message to its keeper there, and will have been directed to return by him, probably with a reply message. This system, besides necessitating the training of a much larger staff of keepers in the first instance, also entails a considerably greater wastage of life, both among the men themselves and the dogs, as the position of the keeper in the front line is fraught with risk, and the dogs are also required to run a double journey over the danger area.

When the work was officially commenced of training these dogs the man-power question was already becoming serious, and became much more acute later on, so that the second difficulty alone would have made the simpler system more advisable. In commenting on the two systems, I would say that, were training to be kept up permanently in our Army in peace time, I would certainly advise that a certain number of liaison dogs should always be kept in training. At the same time, I still believe that the bulk of the dogs, as a whole, should be trained for active warfare on the simpler principle, and in the event of large quantities of messenger dogs being hurriedly required again, and no training having been carried on in peace time, the one direction-trained dog is unquestionably the best for the emergency, as it can be trained quickly and reliably, and many dogs can be utilized that will do this method well, but would be incapable of the other more difficult system.

The hour of training is eagerly anticipated by the dogs, and they are in a high state of excitement when led out on to the parade ground by the keepers. It is better, if possible, that each man should concern himself with two dogs only at this time, but in the case of the more advanced classes, it is sometimes necessary, if the number of dogs under training is very large, that each keeper should have three, or even four, which are taken from their kennels on leads. A certain amount of " swank " is evident among those members of the classes who consider their work is approaching that quality known as " *haute école.*" This is for the benefit of the less accomplished, and especially for the last comers, which are drawn up in line on the opposite side, and are attached by their leads to posts. These raw recruits wait until all the dogs which are capable of return-ing from some distance have departed. This morning parade is an excellent time for the officer in charge to conduct a thorough inspection of all the dogs on duty. Signs of sickness are noted, and condition of health in every particular, including coat, skin, and so on.

All dogs are classified according to their work, and those at the same stage of training go out together, with their keepers, in groups. As I have said, they are at this time in such a high state of complacency that their behaviour is apt to get on each other's nerves, and the natural desire " to take each other down a peg or two " sometimes results in squabbles of an undignified nature. These are, however, soon ended, and the next moment the combatants are trotting off quite happily as though nothing had occurred. It may be added that this is the only occasion when a scold-ing is administered.

I might remark here that the best weapon for stopping a dog fight is a heavy stable broom, with good stiff bristles. In the event of two dogs fighting, two keepers should each seize a combatant by the tail, and hold the dog apart as far as it can be drawn. The dogs will probably be holding on to each other's heads by their teeth, but by drawing them apart just to that point where they cannot get further purchase they will not be able to increase their grip. In the meantime the broom is brought into play, and by bringing it down bristle end on the dogs' noses it will be found they will quickly realize the game is up. The broom need not be used heavily, as they dislike the bristles very much, and usually let go without further trouble. It should be pointed out that the dogs must not be drawn roughly apart, as that would only injure them, but they must be drawn out just to that point where they can only hold each other, but not take further grip. If this method is followed it will be found that the dogs will never seriously injure each other. In the event of a good " mix-up " fight, where several are joining in, good play round among them with the broom, thrusting the bristles in between the combatants, will be found quickly effective, and without injury to the dogs, and all hands must be called on to select a tail, and make the owner captive whenever it is separated. Fighting dogs should only be handled by their tails.

The first training each day is the firing drill. The entire parade of dogs, excluding the new arrivals, are led to a large shed, where a certain number of keepers are drawn up with rifles loaded with blank cartridges. Several rounds are fired, and many of the haughty spirits that have been making such a display on the parade ground are now inclined to put up a sorry show. Much gentleness is, however, extended at this lesson, and any dog that shows timidity is taken further off until it gets accustomed to the firing. This they very soon do, and the old hands proudly stand right under the firing keepers. After this there is a system of bomb-firing, which is a further call upon nerve force, and has often to be carried on for some time. The dogs are also trained to run among the keepers who are firing their rifles from a recumbent position across the road by which the dogs have to come. They are also taken to the batteries and accustomed gradually at varying distances to the sound of 18-pounders up to the 12-in. guns. Another lesson is the water training, and in this case the dog has to cross a stream, either by jumping, or swimming, or wading, and there is also the obstacle crossing, which may be barricades of barbed wire, fencing, thorn-hedging. The smoke barrage has also to be met and conquered. This is made by setting alight bundles of straw or hay, or by harmless smoke bombs, and the dogs must run through it.

In all these tests the dog has to do the work voluntarily. It is not coerced or compelled. It must want to do it. For this reason it will be understood how much patience is required, and that no definite time can be laid down for each dog's training. Those that refuse are gently asked to try again, and are this time given a much easier test, and so are led up to the point which was at the time rather beyond their intelligence. The classes are now ready for the running work, and are taken out shorter or longer distances, according to their capabilities, and are slipped back to the training post.

In the meantime the new dogs are dealt with. Each dog is taken singly by a keeper, and slipped back, and this system is carried on over and over again, and at increasing distances. The officer in charge of the training will find it very useful to have a platform erected, from which he surveys the surrounding land sufficiently to inspect the running of the dogs, and note each one's behaviour. The eye soon becomes practised where the training-ground is in open country to distinguish the running dogs from a long distance, and note will be taken as to whether the dog comes steadily or if it stops, and why. This training is carried on twice a day for all the dogs, except those of the highest class, which will probably have been taken out four miles or so in the morning and slipped backwards, thus bringing up their run to about eight miles. In their case, that is sufficient for one day. When the evening hour comes they are all very ready to seek the quiet rest of their individual kennels, and to feel the proud consciousness that they are daily learning a little more of a very honourable task.

The following nominal roll of men and dogs, attached to a sectional kennel, gives a good idea, of the class of dog found most suitable. It brings out the fact, that the gift of intelligence necessary for message carrying, cannot be said to be confined in particular to any one breed. It should be noted, however, that many of these dogs had slight crosses in them, and this is especially so in the case of the Retrievers, many of which had a strain of Collie in them.

MESSENGER DOG SERVICE
NOMINAL ROLL OF DOGS AND KEEPERS No. 3 SECTION
N.C.O. i/c, Sergt. W. Bonney.

No.	DESCRIPTION.	SEX.	NAME.	KEEPER'S NAME.
—	———	—	—	427773 Sergt. W. Bonney.
101	Airedale	Dog ...	Buller	3133 Cpl. J. Coull.
102	Collie	Dog ...	Trick	
103	Setter	Bitch .	Nell	
104	Collie Lurcher	Dog ...	Yellow.....	491793 Pnr. H. Bevington
105	Airedale	Dog ...	Rocket	
106	Airedale	Dog ...	Jame	
107	Airedale	Dog ...	Tags	361465 Pnr. H.Monagham
108	Old English Sheep .	Dog ...	Tweed	
109	Retriever	Bitch .	Lill........	
110	Irish Terrier	Dog ...	Paddy	449951 Pnr.G.L.L.Griffiths
111	Irish Terrier	Dog ...	Mick	,, ,, ,,
112	Irish (Missing)	Dog ...	Cocoa	,, ,, ,,
113	Airedale	Dog ...	Dale.......	432401 Pte.P.M.O.Oldroyd
114	Airedale Lurcher ...	Dog ...	Badger	,, ,, ,,
115	Bloodhound (Missing)	Dog ...	Duke	
116	Retriever Sheep	Bitch .	Curly	234830 Pte. W. T. Rea.
117	Airedale Irish	Dog ...	Gyp	
118	Irish	Dog ...	Dick	
119	Lurcher	Dog ...	Sharp	360178 Pnr. J. Ferriby.

No.	DESCRIPTION.	SEX.	NAME.	KEEPER'S NAME
120	Irish Water Spaniel..	Dog ...	Coffee	360178 Pnr. J. Ferriby.
121	Yellow Lurcher	Dog ...	Vulcan	
122	Lurcher............	Dog ...	Dan	360700 Pnr. R. Young.
123	Retriever	Dog ...	Black Petal	
124	Collie	Dog ...	Flight	
125	Terrier............	Dog ...	Georgie	369186 Pnr. C. Welham.
126	Spaniel	Dog ...	Spotty	,, ,, ,,
127	Retriever	Dog ...	Hanky.....	
128	Brown Setter	Dog ...	Ginger	360167 Pnr. J. Cousall.
129	Collie	Dog ...	Ben	
130	Airedale	Dog ...	Moses	
131	Lurcher	Dog ...	Frolic	443982 Pnr. W. Taylor.
132	Collie	Dog ...	Willard	
133	Spaniel	Dog ...	Drummer ..	
134	Collie	Dog ...	Jim	525929 Pnr. H. Cotton.
135	Old Sheep	Dog ...	Jock	
136	Bedlington	Dog ...	Dick	
137	Irish Bedlington	Dog ...	Paddy	360174 Pnr. T. W. Woo
138	Brown Lurcher	Bitch .	Lady	,, ,, ,,
139	Lurcher	Dog ...	Roger	,, ,, ,,
140	Small Retriever	Dog ...	Darkie.....	210148 Pnr. G.W.Allcoc
141	Retriever Spaniel ...	Dog ...	Prince	,, ,, ,,
142	Collie	Dog ...	Flier	,, ,, ,,
143	Whippet...........	Dog ...	Skim	360173 Pnr. R. Windle.
144	Irish	Dog ...	Links	
145	Whippet	Dog ...	Forest	
146	Lurcher	Dog ...	Slick	360188 Pnr. J. Dunn.
147	Collie Lurcher	Dog ...	Rapid	
148	Lurcher	Dog ...	Sailor......	

The following is a list of breeds sent to France within a certain period for messenger work.

BREED OF DOGS.	No.	BREED OF DOGS.	No.
Collies	74	Bull terriers	5
Lurchers	70	Greyhounds	2
Airedales............	66	Eskimos	2
Sheep dogs...........	36	Dalmatians...........	2
Retrievers...........	33	Bedlingtons	2
Irish terriers	18	Pointers	2
Spaniels	11	Bull dogs	1
Deerhounds	6	Whippets	1
Setters..............	4		
Welsh terriers	5	TOTAL 340	

Roman.

Training war dogs to shell-fire

Type of kennel used.

Training the messenger dog to water

[*To face p.* 81.

It will here be seen that the collies and lurchers take the highest place as regards numbers, and Airedales the next. Some of the other breeds were good at the work, but were of a scarcer breed and therefore more difficult to obtain. Of these I would particularly mention Welsh terriers. Some deerhounds also, showed a great aptitude, but they are of course rather scarce.

It will be observed however, that the first four breeds are all such as have been associated, some of them from prehistoric times, with man, in connection with his work, and therefore have instinctively a sense of calling inherent in their minds. The collie, or the sheep dog, is, as I have shown elsewhere, quite one of the most ancient breeds, and has always been the companion of man, for guarding his person and his flocks. The lurcher is a mixture of working dogs, the greyhound part of him being adapted, on account of the fleetness to be derived from this breed, to the intelligence of the other part of him, which may be a collie or an Airedale, the two portions combining into a very clever, reasoning, working dog. The Airedale has, for many generations, now been adopted as a very personal dog, mostly for the guardian of person and property, and he also takes life as quite a serious business. This natural instinct for work is of course a great point on which to base the training.

CHAPTER IV

MESSENGER DOGS IN THE FIELD

Nay, man may fail, though wise and strong,
Yet God can save.
A brave dog dashes from the throng,
And throws his shaggy length along
The boiling wave.
. . . Back, back, through 'whelming surge, for life or death
His task is done."

Anonymous, 1863.

I N estimating the value of the work of the messenger
dogs in the field, it is necessary to remember certain
essential facts, when comparing this means of communication with others more commonly in vogue. Runners and
telephones may certainly be sure and rapid in peace time,
but the imperfections of these are only too well known to
those who had to depend on them under war conditions.
If, under peace conditions, it may seem that these forms of
communication should take precedence, it will be found
that in the upheaval that takes place in war time, the more
mechanical methods become displaced, and the dog is then
more than equal to any of them. In support of this I
may mention an instance of a Brigade signal officer issuing
instructions, that, as far as possible, all important dispatches were to be sent by dog. On numerous occasions
the dogs were the first to bring back information of im-

portant operations and many urgent messages. On dark and stormy nights they were invaluable, and the time in which they did their work was approximately the same as in the daytime. The average speed of the dog was one-half to one-third of the time taken by runners in the daytime, and at night still less. Runners have come in cut and bleeding from barbed wire and other obstacles after having been lost for several hours in the darkness, while the dogs have come through safely and without delay.

I here give some statements of the work of the messenger dogs in the field, which were sent to me by the keepers when the dogs first went overseas. I have already stated that the importance of their work was not properly understood by either officers or men of the regiments to which they were attached, nor in the army as a whole. Later, when the real service they could render came to be understood, and when the regulations governing the dogs began to be enforced, all ranks were much more ready to assist the dogs. One of the most important rules for the troops to observe was to refrain from enticing or checking a dog on its journey.

Keeper Goodway, who was one of the earliest men to be trained and to go to France, mentions the difficulty for the dog by this regulation not being properly understood.

" The two are doing well, the Black Lurcher Bitch especially, she is splendid, takes no notice of the guns or anything ; they have both been running regularly day and night this last fortnight from advanced H.Q., to the rear —they used to do it in about 7 or 8 minutes where it takes a man over half an hour. The officers think they are splendid, and I know they have sent in a good report. One

6*

thing I was rather afraid of was the runs at night, when there is generally more shelling, but it makes no difference, they run quite as well in the dark as the daylight. The only fault about the big Collie ' Scott ' is, that he is rather a good-looking dog and everybody will make a fuss of him if they get a chance, therefore, if any soldier calls him he will stop to be made a fuss of ; the bitch being a bit savage-looking doesn't get spoken to, and she is absolutely the best."

Keeper Rea, who also went to France in the early days of the movement, makes the same complaint. These men both testify also to the fact, which was amply proved later, that the night time made no difference to the dog when at work.

" Old ' Tray ' is still as steady and faithful as ever, and is as sure as day and night and he can jump as good as any of them. ' Joseph ' is a good one and fast, only not as good as old ' Tray '—in rough ground ' Swallow ' is doing grand. I am keeping him in practice all the time. Pte. Reid, of the 13th R.H. of Canada, is at the same place as myself and we work the dogs between us. I take his and he mine. It is a hard job to keep the lads from making a fuss of them, it seems as though man and dog were made to go together. We are down on our old front again. (The dogs are running from 3 to 6 kilos per day, so keep in good condition. We have snow on the ground and it has been very cold ; to-day it is thawing a little, the ground is covered with snow still. Some very heavy strafing going on— steady here now. We got a bunch of Germans last night all dressed in white overalls and white smocks. I was thinking they would be a good rig for the Salonica dogs at night practice. I have good places for dogs and lots of good food."

Keeper Davis in his statement refers also to the question of night work.

" ' Joe ' and ' Lizzard ' have done some very good work out here both day and night. The dog is as good in the night as he is in the day, he is worth his weight in gold and the bitch is very good. I have had them come three miles at night in 20 mins. and they are just the same on any front that we go to. The dog can always be relied upon."

These statements from the keepers in the field were a great help to us in the training work at the school. For instance, we were not certain as to the effect of gas on the dogs. Keeper Brooks mentions this matter in a report on his dog " Tom." As a matter of fact, they were not so sensitive to this, on the whole, as one would perhaps have imagined.

" The dogs I brought out from England were taken away from me to be distributed amongst the other men, for we have to have 3 dogs each. I had 3 of the first lot sent out and the names are as follows :—' Tom ' (black and white spaniel). ' Moses ' (black, with a little white in neck, sheep dog). ' Fritz ' (the large German sheep dog). I am very pleased with them, they are doing some very good work ; they are running from the front line to Batt. Hdqtrs. which is a good mile and a half, and their average run is from 5 to 8 mins. which the officer thinks is very good. ' Tom ' has been gassed and got a bit of shrapnel but is quite well again.   I am going back on the 25th for 14 days' rest which I think we earned."

A later report on " Tom " is as follows ·

" No. 10 Cross Spaniel has been on the Ypres Sector for the last 12 months, having done some good work bringing back some urgent messages from 9 Division and the Highland Light Infantry, being gassed and wounded in the shoulder and getting some very close shaves from shrapnel going through the barrage, was in the advance until it finished."

Keeper Nicolson seems to have brought his dogs through a gas attack well.

" I have tried my three dogs in the trenches and found them all very satisfactory. The first time I sent them forward ' Jim,' the dog without a number, did record time ; the journey he did used to take a man one hour and 10 mins. to walk, and ' Jim ' did it in 22 mins., through barbed wire entanglements, and a large number of batteries. I noticed when he got near home some of the gunners tried to draw his attention, but he took no notice and came straight to the pill-box where I was billeted. It was very difficult ground he had to travel, the other two dogs were a bit slow. We are in again for the second time and I tried all three. ' Jim ' was sent up to the Test Station yesterday afternoon, and did his journey in 17 mins., which would have taken a man three-quarters of an hour to walk, and the little Irish terrier was sent up this morning before day-break and he did the same distance in 14 mins.

" The night before last we had a very nasty attack of gas and my dogs' helmets were not available, so they had to stand bare-faced and took no harm. I think they will stand much better than man. I had a bit of trouble with

Jim,' he got wounded in the head, so I dressed the hair off and got a syringe and some dressing from a Red Cross man, so he is going very well."

Keeper Osbourne gives an interesting instance of his dog " Jim " notifying the approach of gas. This was a small cross-bred retriever spaniel and was a most intelligent little animal, and is a different dog from the "Jim" mentioned in the foregoing statement.

Keeper Osbourne's Statement

" You will be highly gratified to learn that little ' Jim ' by his excellent services and consistency has justly earned our C.O.'s commendation who thinks he is easily the finest dog we have in France.

"One or two of his services to wit. While in the recent offensive in Belgium he carried important dispatches in wonderful quick time, and it is certain no one else could have delivered such dispatches under such terrific and heavy shell-fire without meeting with bodily harm.

" At present we are on a much more quiet part of the front, where long distances of trenches have to be traversed, and invariably little ' Jim ' covers the distance of approx. four kilos in the very good time of fifteen mins. And I feel sure you will agree with me that with his consistency this wonderful little dog is invaluable.

" On another occasion while in the first-line trenches little ' Jim ' was instrumental in first giving the warning of gas, due no doubt to his highly sensitive nose, thereupon he was immediately released with the warning to Hdqtrs., arriving there a little more than three-quarters of an hour earlier than the warning given by wire. His worth is beyond value and his services beyond praise, and I feel honoured to take care of such a very serviceable animal.

" At such times when gas is about I have to see to the putting of ' Jimmy's ' head in a man's P.H. Smoke Helmet, and I should be greatly pleased if you could inform me where to secure a mask for his proper protection, as of course a P.H. Helmet is made solely for the requirements of a man and does not adequately safeguard a dog."

OFFICIAL REPORT OF ABOVE DOG " JIM "

Dog 36.

Black. Cross between RETRIEVER and SPANIEL, about 3 years old. Brought from ENGLAND by Pte. OSBOURNE and worked with 1/6th R. War. R. since August, 1917. The most reliable dog ; has often done distances up to 4½ miles.

The speed in covering this distance was proved to be three or four times the speed of a runner.

Keeper Macleod gives an account of the way the dogs under his control picked up, after being gassed, and of the plucky behaviour of little " Paddy," in reporting himself at Headquarters, although wounded and left for dead. In this will be seen one of the many instances of courage and determination displayed by these dogs. " Paddy " was an Irish terrier.

" I left for France with three dogs in Nov., 1917, and went back to my old Division—34th. The G.O.C. Division appeared to be greatly interested in the dogs—that alone gave me some encouragement to do my best for the dogs.

" I went into the line at the back of Monchy, and kept my dogs beside me for a day,—they were taken up on the second night. They were sent back in the morning with a trial message, and all three of them did well. They were kept there for a fortnight, always running home in the morning. They never made any mistakes at all. We were sent into the line on 27th Dec. until the end of January,— 5 weeks, during which time the dogs ran once every 24 hours, covering the distance—a little over 5 kilos.—in something like 20 mins., over very rough country, which it always took the runner over one hour to get over. The dogs always brought messages, and usually saved a mid-day runner.

" We left on April 14th, 1918, and went up to Haze-brouck with the dogs 'Whitefoot,' 'Prince,' 'Paddy,' 'Mop,' 'Shag,' 'Swift,' 'Lloyd,' 'Jack,' 'Jock,' 'Wolf,' 'Tim' and 'Champion.'

" When the 29th Division came in and relieved the 31st, there was a small advance made then—the dogs did great work then—that was in Nièppe Forest Sector. The G.O.C. 88th Brigade wrote out, and had a note typed of which I got a copy, giving great praise to dogs 83, 84 and 65. The first two were ' Jock ' and ' Bruno,' the other ' Champion.' That was the first official praise we had from anyone. Then came another small advance, which proved the mettle of 3 more dogs, ' Whitefoot,' ' Paddy ' and ' Mop.' The first two were badly gassed, but carried on, they were 3 weeks in hospital after they came out of the line, but during the gas bombardment they never failed to give the greatest satisfaction. Once again there was a slight advance made, in which two other dogs, ' Bruce ' and ' Blue Boy,' were to the fore. Bruce came four different times from the front line to Brigade Hdqtrs. with messages which were of great importance. ' Blue Boy ' was killed in the first attempt to cross over from an outpost to the Hdqtrs.—2 runners had been badly knocked out trying to get through.

" About this time there was another slight advance in the Nièppe Forest Sector, but nothing out of the ordinary took place. At that time, ' Paddy ' was badly gassed in the front line, and came right back to the Section Kennel,—a distance of 17 kilos. When he came in he was totally blind, but went direct to his own kennel and lay there till I went to his assistance. In three hours he had his eyes open again and was as lively as ever. We were then transferred to the 19th Corps Signals in and around Kemmel Hill, and between that and Ypres. The first time that any dogs were in that part they did not do anything worth mentioning. However, there was going to be a big stunt on that front, and all the men and dogs were taken into the line together and placed by the Brigade Signals Officers who were in charge. The first message to come through was brought back by the dog ' Roman.' He brought through a request for reinforcements in men and ammunition, thereby saving a nasty situation. At the same time ' Paddy ' was again in the wars. He was led nearly up to the top of Passchendaele Ridge with the infantry; he was along with an officer and a runner at a farm-house which contained Germans. A German came out and took a revolver and shot the dog, which was left on the field for dead. He had lain there a long time before he came to himself. He reported at Brigade Hdqtrs. and word was sent to me to go and fetch him as he was badly hit."

The dog " Roman," mentioned at the end of Keeper

Macleod's statement, was a pure-bred tri-coloured collie, of the show type, and carrying a splendid coat, and with a long narrow head. He was a curious character, rather self-centred, and fond of taking his time on the journey, but imbued with a strong understanding always, of the absolute necessity of making his way homewards. In this connection I may here remark, that it is instructive and interesting to watch the growing of conscience—the sense of right and wrong—in the dog while under training. As the idea of duty becomes implanted in its mind, the uneasiness at stopping at any point *en route*, becomes gradually more marked. A promising dog that is beginning to understand the high responsibility that is placed upon it, even if it is tempted to linger, will generally make good, by increasing its pace when starting again. It is amusing to come across two or three dogs, at a point some distance from home, and watch them unobserved. They are going back with their messages, and are keeping up a steady lop, generally led by the best dog. Suddenly, something will attract one of them, and they may even all stop for a minute. The dog that knows its work best, however, will not long tolerate delay, and it soon trots off, and now sets the pace at a fast gallop, which the others are bound to follow.

While it is of course better that each dog should make its journey alone, it is impossible, while under training, and when sometimes fifty or sixty dogs are out in various directions, to keep them entirely separate, when they are released to bring their messages home. But in the long run it is a point of not much importance, as even if a promising dog may be momentarily detracted from the path of complete obedience, by one less trained or less conscientious, he himself will sooner or later come to see that it is much better to go straight, and will assist in impressing this on his more faulty comrade.

The dogs " Paddy " and " Roman " are both mentioned in the following official report.

OFFICIAL REPORT

" *DOGS*."

These were most useful. In the right Brigade the first intimation received that the final objective was reached was brought back by a dog in 40 mins. Dog 54 was shot at and wounded by a German Officer, who in turn was shot dead by an Officer of the 6th Wiltshire Regiment. This dog was reported killed in error by the Brigade as it subsequently turned up. In the left Brigade a message by a dog was received in 50 mins. saying, that the BLUFF had been captured, distance covered 6,000 yards. Another important message came back by dog which was of importance to the Division on our left.

Some of the dogs had never been in the line before, and considering this, their work was good throughout.

Unfortunately poor " Blue Boy " after faithful service laid down his life at Nièppe Forest. Keeper Matheson speaks of him when working under his charge.

STATEMENT OF KEEPER MATHESON

" I had two very good dogs and they did very good work. No. 67, a Bedlington, ' Blue Boy ' by name, he was a very reliable dog, he did very good work when the enemy tried to take Mount Kemmel last year. He was shot at Nièppe Forest bringing a very important message as the 31st Division was held up. The poor dog was liberated under a barrage of machine-gun fire and was killed on me.

" Poor old ' Mop,' No. 60, did very good and would run a message, say 4 miles, in 12 mins.—she was very reliable."

To revert once more to the subject of pure-bred dogs I may mention a collie called " Nell," which was one of the first to go to France. This was a sable and white, perfectly pure-bred dog, sensitive and highly strung, and to look at her one would have thought there was no room in her narrow skull for brains. Nevertheless she developed very wonderful intelligence, and worked steadily to the end of the war. It can safely be said that this dog alone saved hundreds of lives. She is now living in honourable seclusion, in the home of her keeper to whom she was devoted.

My object in specially mentioning again the subject of pure-bred dogs, is that a very general idea prevails, that only mongrels have any real sense of cleverness. My own experience goes to show, however, that while one comes across many extraordinarily clever mongrels, there are also quite as many clever dogs of the pure-bred varieties. These may sometimes individually need greater care and patience in training, as they are occasionally somewhat highly strung, but to suppose that pure-bred dogs are necessarily lacking in intelligence is a mistake.

Keeper Dowdeswell tells of the wonderful sense of duty displayed by his dog " Smiler," which was a lurcher cross. The dog brought his message in safely although severely wounded.

" I am sorry to have to tell you that I have lost poor old ' Smiler.' The Staff Capt. had taken him up the line and sent him back with a message which he brought back in 20 mins.,—a distance of 3 kilos. The poor old fellow's jaw was hanging down, being fractured by a bullet—I knew there was not much hope for him, but I took him to the A.V.C., after binding him up, and they immediately shot him. He had been going up the line with the General each morning and bringing his messages back in good time always. The General was very fond of him and told me yesterday he was sorry I had lost him."

After the first few months of experimenting, I was able to bring the training of the dogs to gunfire up to a much more effective standard, and shell-shock became much the exception. Keeper " Swankie," who went out early with two dogs, " Creamy " and " Ginger," mentions an unpleasant experience whereby " Ginger " suffered from shell-shock.

" I left here in September for Poperinghe—was there for 5 days, then went to Canal Bank with the 18th Divisioual Hdqtrs., from there to VARNA FARM, where I was attached to the 54th and 55th Brigades. It was there both my dogs were blown up by a shell. I found one that night but lost the other one for 3 days. My first night there, which was by no means comfortable for me or my dogs, I had to stand all night with my dog by my side. Next morning ' Creamy ' was taken out by the Brigade Major to the front line trenches, leaving at 7.30 a.m. Released at 1 p.m., arriving back 1.25 p.m., with a few messages and a map of the new position taken that morning, POEL CAPELLE BREWERY, approx. distance 6 kilos., time taken

25 mins. The 3rd day ' Ginger,' my other dog, was brought back to me and I found he had shell-shock. I tried my best to cure him but without success."

" Ginger," however, greatly recovered later on and was constantly in use in the field. Keeper Swankie's report continues :

" On one occasion the Div. General came to see the dogs work. Their duty that day was to carry 2 messages sent out by Message Rocket back to Brigade Hdqtrs., a distance of 1,000 yds.—time taken 3½ mins.

" After we had got the kennels fixed up, orders came for 8 men and 24 dogs to go up the line. I was amongst them and next morning went to Gentilles Wood, where I was attached to the 47th London Div. The dogs did splendid work there, and were working day and night. I lost one dog there, an old collie—he had carried 5 messages that day and was on his way back with his 6th one, when he was killed by shrapnel. By this time the French had taken over that part of the line, and we had to go to a place called Vignecourt where we were attached to the Australian Corps. My first trip up the line from there was to a place called Villers Bretonneux, where I was for 7 days, and during that time my dogs were working day and night. From there I went back to the Compound for 7 days' rest, then back to Villers Bretonneux for another 7. This time it was pretty rough in this part and the dogs had plenty of work and did it well."

The dog " Creamy " was a cream-coloured cross-bred lurcher with a semi-rough coat—a most affectionate and intelligent messenger. It did most of its work under Keeper

Swankie, to whom it was greatly attached. A further statement as to its work is as follows ·

" The last time this Div. (18th) was in action, I was sent to Brigade Hdqtrs. After being there for one night, my dog ' Creamy ' was taken out during an attack and carried a map of —— also a message from the front-line trenches back to Brigade Hdqtrs. Time taken was 25 mins., whereas a man took from 2½ to 3 hours. Under the conditions and heavy shell fire, it was very good, and my Officers were highly pleased with it, for the map and message were very important, and all other means of communication at the time failed."

Further testimony as to " Creamy's " sagacity is sent by Keeper Reid :

" I may say that Swankie's bitch ' Creamy ' helped the 3rd Londoners from being cut off on the right of Villers Bretonneux. She and ' Tweed' kept the Battalion in touch with Brigade Hdqtrs. There was no way of getting a message through only by a runner or a dog and the dog kept the way open."

Keeper Reid makes the following statement regarding his own dogs :

" I am writing this to let you know how my dogs are doing. I may say I have tried them all ways and they come home. To-day I had ' Tweed ' and ' Jock ' acting Batt. Runners from Batt. Hdqtrs. to Transport Lines, and they have done splendid. I had ' Tweed ' up the line and

Keeper Reid with Tweed (left).

[To face p. 96.

brought back a very important message through heavy shell fire. I am highly satisfied with my dogs.

" On May 2nd, 1918, I was sent to the 18th Div. There were no dogs that had been up before. On May 2nd at 10 p.m. the Hun came over on the Q.V.R.—my dog was up at their Batt. Hdqtrs. They were cut off from the London Regt.; they released ' Tweed ' with the message ' Send up reinforcements and small round ammunition.' He came through a Boche barrage—three kilos. in 10 mins. The French were sent up and filled the gaps, and straightened out the line, otherwise Amiens would be in the hands of the Germans. On May 8th I was with the Australians 48th Batt. They had moved forward, no runner could cross the open in the daytime—pigeons could not fly at night, they were in a bad place, so they sent for ' Tweed.' He made three runs at night, and one of the runs he was out on patrol ; they sent him back with a message ' The Germans are preparing for a raid ' and spoiled the Huns' plans."

The dog " Tweed " mentioned in the above statement performed some wonderful services. He was a Highland sheep dog, and took rather longer to train than usual, owing to his highly sensitive nature, in fact he was nearly rejected altogether, and it was only through the urgent representations of Mrs. Richardson, who discerned " Tweed's " fine character through his shyness, that he was retained and his training persevered with. Patience and great gentleness in handling eventually overcame his reluctance and timidity, and the clever management of " Tweed " in the field by his keeper brought this dog up to a very high standard.

A further account by Keeper Reid shows that the messages brought by the dogs, besides being frequently of the most vital importance, were at times of comparatively minor value, such as this one with the request for socks, but which nevertheless would make the greatest difference to the comfort of the troops ·

" For six months the three dogs were in constant work from the line. This same dog was with my Batt. 13th R.H.C., at Passchandaele on Nov. 8th, 1917. The Batt. had to go in and support the 3rd Canadian division. The O.C. wished dry socks for his men. There was no way to get a message back in daytime, he released ' Tweed ' with message ' Moving forward to-night. Send socks for men and some S.O.S. Lights.' "

" Tweed's " fine behaviour at Amiens, mentioned by Keeper Reid, deserves special commendation, and there are other occasions that stand out particularly, when other dogs did specially brilliant service. The attack at Kemmel Hill brought many of them into prominence. Amongst others, two dogs called " Flash " and " Boxer " deserve mention. The former was a brindle lurcher, the latter was a large, powerful Airedale. They were devoted to their keeper, Dixon. He reported on these two dogs as follows, soon after he arrived in France with them ·

" The two dogs I took out are doing well, I should say exceptionally well. I have not the least hesitation in saying there is not a brace of better dogs in this or any other country as Messenger Dogs. ' Boxer ' the Airedale is running like an engine. The lurcher bitch ' Flash ' beats him on this week's running by 20 mins., which is not a lot considering the breeds. The General of the

—— Division said that the Airedale was the best dog he had seen. ' Boxer ' was a bit long on Thursday, he had been at some carcase and tried to steal past into his bed but I saw him—he knew he had done wrong. The conditions are very bad for running dogs, such a lot of rubbish and dead carcases and abandoned cook houses, etc."

In this report will be seen the temptations which confront the messenger dog in the field and to which poor " Boxer " at first succumbed. The distinguishing sense of right and wrong is very highly developed in many dogs, especially in those which are trained, and " Boxer's " sense of duty evidently rose above the temptations of the flesh, as Keeper Dixon later reports on him :

" A staunch reliable dog, ran steadily and never let me down. Best time 3 miles in 10 minutes. On one occasion he went over the top with the Kents. Released at 5 a.m. with important message. He jumped at me at 5.25. A tip-top performance, about 4 miles. A great dog ! "

" Flash " was a very fast, clever dog, and Dixon reports :

" She ran every alternate week except two and was never once behind time."

These two dogs were both at Kemmel Hill. Dixon states in this connection :

" About the best week's running I did in my opinion was at Kemmel Hill in October with the 34th Division, when all my dogs did well. The times seem slow but they were really good, as the dogs were running belly deep in mud. It took a man two hours to go to the line. The conditions were horrible."

Keeper Hedley testifies to the good work of his dogs at this time and also during the last offensive of the war:

" I can faithfully say my dogs did excellent work, especially on two occasions. The first offensive which the Germans made on Kemmel Hill between the dates of 16th April and the 25th April, 1918, and the second was when we made the large offensive commencing Sept. 28th, 1919, at Ypres. They came back in splendid time."

Keeper Young had in his charge a very good cross-bred dog called " Dane." He was a powerful dog and did his work faithfully and well:

" 'Dane,' No. 29, he did good work all the time but I did not know what the messages contained, but during the German offensive on Kemmel in April, 1918, he fetched the situation reports every morning for 10 days, sometimes when all other communications were broken and very heavy shelling going on."

Keeper Brown had two good dogs, but unfortunately there is a tragedy in his report following the dog's good work at Kemmel Hill:

" My dogs have done very good work in the field. I was on the Hazebrouck Sector part of last summer and my dogs, ' Trusty,' No. 79 and ' Peter,' No. 78 were doing good work there taking messages and then I went to Kemmel Hill where they were taking in messages day and night. The Officer i/c Signals there was highly pleased with the work the dogs had done taking in messages day and night, and I went from Kemmel Hill to the Ypres Sector where my 2 dogs were killed with one shell, also the runner that was taking them to the front line—that was on 28th September. I was very sorry to have them killed as they were very good dogs."

The official report on the work of the dogs at Kemmel is as follows :

" On 17th April during the German attacks on Kemmel Hill, three more Messenger Dog Groups were sent up by road to XXII. Corps, and reallotted straight away by them to the 9th Division. These dogs were sent to Scherpenberg, which was the advanced 9th Divisional Headquarters. When they arrived, however, the Division was already retiring, and the groups were left for the use of the Brigade. It is of interest to note, that these dogs did sterling work, between Kemmel and Scherpenberg, during the whole of the German attack on Kemmel Hill."

The Report continues :

" The Messenger Dog Groups, which had been allotted to the XV. Corps had been reallotted by them, two Groups to 1st Australian Division, and two Groups to 1st Guards' Brigade. The Australian Division reallotted one group for use with their Brigade at Flêtre, and one group was used with the 2nd Brigade at Borre. The 1st Life Guards used their two groups in the Forest of Nièppe. These two groups were used by the 1st Guards' Brigade during the heavy mustard gas attacks on 22nd April, which caused so many casualties. Two out' of the twelve dogs were badly wounded, and all the dogs suffered from the gas, although they ultimately recovered.

" Exceptionally good work was done by these dogs through the Forest of Nièppe, and interest in the messenger dogs, as a means of communication in heavily shelled areas, was aroused."

I may say here, that during a tour of inspection which I made during the war, I myself saw the dogs working through the Nièppe Forest, and was greatly pleased with the manner in which they negotiated this difficult sector.

Since the Armistice, I have again made an entire and close inspection of the entire battlefields, with the object of studying the various sorts of surfaces the messenger dogs had to traverse. The Ypres sector is, of course, one of the worst, and in this shell-torn ground the dogs must have had all their energies called out. In wet weather, when every step brought a risk of drowning in the terrific shell holes to the human runner—and this apart from the cease-less firing—a message would have a far greater chance of being brought through safely by a dog. If the dog fell into a hole, it could easily swim and scramble out, and it would certainly be able to negotiate these obstacles much more quickly, creeping lightly along the lip of the craters.

At Passchendaele also, the terrible slope presented un-ending dangers to anyone forced to move rapidly, and here, too, excellent work was done by the dogs, which would have been appallingly difficult, if not impossible to runners.

Other parts of the line presented different features, but in every sector I came to the conclusion that message carrying could be carried out with far greater dispatch and certainty, as long as the rules for working were enforced, and the troops given a good understanding of the work the dogs were doing.

As showing the tremendous amount of ground covered by

the messenger dogs during their work in the war, I may quote from the official report on this point, which even then only deals with the time after the formation of the dogs into concentrated service, and does not take into account the period previous to that, when they were allotted to battalions.

" During the nine months the Messenger Dog Service was working as a service, the three section kennels were moved thirteen times, and shifted practically from one end of the line to the other.

" During this period section kennels were placed at Kruistraatt, Kemmel, Noordpeene, Wallon Capell, Morbeque, Hinges, Villers au Bois, Viller Bocage, Vaux, Dury, Menin, Blandain, Lille.

" Both at Lens and Villers Bretonneux, dogs had to run through towns, which the enemy daily saturated with mustard gas. At Lens especially, the dogs were called upon to use their intelligence."

Another portion of the official report reads :

" Proceeded to Battalion Headquarters of 1/14 Rifle Brigade. The C.O. who had been using messenger dogs from the front line trenches back to the ramparts at Ypres, told me that all the dogs he had used had done extremely well and proved very reliable.

" Visited A.D. Signals XIX. Corps, who showed me some reports which had just arrived in from different divisions, on Messenger Dogs. The Divisions continue using their dogs, and taking them up with them as the troops advance. Excellent use is being made of the dogs, and in two cases, the first news that their objectives had been taken, was brought in by Messenger Dogs."

Keeper Errington in the following report gives an account of his three dogs " Jack," " Whitefoot " and " Lloyd." " Jack " was an Airedale, and the other two were Welsh terriers of a large size :

" I started running these dogs in difficult circumstances at Strazeele on April 14th, 1918. The roads were busy with traffic and stray dogs in abundance, cattle, sheep and poultry were being killed by the heavy shelling. We had 10 dogs running, in which the dogs were thoroughly tested —I found the greatest difficulty at first was the Relay Post. The dogs were sent to this post, a distance of 2 kilos., and had to wait there until another runner came to take them to the front line 1½ kilos., the waiting here was from 30 mins. to 2 hours, therefore the dogs usually stopped at this point the first few runs, but with practice it was soon all right. I started at Nièppe Forest (Hazebrouck Front) in May, the dogs did some excellent running—the distance was 5 kilos. at first, the average time 45 mins. ; the front got quieter and the distance was reduced to 3½ kilos. ' Whitefoot ' acted as runner for Brig.-Gen. Taylor, who personally took the dog to visit his Battalions in the line. After receiving the Intelligence Report, he released the dog, which ran to Brigade Hdqtrs. 7 runs in succession. This dog's time was 23 and 25 mins. The greatest difficulty here was gas which affected the pads of the feet, especially during damp or wet weather ' Jack ' was killed and ' Whitefoot ' and ' Lloyd ' were footsore, but soon were running again.

" During damp weather and when it was muddy and heavy running for dogs, I used to clip the hair between the toes (pads) that prevented any gas in the mud from adhering to the feet and causing inflammation.

" At the taking of Villers Bretonneux in August ' Lloyd ' arrived in 10 mins. 1½ kilos. after being released and was slightly wounded in fore leg, the message stating that ' their objective had been taken.' ' Whitefoot ' ran the distance in 12 mins. with a message asking for stretcher bearers or R.A.M.C. men.

" During October the enemy was falling back, and we were moving every other day although we still kept running the dogs. On Oct. 14th the dogs were taken to the firing line and had to cross the Canal by boat. They were liberated on the 16th by the Scottish Rifles. No. 59 message was ' they were still advancing.' Time 65 mins. —distance unknown. ' Lloyd ' was killed by shell and was found several days later. During this running, I found that dogs ran faster and keener if they were on strange ground, but should as far as possible have at least 10 hours in their new home to give good results, but in cases we have run them after only 2 hours and with good results. ' Whitefoot ' never failed once and was very reliable and fast. ' Lloyd ' was also a good dog but not so fast.

" In one Division on certain days there was no communication by telephone, as they suspected the enemy of tapping the wire with some instrument and the dogs did the running, which was usually a list of requirements to be taken up at dark as no one was allowed to travel during daylight.

" The dogs kept in good health and the food was all right, and the Veterinary Surgeons were always ready to give any help."

Keeper Errington's remark on the length of time which the dogs should be given in a station should be commented upon. What he says is I think perfectly sound, namely

that the dogs should be given a day in a new point.
He however has found, he says, that they have worked with
good results after only two hours in a new place.   This
rapidity of adapting themselves to a new environment
has been confirmed by other keepers.   On many occasions the dogs have arrived at night and within an
hour or two have been taken up through the darkness to
the front line to be released in the early morning.   This
sense of direction and remembrance of where they last left
their keepers is certainly marvellous.   It points to a sense
of location which in the human being is much less developed.

The rate of speed with which the dogs accomplished their
journeys was of course an important point, and the fol
lowing statements from different keepers touch on this.
While a rapid dog was of greater value than a slow one,
still the question of reliability is the most important point
of all, and a dog which might not make such a brilliant
show on the time sheet, might nevertheless be worth its
weight in gold on account of the absolute certainty of its
steady if somewhat slower return.   On this point Keeper
Macgregor says :

" I wish to let you know that my dogs are doing well
over here.   I have them running from one company to
another.   The retriever did 8 kilos. in a little over half
an hour and the other in 20 minutes."

Keeper Ferriby sends the picture of his dogs with their
running prize, the result of a competition :

" I am writing to let you know that my mate Woof
and I won the silver cups with my three dogs ' Coffee,'

' Vulcan ' and ' Sharp.' The latter is the dog which I brought out with me. He has done one mile in 1 minute 50 seconds."

Keeper Bevington in the following report speaks with pride of the rapidity with which his dogs returned to him, and the trouble to which he went to verify the timing. The fact may also be observed that the dogs had to start their work after being only two hours in their new quarters :

" I was sent up to No. 3 Section at Amiens and all three dogs were sent up with the troops in that big attack on July 4th—you will remember that as the Americans were in it for the first time, two of the dogs were taken over the top in the attack with the Australians and No. 106 did a good run also. 104 he did a very good run for the Artillery Officer, the forward observation post he ran from, and 105 was lost for a time, but in my opinion he was stolen as I found him with some artillerymen on a different part of the front.

" The next important front where they were working was on the Vimy Ridge sector, and they did some very good runs there. In one small attack there, my dogs were sent up in the attack, and it was running on duck-boards that time, not on open country, and they brought back all these messages in very good time, as anyone can see by looking at their records, that should be at the 8th Army Corps.

" They also ran some very good runs at Maroc from Hart's Crater, and Harrison's Crater. Then we began to advance, and our kennels were in Hythe Tunnel. This will show that my dogs were very fair dogs—they were sent out of the tunnel to the forward post Batt. Hdqtrs., a distance of three thousand yards, and came back in four minutes, with what I believe was an important message; it was a map of the German Lines. That four minutes' run was done by 2 dogs, 104, and 106, and you can imagine how they must have run to have done it in that time; it was a night run and was very dark. Anyway, I will convince you that what I have said is true. The two dogs came in to the tunnel, I got the messages out of the carrier and was half way to the Signal Officer, when I was met by the R.E. Corporal who said that my two dogs had been released. Of course I told him that they had reached me—Well! he said, he would not believe it that a dog could beat a telephone message, evidently when the dogs were released the telephone man had telephoned through to say the dogs had been let go. I was not satisfied, I wanted the thing correct, so I went to the Signal Office and asked the man at the forward post what time he released the dogs, and he replied that they had been released exactly six minutes, so as it was a minute's walk from the kennels to the Signal Office and with the time it took to get the messages out of the dog's collar, I say they did their run in four minutes, and there was not a dog beat that time.

"The last important place they ran, was from a wood that the Germans held part of, in front of St. Amand, near to Valenciennes. There was an attack there one night and my three dogs were sent in that. I may add that they had only been with me two hours at this new place before they were sent up to the front-line Company, and they came back in fairly good time. The Officer spoke well of them."

Keeper Waters had two black-and-white collies, " Pierrot " and " Domino." They were both handsome dogs, " Domino " especially. Unfortunately he had to be sent back from the line on account of shell-shock.

" I went to the 15th Corps on the 26/7/18 and went into the line to the 9th Div. near Meteren, and was sent to the 26th Brigade. My dogs were running through Meteren to Fletre, about 6,000 yards. I had a black-and-white collie, ' Pierrot.' He was a good dog, and did some very good work. The black-and-white collie, ' Domino,' was not of much use. He had been with No. 3 Section and had shell-shock, and would not run when there was any shelling going on. I then went to the 30th Div., 93rd Brigade, on the left of Fletre. I went up the line with two dogs ' Pierrot ' and ' Domino.' As there was heavy artillery fire on that front ' Domino ' was useless, but ' Pierrot ' made some good runs."

Keeper Fergusson, in his statement, confesses to his predilection for Airedales for the work. and while it is true that they are remarkably hardy dogs and not inclined to be nervous under fire, still I have convincing recommendations as to other breeds from other keepers in the field.

" I consider the most useful dogs for the work are Airedales, pure or cross-bred. They have not great speed, but they are sure, and soon find their way on strange ground.

" The most outstanding instance of usefulness which I have on record was with my Airedale dog, ' Jock,' No. 73. He on several occasions in the month of June, 1918, was taken forward with the attacking forces, and was sent back with messages stating that the positions had been captured, giving the estimate of casualties, and giving map references of the new line taken up. This dog, also ' Bruno,' dog No. 72, did many other good runs. I have omitted to state that the distance which ' Jock' carried previous mentioned messages was 5 kilos.—times ranging from twenty-three to twenty-eight mins. (5 kilos=3½ miles) over rough ground swept by machine-gun and shell-fire."

Keeper Shayler, who gives the following report, was one of the earliest men to be trained. The whole messenger dog service owes a debt of gratitude to those loyal keepers who gave their whole mind and energy to overcoming great obstacles in the first few months, when the work of the dogs was hardly understood at all by those in the field. It will be observed, from his statement, how much easier it was for both dogs and keeper to work, where they were received with sympathy and interest.

" After one month's training of Messenger Dogs at Shoeburyness, I proceeded to France on the 13th July, 1917, with two dogs, one an old English sheep dog, ' Betsy,' and an Airedale, ' Jim.' Landing at Le Hâvre, we entrained for Poperinghe, Belgium. I reported to the 14th Corps H.Qrs. After four days there I went forward to Brig. H.Qrs. at a village named Elverdingh. This place was heavily shelled, but the dogs ran very satisfactorily for the first time under shell-fire. I stayed there for about seven weeks. I then reported to the 19th Corps H.Qrs. and then went forward to Ypres. I stayed there for two months. My dog ' Jim' was killed by a shell. He had been a good reliable dog. At this time of the Dog Service it was uphill work for both men and dogs, there being no one directly in charge in France. From Ypres I came out for a rest. The next move was to Flesquières, near Bourlon

Wood, but only staying here for a few days. The continual movements made it nearly impossible to use the dogs on this sector very much. In February I received orders for Central Kennels, Etaples. At this place men and dogs of the service were made into sections of sixteen men and forty-eight dogs, with one sergeant. I was placed in No. 1 Section. On April 15th, four men, including myself and dogs, proceeded to Nièppe Forest, Hazebrouck Section. These were the first to leave Etaples, and were for trial before the full sections were settled. I stayed in this sector for ten days ; the dogs proved satisfactory. They were sent forward a few hours after arriving at Brig. H.Qrs. to the 2nd Australian Brigade. This position was heavily shelled, more especially with gas shells. I then returned to the 22nd Corps H.Qrs., at which place we made a Section Compound, other men and dogs being sent up to form this section. We only stayed there for three weeks, and then went to the 22nd Corps H.Qrs. at Houtkerk, which was the position of No. 1 Compound for some time. I went forward from Section Compound to Kemmel Hill sector, 18th Bgde., 5th Div. At this position my dog 'Betsy' ran well and in good and regular time. I was relieved after seven days' work here and returned to the compound, where the dogs were kept in training. My next week's work was at Ypres, where the dogs had a very difficult place to work, as they had only two ways of returning, either by going round to a bridge or through a tunnel under the Canal bank. At this place my dogs worked for the York and Lancs. Battalions, for whom they carried good messages. My next place after a week at the compound was at Batt. H.Qrs., between Ypres and Kemmel Hill. This place was well under the observation of the enemy and heavily shelled, causing communication by wire to be frequently cut off, and making it impossible for runners to be used in the daylight, and so the dogs were very much called for. I was working here for the A. and S. Highlanders, 33rd Div. These men were good with the dogs, and my dogs carried good messages for this battalion. At this time I was doing fourteen days in the line and fourteen out. During these fourteen days, my dogs worked for the Cameronians and Scottish Rifles, two good battalions for dogs. My next fourteen days was the same position with the 1st Middlesex Batt. and 1st Queen's. At this time I had a new dog called ' Tiger,' who was a good reliable dog. I never knew him to fail. He carried good messages in very regular time. The route he ran over was very heavily shelled. At the end of fourteen days, I returned to the compound, which was still at Houtkerk. I went forward again to the same place, reporting to the A. and S. H. Batt. H.Qrs. and the 1st Batt. 119th Regt. U.S.A., where ' Betsy ' did some fine work. Always doing 12-15 hours' forward duty and returning in good and regular time. Usual time 10-15 minutes, often wet and covered in mud. The U.S.A. troops were good with the dogs. My dogs carried Sealed Code, Maps and other messages from raiding troops. After being buried in this sector by a shell, I returned to Etaples, not going up again as the Armistice was signed."

Keeper Dempsey gives a graphic description of his work in the field. Conditions were, by now, getting much easier for the keepers, as the work of the dogs was understood by the officers under whom they had to work. At the same time it is extraordinary the amount of prejudice there has been to overcome. I have come across officers with a pile of official reports on successful dog work in front of them,

Messenger dog bringing a message across a canal on the Western Front.

Messenger dog.   Putting the message in the dog's collar.

Messenger dog on Western Front going over shell holes.

[*To face p.* 113.

and who have never themselves, tested them, who blandly remarked that they did not believe in dogs. It is this unreceptive attitude to new ideas, that has been at the bottom of so many mistakes of the war.

" My first turn in action was on the Kemmel front, where the dogs did very well, although the ground was very rough, in fact the conditions were very bad indeed. I stayed there for seven days, and was then relieved, and went back to Corps Headquarters for seven days. Then from there I went to Ypres Ramparts. During my seven days there, my dogs carried very important messages day and night. On one occasion, when with the York and Lancs. Regt., ' Paddy,' one of my dogs, carried a message, when all other means of communication failed. This message was about the artillery. Another of my dogs, ' Prince,' also carried sealed messages. I do not know what they were about, for the signal officer was awaiting the dogs coming in, and took the messages out. The time taken by ' Prince ' was fifteen to seventeen minutes, while ' Paddy ' did it in ten to eleven minutes. The distance was $3\frac{1}{2}$ to 4 kilos. The ground was very rough for dogs. ' Paddy ' was gassed here, and still he carried on with his work day and night without fail. After my seven days there I went back to Ypres again, and stayed in for fourteen days with the 49th Division, my dogs carrying messages all the time. Sometimes the dogs were taken away in the morning, and released at night, then they would change, and would take them at night and release them in the morning. My dogs ' Prince ' and ' Paddy ' always brought important messages. Most of them were sealed. The signal officer was always eager for the dogs to come in. In fact the officers, N.C.O.'s and men of the division were all interested

8

in the dogs, and would trust them with all sorts of important messages. It took the runners one hour and five minutes to go from my dug-out, whereas it only took 'Paddy' eleven and 'Prince' fifteen minutes. The dogs can get over rough ground far quicker than can a man. Later I got a very good dog called 'Rags.'

"I then went back to Ypres and got attached to the 29th Div. I used my three dogs there. Each of the three bringing important messages, and coming in first-class time. I worked there for the Royal Dublin Fusiliers, Leinster Regt. and K.O.S.B.'s, and they were all very well pleased with the dogs, as there was always a heavy bombardment on, and it would not be safe for a man to bring the messages. I then got relieved for seven days. I went back to the same Div. on the same front. They were preparing for a big push. It began on the 28th Sept. The Royal Fusiliers took two dogs, 'Prince' and 'Paddy,' they were away for two and a half days, as all the lines of communication kept good, but they got cut with shell-fire and both dogs were released with messages and returned all right. I do not know what the distance was to be exact. The officer told me he thought it was about nine kilos. It was raining very hard during that time, and that made the ground very difficult to get over with the heavy shell-fire and troops advancing. I then got relieved and came back to Houtkerk. I stayed there ten days training and exercising the dogs. I then got orders to go up the line and got attached to the 36th Div. I joined the 107 Bde., 36th Div., two miles from Dadeszeele and stayed for one night and marched into Dadeszeele next morning at 3.30 with Bdg. H.Q. My dogs were taken away at 4 p.m., the Div. advanced about ten kilos. Oct. 14th. On the 16th two of my dogs, 'Prince' and 'Rags,' arrived with messages. While I was with the 107th Brigade, Keeper Buckingham was with the 108th Brigade. On the morning of the 14th this division advanced and the enemy put up a terrific barrage. All the lines of communication were cut and a battalion of the Inniskilling Fusiliers were cut off. This battalion released a dog, which returned to Buckingham, and thus gave news of the plight of this battalion. The dog was thus the means of getting reinforcements sent up to the relief of the Inniskillings and that gallant body were saved from being wiped out. The Brigadier-General was delighted with the dogs' performance and congratulated Buckingham on his management of them."

The "Paddy" mentioned by Keeper Dempsey is a different one from that in Keeper Macleod's possession, and which has been mentioned earlier. There were several Irish terriers in the service, and I am afraid the tendency to call them all "Paddies" was too strong to overcome, although there were also a number of "Mikes" and "Mickies." Keeper Hammond had a "Paddy" on which he reports favourably ·

"I left Shoeburyness the first week in October, 1917, taking with me two dogs, 'Paddy' and 'Nansen.' I first ran them at Passchendaele, and was on that sector until the beginning of March; 1918. 'Nansen' was killed on the first run, but 'Paddy' was a splendid dog, and never made a mistake during the six months I had him. I consider his best record was carrying a message from Batt. H. Qrs. on Passchendaele down nearly to Ypres, a distance of five miles over about three miles of duck-boards You can imagine the time saved, when 'Paddy' did it in 27–30 minutes and the Batt. runners were doing it in

8*

nearly two hours. After being transferred to the Messenger Dog Service, I did not go up the line again, as I had suffered severely from shell-shock, and my health gave way. Ramsey took ' Paddy ' and I have no doubt at all that he is one of the best dogs that ever went to France."

Keeper Alcock gives an account of a very nice collie he had :

" *Re* No. 140. This dog went over the top with three or four Brigades of Australians on several occasions. One occasion in particular was when an attack was made on Villers-Bretonneux on the Somme. He came back with a dispatch ' Urgent ' which contained the details of the attack,—a distance of $4\frac{1}{2}$ kilos. in 18 minutes. There was very heavy shell-fire at the time. While in front of Douai this dog advanced roughly seven miles, and brought the only message received when Douai was captured, as all the wires were broken. He completed his journey in 55 minutes. The other dogs I had were taken out in attacks and did good work also. I am sure they must have saved a large amount of life."

Another of the men was Keeper Corporal Coull. He took a very intelligent and conscientious interest in his work, helping to educate public opinion, as well as working the dogs. He states :

" Directly under my personal care were ' Buller ' (Airedale), ' Trick ' (collie), and ' Nell ' (setter bitch). At the outset ' Buller ' was somewhat inconsistent, but in a very short time he blossomed out into a very fine working dog, and did some very fine running. He carried messages, such as requisitions for ammunition, material, food, and the most common, but not the least important—the situation reports.

" When the Australian troops were making repeated attacks on the fronts between Villers-Bretonneux about April and May the service of ' Trick ' was repeatedly and specially in demand, and on various occasions on that front he brought back the first messages of the progress of the attacks, and also requests for further materials necessary for the successful carrying out of operations. On one occasion special mention was made in divisional orders of the good work done by ' Trick ' and another dog, called ' Willard,' on the front of the left of Corbie. On that occasion ' Trick ' and ' Willard ' brought back the first message of an important and successful operation by the Australian troops. By his good work ' Trick ' was always sought out by any signalling officer when any message of importance and urgency was to be sent, and never once did he prove untrustworthy.

" A black retriever dog called ' Dick ' had a wonderful record, worthy of the V.C. While carrying a message in the Villers-Bretonneux sector he was wounded very severely in the back and shoulder. The dog completed his run in good spirit, and was ultimately sent to the section kennel for treatment from the veterinary officer. As no foreign bodies could be located in the wounds they were stitched up, and he was soon healed up and at work again. He did his runs in the line as well as before, and seemed all right when we moved to the 8th Corps. A day or two after moving the dog was seen to be suffering, and the attention of the vet. was called to his state. After a few days' observation, the veterinary officer concluded there was some foreign body in the wound, and so, as poor Dick was on the point of death, he was ordered to be destroyed.

" At the post-mortem examination it was discovered that a rifle bullet was resting between the shoulder and body, while near the small of the back a piece of shrapnel was found lodged close to the spine.   Through all his suffer ings the dog carried out his duties cheerfully and most faithfully until he was overtaken by death."

The keepers found considerable difficulty at first in working the dogs with the Australian troops, as the latter were somewhat indifferent in observing the regulations with regard to the dogs in the field. When, however, a commanding officer possessed the gift of discernment and recognized the real benefit of using the dogs and seeing that they received proper treatment, the result appears to have been satisfactory.

Lieut.-Colonel Owen H. Read, Canterbury Regiment, sends the following report :

" WAR DOGS

" During the winter of 1917–1918, while the Division was in the Ypres Sector, I had two of these attached to my battalion.

" Owing to the broken nature of the ground we were holding and the bad weather which was experienced, communication between the Company and Battalion Headquarters was exceptionally difficult, and the dogs on several occasions proved of great value in conveying messages when other means of communication failed, being far more rapid than runners, who in some cases were unable, owing to heavy shell-fire, to deliver their messages.

" Although the conditions in this sector were very trying, the dogs always carried out their work in a thoroughly satisfactory manner and were on many occasions of great assistance.

" (Signed) OWEN H. READ, Lieut.-Colonel,
" Canterbury Regiment,
" N. Z. E. F."

Another Australian officer told me that one of the sights that impressed him most was his first sight of a messenger dog. He saw it first coming from the direction of the front-line trenches—a little Welsh terrier. The ground it was going over was in a terrible condition and was absolutely waterlogged. The little creature was running along hopping, jumping, plunging, and with the most obvious concentration of purpose. He could not imagine what it was doing until it came near, and he saw the message carrier on its neck. As the dog sped past him he noticed the earnest expression in its face.

Keeper Sergeant Brown was a very intelligent handler of the dogs, and he not only worked them in a scientific manner, but he also did excellently in educating the men in the understanding of the benefit to be obtained by adhering to the regulations governing the dogs. He says:

" When the men understood the use of the dogs, I had no trouble, but before that they did not know they were being used as messengers. I got permission to go to the battalions in my division and give the men a lecture about them, and after that all went well. We then moved to another front. I looked over the ground and found it very rough, with holes and wire, and a great distance from the line—about 6 miles. The officer wanted me to work the dogs over this, which I did for a few times till my dogs were getting very bruised and cut, so I stopped them. The officer found the great use they were, as the men were taking about three times as long. I then worked my dogs in a very dangerous part from the battalion to the post, as it was not safe for a man even at night, and the dogs worked at night. When the Brigadier heard the work the dogs were doing, he wanted a great many more. I was then called back to the base, and they were anxious for me to leave the dogs behind, as they knew they had been the means of saving scores of lives. The runners were more than sorry, as they were always asking for more dogs. The old idea was that a dog's life was nothing, but after the experience I have had with them in the field it has taught me to love and respect them as never before.

" I was moved to another sector, and after I had explained the use of the dogs to the men all went well, and one and all were surprised at their good work, as they had to run about three miles through a forest with streams and ditches. They were in the open and on the move all the time, and it was quite impossible for a man to get through the gas sometimes. The dogs worked there for three days, and then they required rest as they were done up and some were wounded. One little bitch, 'Sulky,' nearly had her leg cut off, but it did not prevent her from coming in, and as it happened, she was carrying a very important message. On one occasion I sent a dog with an officer and his runner who was going out on patrol, and when out on No Man's Land the officer was killed. The dog brought back the message and the position, so that another officer could be sent out. I also remember a dog being taken on a bombing raid, which was undertaken with the object of finding out just who was in front of us. The dog 'Vulcan' came back with some papers and a shoulder strap off a German's coat with the regimental number on it.

"On another occasion in the advance on the Ypres sector (1918) the same dog was taken over by the Colonel of a battalion, but he was out of touch with the corps I was with, till the dog came in. I did not know what the message contained, but it was an important one, as this particular battalion wanted to keep up the advance, and they wanted the Belgians to advance as well, in order to make it a success, as they found little opposition in front of them and were well through.

"I understand also that the first news of the capture of Hill 60 was brought in by one of the dogs. On one occasion we had attacked a German sap, and were trying to hold it. We had run out of bombs, and the doggie was sent back with the casualty report, and for more bombs to be sent up."

The Americans had no dogs of their own and viewed the messenger dogs with envy. Keeper Sergeant Brown says on this point :

"I had great trouble to prevent the Americans from appropriating the dogs, as they had no dogs of their own, and they all spoke of the great success of them everywhere."

Corporal Taylor sends the following report, in which will be seen the difference it made to the men when they came under an officer who took genuine interest in the work of the dogs, and also the difficulties experienced in working them, when the troops were not sufficiently instructed as to the importance of refraining from petting and feeding the dogs. This was constituted a disciplinary offence in the German army, and was severely punished.

" I landed in France with my two dogs, ' Major ' and ' Maggie,' and was sent to my old Brigade. Their headquarters were in an old slag heap, just to the rear of Hermies village. I did not get much help, nor did I find anyone very interested in the dogs at first, but on coming out of the line for a rest, I was taken over by the Brigade Signal Officer, Lieut. Parkes. He was very interested in the dogs, and did a lot for me. The consequence was, that next time we were in the line, the dogs were used night and day, with good results. We were in the line from Jan. 25th till Feb. 21st, and the dogs were running from the front line to advanced Brigade Headquarters.

" At different times, our officer had silent days, when no wires were used, only runners and dogs. Of course the dogs beat the runners every time, and never made one mistake. It was a very unhealthy spot—a lot of shelling. Poor ' Maggie ' was shell-shocked. I buried her in a little hut I used to keep her in. It would have been a great thing, if all officers had taken the same interest in their dogs as did Lieut. Parkes.

" I returned to Etaples when the dog service was reorganized, and my next venture was at Kemmel Hill, April 16th, 1918, and went up with Keepers Young, Headly, Ferriby, Radford, and Ferris with eighteen dogs. The men had nearly all the same dogs they brought from England. We went to the 9th Division, and ran the dogs for the 26th and 27th Brigade. Their Headquarters were just to the right of La Clythé. Here I found I was wanted to run dogs from Spoil Bank, close to the Canal, through Voormazeele, a distance of 14 kilos., so made a relay post, at Ridge Wood, leaving Keepers Young and Ferris at

Headquarters. It was here men and dogs had a rough time, as the enemy was doing a lot of heavy shelling, ready for his attack and capture of Kemmel Hill, 10 days later. My own dogs were ' Major,' ' Rab,' and an unregistered dog. The work was difficult for the dogs, as Brigade Headquarters moved about so much, on account of so much shifting. After the dogs had done about 6 journeys, Headquarters moved, so that the dogs had to turn to the right on the Dickebusch Road, instead of to the left, where they had been running before, but four out of the six dogs did it all right. My bitch ' Rab ' was hit by a piece of shell on her second journey. She managed to stagger in with her message, but I could see there was not much hope for her. I bound her up, and carried her down to Brigade Head-quarters, but she died the next day.

" I was watching for the dogs the next day, to come in, and saw ' Major ' and that fast bitch of Ferriby's, I forget her name, racing back over the ridge. As they were passing a battery of artillery, the enemy opened out with eight-inch stuff.

Ferriby's bitch was killed, but ' Major ' got through· I could see that ' Major ' was actually dodging the shells. He took a wide sweep from where the first shell fell, and kept working out further. The time for that run was a record, about 6 minutes. It took me an hour to walk and run the distance. Radford's dogs were doing the night duty, also Ferriby's, and never made a mistake. Hedley's dogs also did all that was asked of them. They were on day duty.

" I might mention here, that I found one or two of the dogs were losing time, so I went forward to find out the cause, and found them in a trench, on their chains, and a lot of pieces of bully beef put in a tin in front of them.

Very kind, of course, but spoiling the dogs. I at once informed the signal officers of both Brigades, and it was stopped. That was one of our greatest troubles—troops feeding and fussing about the dogs.

" On the 25th of April, I was wounded in the attack by the enemy on Kemmel Hill, and was in hospital some time. I returned to No. 1 Section early in October. I only had one turn in the line however, with my three dogs, as ' Jerry ' threw up the sponge. I might say, that ' Major ' was given to Keeper Hunt, when I was in hospital, and he did hundreds of runs for him. One run he did for Hunt is worth telling. Taken forward in an attack, an advance was made of 17 kilos., without much opposition. ' Major ' was then released by the Brig.-General's orders with a message asking for help at once. ' Major ' did the 17 kilos. in one hour. He isn't much to look at—a cross lurcher and deerhound, but a heart of gold."

The following Report given me is of interest ·

" In July, 1918, when the main force of the German attack had subsided, and our policy appeared to be to cut off small portions of German salients, preparatory to the great general advance, small battalion offensives were in vogue, with a view to taking and consolidating strong points, from which larger offensives were eventually pressed forward. In these small offensives (which were more than raids, inasmuch that the ground taken was consolidated and held), the messenger dogs proved of invaluable service. Telephone wires were almost impossible from the front lines of newly-acquired territory, and as these offensives were carried out invariably by night, pigeons were useless. The result of a raid, or minor offensive, giving the line captured and consolidated had to be returned to Higher Command by runners, or dogs.

" In one instance in an attack on a small factory, half a mile west of Vieux Berquin, the attack had to cross very flat, swampy ground, with two small streams, the advance originating from the western edge of the Forêt de Nièppe. The report that the attack had been successful, and a plan showing the line consolidated, reached Corps Head-quarters by messenger dog in 50 minutes, the total distance being 13½ miles. (I regret I do not know how far from the Corps Headquarters were the Kennels, and how much of the distance was done by the telephone, but I should say very little). The next report, which was a duplicate, sent off at the same hour by runner to Brigade Headquarters, and thence by telephone, arrived at Corps Headquarters one hour and thirty-five minutes after the messenger dog report arrived. This statement was pub lished in Corps intelligence, and in the 29th Divisional Orders of that month.

" (Signed) K. E. MILFORD,

" (Major R.F.A.)."

The record of the dogs' work, was kept by the keepers when on duty at the front, on time sheets, of which the following are specimens :

KEEPER'S TIME SHEET FOR DOGS

Dog's No.	Time left Kennels.	Time sent.	Time arrived back.	Distances	Time to run. Minutes.	Date.	Remarks.
111	10.0 p.m.	10.55 p.m.	4.55 a.m.	3 kilos	—	July 27	All Trench running.
110	11.30 a.m.	1.0 p.m.	1.15 p.m.	3 ,, S. Bn.	15	,, 28	Wea' & good.
112	11.30 a.m.	1.10 p.m.	1.30 p.m.	3 ,, L. Bn.	20	,, 28	,,
110	3.20 p.m.	5.25 p.m.	5.40 p.m.	3 ,, R. Bn.	15	,, 28	,,
112	3.20 p.m.	6.40 p.m.	7.5 p.m.	3 ,, L. Bn.	25	,, 28	,,
111	10.15 p.m.	—	1.40 a.m.	4 ,, S. Bn	—	,, 28	Weather good.
110	12.0 midnight	4.27 a.m.	4.55 a.m.	4 ,, L. Bn.	27	,, 30	
112	12.0 midnight	—	3.25 a.m.	3 ,, S. Bn.	—	,, 30	
111	5.30 p.m.	7.4 p.m.	7.31 p.m.	3 ,, R. Bn.	20	,, 30	Kept to lorry.
110	9.50 p.m.	9.45 a.m.	10.30 a.m.	4 ,, L. Bn.	45	,, 30	Weather fair.
112	12.0 noon	3.0 p.m.	3.30 p.m.	3 ,, S. Bn.	35	,, 30	,,
111	12.0 noon	2.5 p.m.	2.18 p.m.	4 ,, R. Bn.	13	,, 31	Gd.
110	4.20 p.m.	9.25 p.m.	9.55 p.m.	3 ,, S. Bn.	30	,, 31	G d.o
111	4.20 p.m.	8.5 p.m.	8.20 p.m.	4 ,, L. Bn.	15	,, 31	Weather fair.
112	11.15 a.m.	2.47 p.m.	3.17 p.m.	3 ,, S. Bn.	30	Aug. 1	G d.o
110	11.15 a.m.	2.26 p.m.	2.40 p.m.	3 ,, R. Bn.	14	,, 1	G d.o
111	4.15 a.m.	8.55 p.m.	9.15 p.m.	3 ,, L. Bn.	20	,, 1	Wea fair.
110	12.20 a.m.	2.32 p.m.	3.5 p.m.	4 ,, L. Bn.	33	,, 2	
111	11.0 p.m.	—	6.30 p.m.	4 ,, L. Bn.	—	,, 2	,,
112	11.0 p.m.	6.30 a.m.	7.5 a.m.	3 ,, S. Bn.	35	,, 2	
110	12.0 noon	4.6 p.m.	4.20 p.m.	4 ,, L. Bn.	14	,, 3	Wea ,, fair.
112	4.40 p.m.	8.50 a.m.	9.5 a.m.	4 ,, L. Bn.	15	,, 3	,,
111	5.0 a.m.	7.30 p.m.	8.5 p.m.	3 ,, R. Bn.	35	,, 3	6oth Brigade.

Dog's No.	Time left Kennels	To Unit	Time sent	Time arrived back	Time taken (Minutes)	Time kept away (Hours)	Date	Remarks
110	6.0 p.m.	R. Battn.	6.55 p.m.	7.7 p.m.	12	1	September 8	Very good.
111	6.0 p.m.	L. Battn.	7.16 p.m.	7.35 p.m.	19	1¼	8	Good.
110	10.0 p.m.	R. Battn.	12.0 a.m.	12.10 a.m.	10	14	9	Too long.
111	10.0 p.m.	L. Battn.	9.25 a.m.	9.36 a.m.	11	11½	9	Too long.
112	6.0 p.m.	R. Battn.	4.55 a.m.	5.15 a.m.	20	11	10	G. d.o
111	6.0 p.m.	L. Battn.	5.42 a.m.	6.0 a.m.	18	11¾	10	Very good.
110	8.0 a.m.	L. Battn.	1.45 p.m.	2.0 p.m.	15	5¼	10	Very good.
111	2.0 p.m.	R. Battn.	7.30 p.m.	8.25 p.m.	55	5½	10	G. d.o
112	2.0 p.m.	R. Battn.	8.5 p.m.	8.10 p.m.	5	6	11	Very good.
110	2.0 p.m.	L. Battn.	6.40 a.m.	6.50 a.m.	10	9¾	11	Very good.
112	8.0 a.m.	R. F. Coy.	2.0 p.m.	2.10 p.m.	10	6	11	V'y good.
111	8.0 a.m.	R. Battn.	11.56 a.m.	12.30 p.m.	34	4	12	Very good.
112	6.30 p.m.	L. Battn.	10.7 p.m.	10.15 p.m.	8	3	12	V'y good.
110	6.30 p.m.	R. Battn.	9.30 a.m.	9.42 a.m.	12	15	12	Very good.
112	9.0 p.m.	L. Battn.	5.50 a.m.	6.0 a.m.	10	7¾	12	Very good.
111	12.15 p.m.	R. Battn.	7.23 p.m.	7.35 p.m.	12	7	13	Very good.
112	12.15 p.m.	L. Battn.	7.7 p.m.	7.15 p.m.	8	7	13	Very good.
111	8.15 a.m.	R.F.Coy.	12.55 p.m.	1.48 p.m.	53	4½	13	G. d.o
110	8.15 a.m.	L. Battn.	2.20 p.m.	2.30 p.m.	10	6	14	Very good.
111	6.0 p.m.	R. Battn	10.12 a.m.	10.20 a.m.	8	4	14	Very good.
112	9.0 p.m.	L. Battn.	9.15 a.m.	9.30 a.m.	15	12	14	Very good.
111	8.0 p.m.	R. Battn.	6.23 a.m.	6.30 a.m.	7	2	14	Very good.
112	12.30 p.m.	L. Battn.	7.14 p.m.	7.16 p.m.	2	7	15	Ext. good.
111	7.0 p.m.	L. Battn.	9.45 p.m.	9.55 p.m.	10	2½	15	V'y good.
110	7.0 p.m.	L. Battn.	5.0 a.m.	5.25 a.m.	25	10	15	G. d.o
112	8.0 a.m.	R.F.Coy.	12.2 a.m.	12.48 a.m.	46	4	15	Good.
111	8.0 a.m.	L. Battn.	12.18 a.m.	12.35 a.m.	17	4	15	Very good.
110	6.0 p.m.	R. Battn.	10.30 p.m.	10.45 p.m.	15	11	16	Very good.
112	6.0 p.m.	—	5.0 a.m.	5.20 p.m.	20	11	16	Very good.
111	8.30 p.m.	L. Battn.	7.0 am.	7.10 a.m.	10	10½	16	Very good.

Distances: R. Battn., 1,200 yards. L. Battn., 2,200 yards. R. F. Coy., 5 to 6 kilos by Trench.

I here give an extract from the instructions laid down by the British Army for the management of the messenger dogs in the field :

TRAINING AND EMPLOYMENT OF MESSENGER DOGS

5. By the use of trained dogs as message carriers, runners can be saved and better communication obtained.

The messenger dog is trained to return to his keeper from any point to which he may have been led.

A dog will not return to any keeper except his own.

A dog can travel by day or night fairly rapidly over ground where a man cannot go at all, or only very slowly ; and because he travels faster, and is a smaller target, a dog has a much better chance of getting through a barrage than a man.

The reliability of the dog as a message carrier depends on his being trained to go with certainty to his destination without paying any attention to bombardment, rifle fire, etc.

The best trained dogs will, however, be quickly rendered unreliable by injudicious handling when sent up for work in the front line, and it is essential that the instructions for their use should be strictly adhered to.

6. The procedure as regards the employment of messenger dogs is for the keeper to go up with his three dogs to, say, a Battalion Headquarters, where the keeper remains. This point is called the " Back Station." The three dogs are then led away by any soldier, from the keeper to, say, Company Headquarters. This point is called the " Forward Station." Then when a message has to be sent back, it is put in the carrier on the dog's collar and the dog released. It is advisable to train a dog on a particular

Tr ining messenger dogs to rifle fir

Training messenger dogs to cross barbed wire entanglements.

route, taking him out a short way and letting him go at once, and then repeating at greater distances till his final station is reached. After that, he should be retained for, say, an hour before being released, and subsequently the time of retention should be increased until he will return to where his keeper is by day or night after 12 hours' stay at his forward station.

This training to a particular route takes some time and trouble, and should be done both by day and night, and the extent to which it is necessary will depend somewhat on the intelligence of the dog. The keeper should be able to give information on this point.

7. To ensure success in getting dogs to return from the forward station to the keeper it is essential that :—

(i.) The dog or dogs should be led up on a chain by a man who is a stranger to the dog.

(ii.) At the forward station the dogs should be kept chained up ; if possible, they should be sheltered from wind and weather, and they should be given water but no food.

(iii.) The men who lead up the dogs should not make friends with them, and the dogs should on no account be petted or made much of.

8. Dogs should not be kept at a forward station for more than 12 hours away from their keepers ; consequently, not more than one keeper and his three dogs from any one Group should be on duty at the same time. After a period of 12 hours the keeper and his three dogs will be replaced by the remaining keeper and his three dogs of the Group. During the 12 hours a dog is on duty he can, after making a run back, be again sent forward as often as opportunity offers for leading him forward.

After a tour of seven days in the front line (during which

9

period each keeper and his three dogs have been doing 12 hours on duty and 12 hours off duty) the whole-Group should be sent back and replaced by another Group from the Section Kennel.

9. It is most important that when dogs are sent forward from their keeper they should be allotted to definite Commanders of Companies or Posts, who then become responsible for the care of the dogs while at their forward stations and for the messages sent back by the dogs to the back station.

10. (*a*) A dog released from a forward station should invariably carry a message, and each message must state the hour at which the dog is released.

(*b*) Dogs should always be released separately; that is, with an interval between each. They must not be released together.

FEEDING DOGS

11. Dogs should be fed once in 24 hours.

No food of any sort must be given to them whilst they are on duty away from their keeper.

At the station where their keeper is, they will only be fed after they have completed their 12 hours' turn of duty.

The authorized daily ration of a dog is 1¼ lbs. food, composed of :—

> ¾ lb. broken biscuit or bread.
> ½ lb. horse flesh.

¾ lb. maize meal per week is also issued for each dog.

If it is impossible to obtain the authorized rations for dogs at forward stations, the dogs should be fed on broken bread or scraps obtained from the Battalion cook.

Each keeper will take up with him two days' rations for his dogs.

To prepare the food, the meat should be cut up into small pieces, then boiled, and the meat and the water in which it was boiled should be poured over the biscuits and allowed to soak for at least half an hour.

PROTECTION OF DOGS FROM GAS

12. Dogs are not so susceptible as human beings to gas poison, and a dog will run and arrive at his destination through gas which an unprotected man could not traverse.

The gas has, however, a certain amount of effect, and a dog who has been subjected to strong gas may be incapacitated for a considerable time, or die from the effects.

It is not practicable to provide a dog with a gas mask. Every effort should be made to protect the dogs until their services are necessary, and on the first sign of gas they should be placed in a shelter protected by a gas-proof curtain and kept there till required. If in forward areas this is not possible, they should be released and allowed to make their way back.

Tests made with " Mustard Gas " show that such gas has little permanent effect on dogs, and practically no effect on their feet.

Commanders of formation or units to whom dogs are allotted will issue orders as to what is to be done with the dogs when the gas alarm sounds.

CASUALTIES

13. If a keeper becomes a casualty, his dogs should at once be returned to the Section Kennel and a report made

9*

to the Officer i/c Messenger Dog Service of the Corps who will detail a keeper and three more dogs to replace the dogs returned to the Section Kennel.

14. If more than one of the dogs of a keeper become casualties, the keeper and any remaining dog should be returned to the Section Kennel and a report made to the Officer i/c Messenger Dog Service of the Corps asking that a keeper with his three dogs should be sent up.

15. Dogs so seriously wounded or sick that recovery is improbable may be destroyed at once and the collar and any other equipment returned to the Section Kennel.

Veterinary Arrangements

16. The arrival of a Section Kennel in any Corps area is at once to be reported to the nearest Mobile Veterinary Hospital.

Dog Collars, Message Carriers, Chains and Muzzles

17. Every Messenger Dog has a *leather collar* on which are his registered number and a message carrier.

18. The *message carrier* (which is always to be kept on the collar) is made in two parts which fit one into the other ; the two parts are held together by a piece of string. When a message is to be placed in the carrier, the dog's collar should be pulled round so that the carrier is uppermost, the two halves of the carrier pulled apart, the message inserted, the two halves pushed well home and tied together and the collar slipped round so that the carrier is under the dog's neck. The dog should then be released without his chain.

19. The Officer to whom the dog is allotted will give

instructions for the *chain* of the dog released to be kept to fasten up a dog replacing him ; or, if the dog is not replaced, for the chain to be returned at first opportunity to the keeper at formation or unit Headquarters.

Dogs sent up to a forward station to which a chain has already been sent will be led up on a rope or other lead and chained up on arrival.

20. Dogs which are sent up muzzled are those which are liable to be savage. The *muzzle* is not to be removed and the dog is to be run with his muzzle on.

ORDERS FOR TROOPS IN THE FRONT LINE

21. A Messenger Dog may be recognized by his collar, on which is a tin cylinder in which the message is carried.

Messenger Dogs will be distinguished by some device such as a scarlet tally, which can be easily seen. These distinguishing marks will be promulgated in orders.

Messenger dogs are not to be hindered when on a run.

At no time are they to be petted or offered food ; if found near a cook-house, they should be hunted away.

Any dogs who fight messenger dogs, and bitches on heat, must be sent out of the area in which messenger dogs are working.

LOST MESSENGER DOGS

Lost Messenger Dogs should be taken to the nearest Signal Service Unit.

CHAPTER V

" Shall damned oblivion ever quench that flame ?
N° ! that viewless essence shall outlive the world,
Immortal as the soul of man it served."

POPE.

THOSE persons who desire to instruct the growing thought of the young in a successful and harmonious manner will usually, if they are wise, study the metaphysical aspect of the subject. This is also true advice, with regard to the training of all animals, and, in proportion as the instructor does this, will he be successful or the reverse. A close study of the relationship of man to the animal kingdom through the ages, discloses many interesting facts and salutary lessons. It reveals the fact, that wherever, and in whatever, man recognizes the presence of good,—cherishing and cultivating it,—the object of his care, from that time, becomes useful and harmless. This applies, as anyone can see, to the Vegetable Kingdom, in which all carefully cultivated species, immediately excel the properties of the wild varieties. And it also, with equal truth, applies to the animals.

Had man at all times recognized this, and realized his tremendous responsibility towards the Animal Kingdom, we should not now have large numbers of savage, dangerous animals, nor vast collections of timid, nay, terrified, creatures. Where man has set foot in newly-explored territory, seldom or never trodden, the animals are tame, and advance to meet him with charming confidence, which is only dispelled, when they find their trust is betrayed.

In confirmation of this conviction that this sense of fear in the animals for man must have been acquired, and is not in any way natural, I may quote Mr. Darwin, who says: " I have already discussed the hereditary tameness of our domestic animals. From what follows, I have no doubt, that the fear of man has always first to be acquired in a state of nature, and that under domesticity it is nearly lost. In all the few archipelagoes and islands inhabited by man, of which I have been able to find an early account, the native animals were entirely void of fear of man ; I have ascertained this in six cases, in the most distant part of the world, and with birds and in animals of the most different kinds. At the Galapagos Islands, I pushed a hawk off a tree with the muzzle of my gun, and the little birds drank water out of a vessel which I held in my hand. These wolf-like foxes were here as fearless of man as were the birds, and the sailors in Byron's voyage, mistaking their curiosity for fierceness, ran into the water to avoid them. In all old civilized countries, the wariness and fear of even young foxes and wolves are well known. At the Galapagos Islands, the great land lizards were extremely tame, so that I could pull them by the tail, whereas, in other parts of the world, large lizards are wary enough. The aquatic lizard of the same genus, lives on the coast, is adapted to swim and to dive perfectly, and feeds on submerged algæ. No doubt it must be exposed to danger from sharks, and, consequently, though quite tame on the land, I could not drive them into the water, and when I threw them in, they always swam directly back to the shore.   See what a contrast to all the amphibious animals in Europe, which, when disturbed by the most dangerous animal, man, instinctively and instantly take to the water !

" The tameness of the birds in the Falkland Islands is particularly interesting, because most of the very same species, more especially the larger birds, are excessively wild in Tierra del Fuego, where for generations they have been persecuted by the savages.   Both at these islands, and at the Galapagos, it is particularly noteworthy, as I have shown in my journal, by the comparison of the several accounts up to the time when we visited these islands, that the birds are gradually getting less and less tame, and it is surprising, considering the degree of persecution which they have occasionally suffered, during the last one or two centuries, that they have not become wilder ; it shows that the fear of man is not too soon acquired."

The French naturalist, Gaede, says :

" It is with the Bible in the hand that we must enter into the great temple of Nature to understand the voice of the Creator."

If this method of research had been more frequently followed by students of nature in the past, there would not be to-day such a host of theories in connection with creation, which lead up to a certain point, but are incapable of any definite conclusion, because most of them are based on faulty premise.

The instruction in Genesis, in the first chapter, on the subject of nourishment for both man and beast is as follows :

" Behold, I have given you every herb bearing seed, which is upon the face of all the earth, and every tree, in the which is the fruit of the tree yielding seed, and to you it shall be for meat. And to every beast of the earth, and to every fowl of the air, and to everything that creepeth upon the earth, wherein there is life, I have given every green herb for meat, and it was so."

The dominion over the fish of the sea, and over the fowl of the air, and over every living thing that moveth upon the earth, could not have been, therefore, based upon that system of compulsion and slaughter, to which man has reduced the original mandate. " God saw everything that he had made and behold! it was very good." Therefore, the power of the dominion must have been one of love.

This strange and terrible misunderstanding of the loving intention of the Great Creator of all things is announced later in Genesis :

" And the fear of you and the dread of you shall be upon every beast of the earth, and upon every fowl of the air, upon all that moveth upon the earth, and upon all the fishes of the sea ; into your hand are they delivered."

But this degraded concept of man's duty towards the animal kingdom, only came after that debased condition of mind, which is known as the fall of man, had become manifest. It would seem, therefore, as though man will have to alter this attitude, and return once more to his original understanding, in which the animals are given into his care to receive love and protection. Until his mental outlook on this particular point is adjusted, just so much proportionally is he excluding himself from that state of mind which is called Heaven, and from which he will continue to exclude himself, until he does justice to the rest of creation.

Milton says :

> " Discord first.
>   Daughter of Sin, among the irrational
>   Death introduced, through fierce antipathy :
>   Beast now with beast 'gan war, and fowl with fowl
>   And fish with fish ; to graze the herb all leaving,
>   Devoured each other ; nor stood much in awe
>   Of man, but fled him, or with count'nance grim
>   Glared on him passing.   These were from without
>   The growing miseries which Adam saw.'

How different is the picture of creation, as shown forth in the first chapter of Genesis, when love reigned supreme between man and beast, and when that understanding must have obtained, which is graphically described in the Book of Wisdom (Apocrypha)

" God made not death, neither hath He pleasure in the destruction of the living. For He created all things, that they might have their being ; and the generations of the world were healthful ; and there is no poison of destruction in them, nor the kingdom of death upon the earth."

It would be as well if this generation awoke to the great obligation placed upon it, of bringing this happy condition to pass once more. That it will have to be done sooner or later, there is no question of doubt, and God's immutable laws, which grind " exceeding small," will, metaphorically speaking, reduce to " powder " that mental attitude, which resists the mandate.

Love for, and the protection of animals, should be taught in all schools, and the churches might easily take a more energetic attitude on this point, than they have done in the past.

So far is this from being done, however, that we find the children instructed to assist in destroying whole communities of animals, such as sparrows, flies, rats, etc. These irregularities of production among the animals, nearly always result from some disorderly or insanitary method of man himself, or by his interference in some way, with the laws of Nature. It would be well, therefore, if he remedies his mistakes himself, without blunting the natural instincts of love and pity for the animals, in the minds of the children, which are infinitely more valuable to the race, than are any material expediencies.

It will be remembered that the Covenant was made with the animal creation, as well as with man, and reads in Genesis : " And God said, This is the token of the covenant which I make between Me and you, and *every living creature.* . . . And I will remember my Covenant which is between Me and you, and every *living creature of all flesh.* "

The egotistical point of view, which man has adopte in allotting to himself the promises of the Bible, and of leaving the animal kingdom without them, is indefensible. Some of the greatest thinkers on this subject uphold the standard of the animal kingdom, and I may quote Professor Romanes—the great authority on animal instinct. He says :

" Just as the theologians tell us, and, logically enough,— that if there is a Divine Mind, the best, and indeed only, conception we can form of it, is that which is formed on the analogy, however imperfect, supplied by the human mind ; so with inverted anthropomorphism we must apply a similar consideration to the animal mind. . . . And this consideration, it is needless to point out, has a special validity to the evolutionist, inasmuch, as upon his theory, there must be a psychological, no less than a physiological, continuity extending throughout the length and breadth of the animal kingdom."

Addison, when writing on the subject of instinct, says :

" I look upon instinct, as upon the principle of gravitation in bodies, which is not to be explained by any known qualities inherent in the bodies themselves, nor from any laws of mechanism, but as an immediate impression from the first Mover, and the Divine energy acting in the creatures."

The above illuminating statement is especially interesting, when we notice that one of the definitions of the word "instinct" means "urged from within," and yet another explanation is "animated," derived from *anima* —soul.

The description of the animal kingdom, pictured by Isaiah, is certainly a state which has previously existed · " The wolf also shall dwell with the lamb, and the leopard shall lie down with the kid ; the calf and the young lion and the fatling together ; and a little child shall lead them.

" And the cow and the bear shall feed ; their young ones shall lie down together ; and the lion shall eat straw like the ox ;

"And the sucking child shall play on the hole of the asp ; and the weaned child shall put his hand on the cockatrice den."

" They shall not hurt nor destroy in all My holy mountain ; for the earth shall be full of the knowledge of the Lord, as the waters cover the sea."

This prophecy, as to the return of this harmonious understanding between man and beast, has not yet been fulfilled, but in the insistence by man for more humane treatment for all animals, one sees the gleam of the dawn, and one knows that, as thought in this direction progresses, as it is certain to do, the entire prophecy will be completely fulfilled. The time will come, when the commandment,

" Thou shalt not kill," will not be accepted in the watered-down rendering, " Thou shalt do no murder," but will be taken as a solemn injunction as it stands in the Bible, and as it is certainly meant to be understood. Those of tender heart who yearn for the driven steer, the dumb, bewildered sheep at the shambles, the little stricken mass of feathers falling from the skies, the terrified dog on the vivisection table, may take comfort, that the age is not far distant, when man will awaken to the awful responsibility he assumes, when he misuses or takes the life of any one of God's creatures. He will then understand, that the Giver of all Good loves all the animals, and that they are *His* creatures, and that if left unmolested, and, on the contrary, protected and tamed, they will all begin to reflect this love, of which man will be the channel, and will be gentle and affectionate both to man himself, and to each other. If man is obedient to this commandment, " Thou shalt not kill," and discards his wilful and limited interpretation of it, he will then begin to find countless other sources of food-supply coming to him, of which he has been hitherto unaware, and the seeming necessity for taking the life of any animal, in order to minister to his own needs, will be no longer apparent. The animals themselves will then also find other sources of supply, in place of preying on each other.

This latter statement may seem difficult to credit, but if anyone likes to make a close study, they will find, that it is even now extraordinarily apparent, how strongly animals,—dogs especially,—reflect the mentality of those with whom they associate. This can be seen in the dogs of different nations. The bulldog and the fox-terrier, may be said to represent the tenacious, and also the sociable qualities of the English race, the Dandie Dinmont and the Scotch terrier, the independent and argumentative characteristics of the Scotch, and the Irish terrier partakes to a remarkable degree of the impulsiveness and relish for " a bit of a shcrap," of his master. The underlying ferocity in the Prussian character, is strongly reflected by the Great Dane—the favourite breed of the German students, —and, until well tamed by long residence in this country, is always capable of unexpected outbursts of anger.

When travelling in Norway and Sweden, I have been struck with the sedate and aloof demeanour of the dogs, which so closely resembles the human inhabitants of these countries. The very puppies disport themselves in a more dignified manner, than is usually seen elsewhere. The gay insouciance of the French, is well represented in the poodle, the inscrutability of the Chinese in the chow, the wild and lawless spirit of the mountainous races of middle Europe, in the savage sheep dogs of these regions,—and so on, in varying degrees all over the world one can see, that the dog, the closest associate of man, partakes of his master's qualities.

Coming down to individuals, this is even more apparent, and one can almost judge the character of any person, by noticing the sort of dog they keep, or, to put it the other way, the dog has been selected and trained according to the tastes of the master or mistress, and reflects these attributes of mind whatever they may be. Thus, at opposite ends of the scale, one gets the keeper's night dog, and the timid and circumscribed little lap-dog of the old lady. In pondering this matter, therefore, it is perfectly apparent, that the dog, owing to this intimate association with man, very closely assimilates the characteristics of the governing human race ; and, therefore, the most solemn obligation rests with the latter to reflect only those qualities which are desirable of perpetuation. This applies in relation to all the animal kingdom, and as man ceases to kill, so will the animals cease to do so also.

It may be asked what has all this to do with the training of War Dogs ? The answer is—*a great deal*, for the study of the metaphysical aspect of the subject ; that is to say, the research into character training, which is really mind training, assists one very greatly in the education of animals—and enables one to perceive the soul in the creature.

As I will show in other parts of this book, and especially in the chapter on the homing training, that the most successful results are obtained when the dog is taught to rely on this intuitive prompting from within, rather than on any material guides it may find without, and it can perhaps be understood how important it is for the trainer, to comprehend the original psychology of the dog.

It is a great compliment to man, that when he does find the soul of anything, and uses it well, how wonderful is the response ! It may be said, that, as a whole, this happy state has, to a great extent, been reached in regard to the dog, which, as I have shown, is so closely in touch with the mind of his master, and we are beginning to perceive that many characteristics which we have hitherto considered as belonging exclusively to human beings, and far above the animals, are really as much within the possession of our dogs as of ourselves.

Admitting, therefore, that the dog is capable of reflecting and manifesting the attributes of mind, by teaching it (and expecting to see the result of this teaching), the highest qualities in man, such as honesty, reliability, endurance, patience—in fact, the qualities of soul,—the trainer starts his work, cleared of many limitations that have been held over dogs, and, indeed, over the entire animal kingdom, but which are now, thank God, rapidly breaking down.

It is often considered a curious fact, that the dog receives such unfair treatment in the Bible, and those who love the " Good Book " and also the dog, find it difficult to reconcile the two points of view. This is easily explained, however, especially when what I have already pointed out is considered, in connection with the relationship of the dog to the mind of his master, and when it is remembered that the Bible is a Jewish book, and that the dog was held to be unclean by this race.

In spite of this attitude, however, on the part of the Jews, it would appear that at one time they must have had a high understanding of the dog, as we find that Caleb, the faithful and discerning spy of Israel, seems to have had the sense of faithfulness attached to him, and that his name means " Dog of God."

Renan, writing on this in his " History of the People of Israel," says :

" Often with names of this kind, ' El ' " (which means God) " was omitted, Irham being used instead of Irhamel, Caleb instead of Calbel. This last name, irregular as it is, need not create any surprise, for Dog of El was an energetic way of expressing the faithful attachment of a tribe to the God to which it had devoted itself."

It will be remembered, that when Moses sent a representative of each of the tribes to spy out the land, " flowing with milk and honey," Caleb was the only one of them, who showed fidelity to the Lord's command, and recommended that the children of Israel should go forward and possess it, and also the courage to believe it could be done. Whereas, the other spies allowed their fear of the fierce and gigantic people of the land, completely to obscure the remembrance of the solemn trust and injunction placed on them as a people. On account of this fidelity of attitude on the part of Caleb, we find the following promise given to him :

" But my servant Caleb, because he had another spirit with him, and hath followed me fully, him will I bring unto the land whereinto he went and his seed shall possess it."

The fulfilment of this promise is later on spoken of :

" And Joshua blessed him, and gave unto Caleb the son of Jephunneh, Hebron for an inheritance.

" Hebron therefore became the inheritance of Caleb, the son of Jephunneh the Kenezite, unto this day, because he wholly followed the Lord God of Israel."

The object of quoting this at length, is to accentuate the fact, that the fidelity of this Jewish hero is inevitably associated with the dog, as it was the custom of this race to bestow names on individuals according to certain mental characteristics manifested by the person. Companionship from the dog is, however, hardly ever mentioned in Jewish writings, one exception being the dog in Tobit (Apocrypha), which is spoken of on two separate occasions, as accompanying the young man Tobias on his journeys : " And the young man's dog went with them."

That it is the fact that certain magnificent qualities of mind have been conserved and perpetuated in the dog through all the ages, from time immemorial, and which explains one's vehement rejection of the Biblical, Jewish attitude towards this animal, is due to the Egyptians, who in times past greatly venerated it, and even worshipped it. Dogs were considered valuable for hunting purposes by the Egyptians, and were also treated as companions and pets. Gazing up into the glittering heavens, the farmer observed a glorious star, whose appearance always coincided with the rising of the Nile, which would bring him all he desired for his land. His simple mind was impressed with the fidelity of the star, and casting about for the most faithful thing he could think of to compare it with, he remembered his dog, and so called Sirius the Dog Star. Blaze, a writer on the dog in 1843, says :

" The dog being a symbol of Vigilance, it was thus intended to warn princes of their constant duty to watch over the welfare of their people. The dog was worshipped principally at Hermopolis the Great, and ultimately in all towns in Egypt."

The city of Cynopolis was built in honour of the dog, and priests celebrated solemn festivals in its honour. All this showed that certain very high qualities were recognized as appertaining to the dog, and while one section of the inhabitants of the world utterly failed to appreciate this, another large portion jealously preserved the high and noble concept of man's friend and comrade. We, therefore, owe a great debt of gratitude to these early dog lovers, as they, without doubt, preserved those qualities in the dog from which we benefit at the present day. The dog in those Eastern countries, where the inhabitants have for centuries looked upon it as an outcast, even to this day shows a lack of sympathy and understanding towards man. These qualities, and also intelligence, courage and fidelity, are all there, and were the attitude of the human being in these countries towards the dog to change, they would revive.

An interesting article by Colonel Hamilton Smith, published in 1861, points out that · " Even the Mohammedans, while they shrink from his touch as defilement, are compelled to recognize the courage and fidelity of the dog.

He, moreover, is lifted into the region of the supernatural by no less an authority than the Koran. Three animals, and only three, are permitted to share the joys and repose of Mohammed's paradise. The camel, on which the prophet rode during his famous flight from Mecca, the ass of Balaam, and Kitmer, the dog of the seven sleepers, who, with his master, entered the cave in which, year after year, they lay wrapped in mysterious slumber, who fell asleep with them, and who, with them, was at last raised to receive the reward of his care and fidelity. The Mohammedan legend asserts, that, as the seven youths were on their way to the cavern, in which they intended to take refuge from their heathen persecutor (the Emperor Decius), they passed Kitmer and attempted to drive him away, upon which God caused him to speak, and he said : ' I love those who are dear unto God ; go to sleep therefore, and I will guard you.' So Kitmer ' stretched forth his legs in the mouth of the cave,' and during his sleep of three hundred years turned himself from side to side like his masters."

The Aryan races were also great dog lovers, and associated the dog with some of the most solemn moments in the human life. Thus we find there was a belief, that a dog accompanied the departing soul on its journey to heavenly places, as companion and guardian, and it was the custom, very often, to introduce a dog into the death-chamber, so that the dying person should be comforted by the sight of the creature of whose race, a member would keep him from loneliness on his journey.

The whole basis of the training of the war dog rests on recognizing, and cultivating, certain qualities of mind in the animal. These are, among others, fidelity, courage, honour, endurance, and the homing instinct. Hearing, sight, and scent, are also all trained and accentuated, but these last attributes must have their origin in the first mentioned instincts, in order to obtain successful results.

FIDELITY

As the Egyptians were amongst the earliest to appreciate and celebrate the fidelity of the dog, so through all the centuries do we find the quality extolled, and all who have had experience of the creature, know that it is true, and that one can hardly exaggerate as to this wonderful instinct, so multitudinous are the proofs in history and in one's own individual experience. As an illustration, I may mention a curious instance I came across, when I stepped into a cinema theatre to see a war film, in the earlier days of the war. As the film was passing, the lecturer asked us to observe the dog, which would shortly appear on the screen. He mentioned, that it belonged to an officer in a certain regiment, and that it was lying beside its dead master, no one being able to induce it to leave, at the time. He mentioned the name of the regiment, and I knew I had sent an Airedale to an officer in this regiment.

As the film moved along, there on the battlefield I saw this Airedale, crouching beside the officer's body !

Fidelity to his master, is certainly one of the most accentuated qualities in the dog. Sir Walter Scott, who had a very great love for dogs, says :

" The Almighty, who gave the dog to be a companion of our pleasures and our toils, hath invested him with a nature noble, and incapable of deceit. He forgets neither friend nor foe ; remembers, and with accuracy, both benefit and injury. He hath a share of man's intelligence, but no share of man's falsehood. You may bribe an assassin to slay a man, or a witness to take his life by false accusation, but you cannot make a dog tear his benefactor. He is the friend of man, save when man incurs his enmity."

George Jesse, in writing on this aspect of the dog's character, touches a note, which I think wonderfully discerning, as to the attitude of the dog to man ·

" It has been well remarked, that the poets of various lands, and different ages, have delighted in commemorating the virtues of this favourite animal, as though they recognized in his devotion to man, something of the love and obedience, with which man should look up to his Heavenly Father and Almighty God."

It always seems to me, as if the dog turns to us, as though, in the meantime, all he knows about God, must come to him, through us.

I have very seldom indeed known a really treacherous dog ; that is to say, one that will bite the hand that cares for it. So rare indeed has this been, as to prove that such a condition of mind in the dog is entirely abnormal, and, as a matter of fact, I have always been of the opinion that such animals were insane.

I remember the case of a very large, fine, bull mastiff, which was offered to the War Dog School. It had never been off the chain for four years, as it was so savage, that no one could approach it with safety. With great difficulty, it was sent to the school, and had to be taken out of the railway van, by means of long poles. On arrival, it was fastened to a kennel, but its behaviour was so outrageous, and as there seemed a risk of its breaking away and attacking the staff, the opinion was formed, that it would have to be destroyed. Preparations were made to this end, when Mrs. Richardson pleaded to have one day more for a final experiment.

For two hours she stood near the dog, speaking to it softly. Gradually she edged nearer still, speaking, but never looking at the animal. She discerned that underneath the creature's savage behaviour, there was a very highly-strung, sensitive nature, and that if confidence could be established, the ferocity, which was really due to soreness of mind and fear, would vanish.

After a time, she was able to lean against the kennel, and then very gently her hand was laid on the large brown head, and permission was given for her to stroke the satin ears. With very quiet movement, she unfastened the chain, and slipped on a lead, and led the poor beast away. Its gratitude and delight, at being treated as an ordinary trustworthy dog was unbounded, and when I was making a round of inspection later in the day, I found the great beast seated at her feet, looking up with adoring eyes at his saviour. After that, this dog was the great favourite with all the staff, and was absolutely reliable, while still retaining its guarding qualifications as regards strangers, and it did some very useful work for its country.

COURAGE

If dogs have lived with people of pluck and courage, they will exhibit these qualities. It is quite natural for dogs to be courageous, and if this instinct has become blunted, it is possible to cultivate it and revive it once more.

In order to do this, an object must be set up in the dog's mind, to attain which, it will seem worth while facing seeming dangers. The War Dog, especially the Messenger Dog, has to have all fear of explosions and firing, smoke clouds, water obstacles, etc., eliminated. This, of course, is done by a very gradual process, and by emulation of fellow-students. The firing drill, of course, demands the greatest effort of self-control ; but when dogs are trained together in bands, and begin to take an interest in the work, a single individual has the greatest dislike of being left out of anything, in which the rest may be taking part, and he will rather face something, that for a time may seem unpleasant, than be left behind.

This factor is a great help in training the instinct of courage. When they get accustomed to the sound, the fear vanishes. And so it is with water and other unpleasant-nesses. Rather than let another furry friend reach the other bank, or scale the barbed wire before him, a dog will force itself to tackle these difficulties, which before, it would have considered insurmountable.

Apart from this trained courage, we can all recall instances of natural pluck and real bravery in dogs, defending some person, or thing they valued, and believed to be in danger.

HONOUR

A sense of right and wrong, or conscience, is very strongly developed in dogs, and the moral sense has to be carefully brought out in the War Dog, as it has to do so much of its work entirely on its own initiative. But it is safe to say, that if you can get a dog to understand a certain duty as a trust, it will rarely fail you. In fact, especially in relation to guarding duties, the dog will often rather lay down life itself than betray its trust, and when there is complete understanding and trust between the messenger dog and its keeper, the honourable return of the dog with the message is assured.

Until this co-operation is attained, however, there are

many temptations to be met and overcome, and sad are
the falls from honourable conduct, before our dispatch-
carrying friend learns to listen to the prompting of his
higher sense. Appetizing food is the most serious temptation. For this reason, messenger dogs should always be
very well fed, so that the allurements on the road are less
likely to trouble them. But, even so, there are some
dogs which find, when under training, great difficulty in
renouncing the delights of the rubbish heap, where such
delicacies as fish and bones of ancient origin are available·
As the training proceeds, and the object of the journey
begins to dawn on the dog's mental horizon, each time it
dishonourably stops at any cherished place of call, it will
feel more and more guilty. In this process of moral pro-
gression, it is greatly aided by a companion of more
advanced rectitude, who may be travelling with him, or
who continues steadily on his way. As I have before
stated, the sense of emulation is very strong in dogs, and
is one of the greatest aids in training them. The greedy
and guilty fellow will be very impressed at his friend passing
such delicious fare, and, furthermore, the usual relish in
partaking of it, will be considerably impaired by the knowledge, that the said friend will reach home before him, to
receive the legitimate reward, and approving caress from
the instructor.

I have seen many amusing instances during this moral
education of the dispatch carrier. On one occasion, a
collie found a workman's dinner, neatly done up in a cotton
handkerchief, under a hedge. He was nearing home and
going along with a steady swing. The delightful scent of
the repast was too much for his half-trained sense of honour,
and he stopped to examine it. Feeling uneasy in his mind,
however, he did not care to delay to eat it there, and

seizing the bundle by the knot, bore it away. He arrived at the training post with a curious expression, which desired to convey the information, that although he realized he had not acted in an absolutely straightforward manner, at all events he had lost no time on the road.

I have sometimes watched a gentlemanly house-dog, sitting expectantly beside the tea-table, keep his head self-consciously turned away from the lower shelves of the tea-basket, on a level with his nose, when the smell of the dainties became rather more attractive than he could conveniently endure.

This sense of honour in dogs, can be cultivated in many directions. The " Ettrick shepherd," Hogg, points this out, when telling of one of his collies, trained to accompany him to the hills, to manage the sheep. " If coming hungry from the hills, and getting into the milk house, he, (the collie), would most likely think of nothing else than filling his belly with the cream," while another dog, perhaps a relative of this same one, which had been trained to remain at home, as the friend and guardian of the shepherd's family and property, is bred to far higher principles of honour in this direction. " I have known such a dog lay night and day among from ten to twenty pails full of milk, and never once break the cream of one of them with the tip of his tongue ; nor would he suffer cat, rat, or any other creature to touch it."

The sense of honour in the guard-dog is very wonderful, and it may be said that the basis of the training rests chiefly on this instinct. I have heard people deride a dog, said to be a very determined guard, because they have met this dog on the road, and it has allowed them to pat its head. But the dog really exhibited greater intelligence than the person, because it was not at the time on duty, and did not consider it necessary to obstruct anyone who had no evil intent, and who had every right to be there. Give this same dog its bit of territory to protect, and its attitude towards the stranger will be very different and " Halt " will be the meaning conveyed in no uncertain manner.

ENDURANCE

This necessary qualification in the War Dog, really results in a combination of the previous qualities, and can only be reached when the training has proceeded so far, as to have taught the dog that its work is very much worth while. That a very high standard of endurance was reached by the messenger dog on the battlefield, is proved by the description of their work under conditions and temptations, that were frequently very trying.

THE HOMING INSTINCT

This subject is of such importance, in regard to the training of messenger dogs, that I have devoted a special chapter to it.

This chapter on Instinct should also include a few remarks on the reasoning powers of the dogs. This question of reason in dogs, takes its starting-point from the recognition of the before-mentioned qualities of soul. Unless these qualities are admitted, it will be difficult for anyone to develop in a really satisfactory manner the reasoning powers, and, finally, that which follows as a natural result, namely, the cultivation of all the senses with which the dog is gifted to a high degree. These senses are guided and controlled by the higher instincts, and must be reached, therefore, primarily through the latter. A good trainer will always remember this, and adjust his training so that love, justice, honour, truth, will be reflected all through the daily lessons. A dog should never be tricked or deceived. There are few human beings who feel such treatment as acutely as the dog. At the same time it can be trained to thoroughly appreciate and enjoy, a joke and friendly "ragging." If one hits a dog quite lightly in anger it resents it, but if one is having a joke, one can play a tune with a stick on the dog's back, and hit it relatively much harder, and it will enter into the fun with great zest, and stand to be hit until the ditty is finished, when it will bound round one in high delight at participating in the joke.

Obedience and discipline, based on reason, are the result of the cultivation of the highest qualities of mind. Both can be attained by compulsion, but the only discipline in which I place any real reliance, is that which is based on spontaneous qualities of good in the dog's mind, such as love for its master, honour, justice, etc.

It is an interesting fact that the story with which we are all familiar of Gelert, the famous dog of Wales, whose grave is still carefully tended to this day on account of his brave and faithful defence of the child from the wolf, is found in varying forms in the folk-lore of most widely-separated countries and races.

The following clipping from the *Times*, of December 18th, 1919, illustrates the development of discipline in a dog, based on its love and trust in its master's judgment and ruling:

" For days past every morning has brought fresh news of wrecks on the coasts of Nova Scotia, and along the Gulf of Saint Lawrence, ships having been driven ashore in terrific gales, accompanied by blinding storms of snow, on barren, rocky coasts, far from human habitation. From Newfoundland this morning comes the story of the wreck of a coasting steamer on a terrible coast. Ninety-two passengers and crew were saved by the intelligence of a New-foundland dog belonging to one of the crew. The ship had gone ashore on a reef of jagged rocks, and it was impossible to get a boat out to her in the boiling sea. Finally, a light line was tied round the dog, which obeyed his master's signs and swam ashore, making it possible to rig a block and tackle, by means of which all the souls in the ship were brought to safety. A baby of eighteen months was taken ashore in a mail bag."

If discipline is inculcated on the right lines, so that reason is cultivated simultaneously, it will be found that an understanding is born into a dog's mind that orders should be obeyed for their own sake, and, therefore, its training in discipline should be along those lines in the first place, which the dog is most easily able to comprehend. To illustrate this, I may mention the case of a young dog I had great faith in. It was a collie, with a strain of spaniel, and displayed extreme intelligence and affection. While joyfully adapting itself to all its duties, it unfortunately had the greatest dislike to any sounds of firing or passing near any explosions. I had arranged a test one day, where "Rob" was asked to run down a trench, on each side of which were exploding powder flashes. Nothing would induce him to do it, and the promise of the most delectable dainties had no effect whatever. He had been brought to this pitch of training gradually, but this final test, which it was essential he should pass, seemed to be one he would never be able to attain. I, however, remembered someone, for whom "Rob" seemed to have conceived a very special affec-tion. This person stood at the other end of the trench,

and in his desire to reach the object of his love, " Rob "
cautiously, and with many qualms, stepped gingerly past
the danger zones, needless to say, to be greatly rewarded
and caressed by his friend. After this first test, there was
no further trouble, and he became accustomed to run down
the trench between the powder flashes, with complete non-
chalance. After a time his special friend was replaced by
one of the ordinary staff, and " Rob " understood that this
test was part of a system of duty, and must be disconnected
with any personal element. This power to reason out
things in connection with their work, and to realize that
the rules must be obeyed for their own sake, as part of
the very high mission, with which they were entrusted,
was borne out in France, when a dog's keeper was wounded
or removed from his own particular charge. It at once
" carried on " with another keeper, accepting the change,
no doubt with deep regret, but as a necessity, due to
circumstances.

A wonderful instance of this sense of discipline is nar-
rated concerning a collie, by the poet Hogg, in the " Shep
herd's Calendar." In this case the strict observance of
what the conscientious animal conceived to be its duty,
overcame even the maternal instinct.

A collie belonged to a man named Steele, who was in
the habit of consigning sheep to her charge without supervision. " On one occasion," says Hogg, " whether Steele
remained behind or took another road, I know not ; but
on arriving home late in the evening, he was astonished to
hear, that his faithful animal had never made its appearance with the drove. He and his son, or servant, instantly
prepared to set out by different paths in search of her ;
but on their going out into the streets, there was she
coming with the drove, not one missing, and, marvellous

to relate, she was carrying a young pup in her mouth. She had been taken in travail on the hills, and how the poor beast had contrived to manage her drove in her state of suffering is beyond human calculation, for her road lay through sheep the whole way. Her master's heart smote him, when he saw what she had suffered and effected ; but she, nothing daunted, and having deposited her young one in a place of safety, again set out full speed to the hills, and brought another, and another, till she brought her whole litter, one by one, but the last one was dead."

It will be observed how cleverly the collie must have reasoned out the needs of her flock, and also of her puppies.

A wonderfully clever Dandie Dinmont, belonging to my family, in a long life of absolutely human intelligence, on one occasion by utilizing his reasoning powers, saved what might have been a very serious disaster. He appeared late at night upstairs in one of the bedrooms, and by his extremely agitated demeanour induced one of the family to accompany him downstairs. Here it was found that a lamp had been left burning, and the wick had in some manner fallen down into the oil, so that the entire lamp was a mass of flame.

There is also a well-known story, which has come down to us from the reign of Charles V. of France, and which shows both the capacities of reasoned judgment, and of tenacity of purpose, in a greyhound.

The dog belonged to an officer of the King's bodyguard, named Aubrey de Montdidier, against whom, another officer, named Macaire, in the same service, had conceived a grudge. The two officers decided to meet in the Forest of Bondy, near Paris. Macaire, however, on meeting Montdidier, treacherously fell on him and murdered him. The latter had brought his dog with him to the scene, and after the murderer had hastily interred his victim, the greyhound lay on top of the grave, remaining there for a lengthy time, until hunger compelled it to return to one of the royal kitchens. Here it was fed, but it did not remain, and slipped back to keep the tryst on its master's grave in the forest. It continued to act in this manner for some days, until the curiosity of the inhabitants of the kitchen was aroused, especially as the dog's master was nowhere to be found. It was, therefore, followed, and on the ground where the dog was lying being turned up, the body of the unfortunate man was found. The story does not end here, however. The greyhound's watch being ended, it returned to the palace, and, on seeing Macaire, immediately evinced the strongest aversion and ferocity towards him. No one could fail to notice the dog's intense hatred, and Charles V., on hearing of it, determined to satisfy himself as to the truth of the matter. The dog, and the man, were brought before him, and immediately the greyhound attempted to seize Macaire by the throat. The latter was closely questioned, but denied his guilt. It was therefore decided to test the matter, as was the custom of those times, by combat. This extraordinary combat took place on the Isle of Notre Dame, in Paris, and was witnessed by the whole Court. Macaire was only allowed a club, as a means of attack and defence. It is stated that the dog seemed perfectly to recognize the situation and its duty. For a short time it circled round Macaire, and then with lightning speed, leapt at his throat, seizing him with such speed, and tenacity, that he was taken unawares and was in danger of being strangled. He cried aloud for mercy, and avowed his crime, on which his assailant was pulled off.

This curious instinct for " sensing " people's characters

on the part of dogs, whereby their reasoning powers are brought into play in the working out of their ideas, is well typified in the well-known story of the mastiff, belonging to Sir Harry Lee, of Ditchly, in Oxfordshire. This dog had been used as a guard for the house and yard, but had never been treated in any way as a companion by Sir Harry, or any other member of the family. The dog would, however, have seen him going about the place as owner and master. One night he was retiring to bed, assisted by his valet, an Italian, and for some unexplained reason, the dog presented itself at the door of the bedroom, where it had never been before. It was ordered downstairs, but returned again, and commenced to scratch so determinedly at the door, that, to save further trouble, it was allowed to enter. It retired under the bed, and remained there quietly. During the night, stealthy footsteps entered the room. Sir Harry started from sleep, and the dog leapt from under the bed, and seized the intruder. When a light was brought, it was discovered that the mastiff was holding the Italian valet, who was armed, and who confessed that his intention had been to attack and rob his master. A full-length picture is still preserved in the family of Sir Harry Lee, with the mastiff by his side, and the words attached : " More faithful than favoured." To cultivate this habit of thinking things out for itself, and of noticing events, and putting two and two together, rather than of waiting for the word of direction, is the object of all those who train military dogs. In the chapters on the work the dogs have actually done in the field, it will be seen how wonderfully the dogs used their reasoning powers.

A sense of justice is to be found, too, in a high degree in some dogs, and is easily affronted. From man it feels such affronts severely, but also from its own comrades.

Messenger dog Nell.   This dog worked throughout the war and saved scores of lives

To face p. 1 l.

I remember an amusing instance of this in the case of a young Dandie Dinmont, of ten months, who accompanied me for a walk. As we approached a certain gate, a fox terrier rushed out and attacked the Dandie savagely, although the latter was not encroaching on the preserves of the fox terrier, but was trotting innocently down the middle of the road. The Dandie carried a very fine silver topknot, which seemed especially to irritate the fox terrier, who concentrated his energies on this ornament, and shook poor Dandie in a most brutal manner. Dandie put up a good fight and managed to shake off his assailant, but being only a young thing, was obviously somewhat shaken in his nerves, and much affronted altogether. On arrival at home, we were met at our gate by the pup's elder brother, and in canine language, the whole story was poured out. Both Dandies manifested intense indignation, bouncing about the garden with stiffened fur and tails, and gurgling loudly to each other. Foreseeing it would be much better to have the matter settled once and for all, as soon as possible, I started out again, accompanied with both Dandies. As we approached the gate of the enemy's residence, both Dandies became much excited, and the elder started ahead, giving directions evidently to his brother to follow behind. He arrived at the gate, and stood stiffly to attention. At that moment, a whirlwind of white fur, hurled itself under the gate. The conflict was short but sharp, and presently, a sorry-looking fox terrier limped back to its home. After that, there was a definite understanding, and while no friendship was attempted between the three, it was admitted that the roadway was a right of way.

I have also seen a strong instance of justice, and honourable dealing, manifested by messenger dogs under training. When two or three dogs arrive at the post together and receive a reward, I have seen one dog take its piece of meat from the ground and step back, and watch the other competitor receive its reward, which would be frequently placed on the ground. There was no attempt to snatch it, and there was evidently a distinct understanding that it was a definite reward for good work done, and, therefore, to interfere, would be a most unsportsmanlike act. At any other time, when feeding a group of dogs with scraps, there would not be this withholding, but a lively scramble would ensue sometimes with exciting results.

This sense of justice is closely allied to that of dignity and a due appreciation of the proportion of things in general. The dog is so undeterred by many of the temptations which assail human nature in certain respects! Mr. Ruskin, in commenting on the Veronese and Venetians, mentions dogs, which are introduced by Paul Veronese into two of his greatest pictures : " The Presentation of his Own Family to the Madonna " and " The Queen of Sheba before Solomon." In the first, the dog is represented as walking away much offended, wondering not a little, as Mr. Ruskin amusingly suggests, as to how the Madonna could possibly have got into the house. In the second picture, while the Queen is quite overcome with emotion, her dog " is wholly unabashed by Solomon's presence, or anybody else's, and stands with his fore-legs well apart, right in front of his mistress, thinking everyone has lost their wits, and barking loudly at one of the attendants, who has set down a gold vase disrespectfully near him."

CHAPTER VI

THE HOMING INSTINCT

" Yea, the stork in the heavens knoweth her appointed times. And the turtle and the crane, and the swallow, observe the time of their coming."—JEREMIAH.

THE homing habit enters so largely into the training of dispatch-carrying dogs, that the instructor will find it of interest, and of assistance, to make some investigations into this subject.

This instinct in the dog teems with interest, not only on account of the wonderful results to be obtained by its exercise, but also because it is one, which man does not possess himself in anything like the same degree. How is it that the dog, without any of the material aids of direction open to man, can find his way homewards, across totally unknown country? How is it that the Messenger Dog, which has been taken up to the front line, through the trenches, will choose very often to return by night, as well as day, and do so successfully, across the open country, often with every sort of obstacle in its path? What is it that guides it? It cannot be sight, or darkness would be an insuperable hindrance, and they work as well at night as by day. It cannot be hearing, nor is it by the sense of scent, as the dog does not necessarily choose the same route for its return, even in the doubtful and in most cases impossible likelihood of there being any trail.

It must be confessed, that in trying to account for the cause of this wonderful instinct in his four-footed friend, man is hopelessly nonplussed, and can only admit with admiring humility, that in this respect at all events, dog beats man completely.

I have instanced how the Messenger Dogs were frequently taken up to the line by night and slipped in the early dawn, with uniform success, and very often they deliberately chose a different way to return. In civilian canine life, also, there are numerous cases of dogs being taken long distances by train, and of their finding their way home by road. An authentic case is that of a dog which belonged to the Royal Kennels at Windsor, in the reign of George III. It was carried to London in a carriage. From there it was taken down into Lincolnshire. Within a month it had escaped, and found its way back to Windsor.

Another case, is of a shooting dog, which was sent to a purchaser sixty miles off, and found its way back whenever it could escape. When I was in the Vosges, visiting the French Army in 1915, a war dog, which had been demobilized, and had been sent to the rear, appeared at its old quarters, apparently highly indignant at its services being dispensed with. One of my own companion dogs, on being taken by road for the first time to a busy town ten miles off, was lost there. A short time after, a little grey, hurrying figure was seen scudding across the high land towards the house,—a way it had never been taken, but which was much shorter than by road.

These last instances are all cases of naturally-developed homing instinct, but all dogs do not have this equally developed. It exists, however, in nearly every dog, and can be cultivated and accentuated. This, of course, has to be done in the case of the Messenger Dogs, and, in fact, the whole trend of their training is on this line. First of all, they are trained from a fixed base, and then from a movable base. It was always interesting to observe how the different dogs thought out the return journey, when under training. Sometimes they would be taken out by a roundabout route by road, and certain dogs would always return by the shortest way, which sometimes took them straight across country. Others, on the other hand, quite as clever, chose to take the longer route back on which they had been brought outwards, because they thought they could run quicker on the smooth road unmolested by obstacles of any sort. I noticed that the most cunning and elderly dogs generally did this. In the field, it was much the same. The most experienced dogs generally took what they judged was the easiest route homewards, even though it might be somewhat longer.

In studying this instinct among animals as a whole, we find, that the habit of migration in many of the species is closely allied to it. The underlying motive does not always seem to be the same, but the method of procedure resulting is the same. The migratory habits of the birds are exceedingly interesting to study, as are those of the fish and many other animals. First of all, however, the attainments of man in this direction must be inquired into, and here it is regrettable that this very wonderful gift is at present practically unused. That man has this instinct, however dormant it may be in the meantime, seems probable, as capabilities of home-finding are still possessed by certain primitive races. Travellers in Arctic regions, for instance, have stated their astonishment as to the manner in which natives were able to find their way amongst the trackless ice-floes, while they themselves were helpless without the aid of a compass. On this point Mr. Alfred Russell Wallace, however, has very definite ideas as to how this home-fiuding is accomplished by human beings. He says :

" Let us consider the fact of Indians finding their way through forests they have never traversed before. This is much misunderstood, for I believe it is only performed under such special conditions, as at once to show that instinct has nothing to do with it. A savage, it is true, can find his way through his native forests in a direction he has never traversed before ; but this is because, in infancy, he has been used to wander in them, and to find his way by indications which he has observed himself, or learned from others. Savages make long journeys in many directions, and their whole faculties being directed to the subject, they gain a wide and accurate knowledge of topography, not only of their own district, but of all the regions round about. Everyone who has travelled in a new direction communicates his knowledge to those who have travelled less, and descriptions of routes and localities and minute incidents of travel, form one of the main staples of conversation round the evening fire. Every wanderer or captive from another tribe adds to the store of information, and as the very existence of individuals, and of whole families and tribes, depends upon the completeness of this knowledge, all the acute, perceptive faculties of the adult savage are devoted to acquiring and perfecting it. The good hunter or warrior thus comes to know the bearing of every hill and mountain range, the directions and functions of all the streams, the situation of each tract characterized by peculiar vegetation, not only within the area he has himself traversed, but perhaps for a hundred miles round it. His acute observation enables him to detect the slightest undulations of the surface, the various changes of subsoil and alterations in the character of the vegetation, that would be quite imperceptible to the stranger. His eye is always open to the direction in which he is going ; the mossy side of the trees, the presence of certain plants under the shade of rocks, the morning and evening flight of birds, are to him indications of direction, almost as sure as the sun in the heavens. Now if such a savage is required to find his way across this country in a direction in which he has never been before, he is quite equal to the task. By however circuitous a route he has come to the point he is to start from, he has observed all the bearings and distances so well, that he knows pretty nearly where he is, the direction of his own home, and that of the place he is required to go to."

Mr. Wallace then explains how he thinks the savage proceeds on his journey, and further states :

" As he approaches any tract of country he has been in or near before, many minute indications guide him ; but he observes them so cautiously, that his white companions cannot perceive by what he has directed his course. To the Europeans whom he guides, he seems to have come without trouble, without any special observation, and by a nearly straight, unchanging course. They are astonished, and ask if he has ever been the same route before, and when he answers ' No,' conclude that some unerring instinct alone could have guided him. But take this same man into another country, very similar to his own, but with other streams and hills, another kind of soil with a somewhat different vegetation and animal life ; and after bringing him by a circuitous route to a given point, ask him to return to his starting-point by a straight line of fifty miles through the forest, and he will certainly decline to attempt it, or, attempting it, will more or less completely fail. His supposed instinct does not act out of his own country. It appears to me, therefore, that to call in the aid of a new and mysterious power to account for savages being able to find that which under similar conditions we could almost all of us perform, although perhaps less perfectly, is ludicrously unnecessary.

" I shall attempt to show that much of what has been attributed to instinct in birds, can be also very well explained by crediting them with those faculties of observation, memory and imitation, and with that limited amount of reason which they undoubtedly exhibit."

Mr. Romanes, however, differs from Mr. Wallace to a certain extent, and says :

" Moreover, it is certain, that in many cases, if not as a general rule, the animals, on their return journey, do not traverse the actual route which they were taking in the outgoing journey, but take the bee line ; so that, for instance, if the outgoing journey has been made over two sides of a triangle, the return journey will probably be made over the third side. The remarkable fact is, that the animals are able to find their way back over immense distances, even though the outgoing journey has been made at night, or in a closed box ; so that it is truly upon some sense of direction, and not merely upon landmarks, that they must rely. Now it is evident that this fact alone— i.e., of animals not requiring to return by the same route— is sufficient to dispose of the hypothesis advanced by Mr. Wallace to the effect, that the return journey is due to a memory of the odours perceived during the outgoing journey, these odours serving as landmarks. Therefore, it seems to me there are only two hypotheses open to us, whereby to meet the facts. First, it has been thought possible, that animals may be endowed with a special sense, enabling them to perceive the magnetic currents of the earth, and so guide themselves as by a compass. There is no inherent impossibility attaching to this hypothesis, but as it is wholly destitute of evidence, we may disregard it. The only other hypothesis is, that animals are able to keep an unconscious register of the turns and curves taken in the outgoing journey, and so to retain a general impression of their bearings."

Mr. Darwin made experiments, and taking a number of bees in a box, released them about two and a half miles from the hive. Most of the bees returned, but Mr. Romanes thinks that as the bees probably frequently flew this distance outwards at ordinary times, that they found their way back by a recognition of the objects *en route.*

Monsieur Fabre also inclines to this point of view.

Sir John Lubbock conducted many experiments with ants, testing their sense of direction by various methods. He was led to believe that these animals possessed this sense in a very definite degree, and observed that they found their way, by observing the direction in which the light was falling. " So that so long as the source of light was stationary, no matter how many times he turns them round upon a rotating table, when the rotation ceased, they renew their road to and from the hive, as well as they did before the rotation ; whereas, if the source of light were shifted, the insects at once became confused as to their bearings, even though not rotated at all."

In commenting on the above experiments, Mr. Romanes says :

" Now if ants thus habitually guide themselves, by observing the direction in which the light is falling, (i.e., the position of the sun), I do not see why migratory birds should not be assisted by similar means."

Where such eminent men are doubtful, and even at variance, it requires considerable courage to venture an opinion on this knotty subject. It may, however, be of some assistance, if I record a few conclusions reached through many years of observation of the habits of the dog in this connection. It is remarkable, however, seeing that so many clever minds have concentrated on this interesting study, so much of their work has been conducted amongst the less intelligent animals of creation, and that, beyond noting the fact that dogs do have a wonderful homing instinct, very little research has been carried on with their aid. Had half the efforts expended on ants, birds, bees, etc., been directed towards training, and also unravelling the mental riddle, which the dog presents in this respect,— we might by now have discovered invaluable clues, by which man himself might be led to understand many things at present hidden from him. But no ! every animal, from a semi-animated particle of jelly, is preferred, and the dog —the most wonderful animal we have, and the nearest to man in intellect and aspiration of all the animal kingdom —is completely ignored. Even in the knowledge obtained by all the years of patient research as to the homing instinct amongst the lower animals, by what comparative degree can the results be compared to those IMMEDIATELY returned by the dog, in the adaptation of this gift to the need of mankind during the war ?

I will, first of all, say, that with regard to the homing or migratory instinct in birds, it appears to me, that the process by which they obtain their end is in some ways more obscure than is the case with dogs. For instance, in the case of homing pigeons, the method of their return is governed entirely by sight. Lieut.-Colonel Osman, who conducted the pigeon section throughout the war, and whose experience is such, that his opinion can be received with respect, informed me that such is the case. This is also confirmed by the fact that these birds cannot fly at night, and although their roosting instincts might, to a certain extent, account for this, still, they are also unable to find their way in mist in the daytime, which would also seem to show that they are entirely influenced by sight. On the other hand, there are certain kinds of birds, which choose the night-time for their flight—such as the quail. One authority believes that swallows always start against the south wind, and that they associate direction with the soft, moist breath of this wind. One would certainly conclude that, with the birds at all events, the homing cause, in the first instance, is the prompting due to climatic conditions, causing a desire to migrate to countries where a greater degree of warmth may be experienced, and also a better food-supply. As to the secondary causes, whereby they are enabled to cross trackless oceans, it certainly seems probable that they are assisted and influenced by light, wind, and by observation of many objects to which they attach some meaning, and to which man has not the clue.

But, granting all this, the whole question is not entirely answered, and especially is this so in the case of the homing instinct in dogs.

Mr. Romanes himself gives an instance of a lady staying at an hotel at Mentone, taking a fancy to a dog belonging to the proprietor, and carrying it with her by rail to Vienna. Not long afterwards it appeared at the hotel at Mentone, having thus run a distance of nearly a thousand miles. A scientific friend of mine describes to me, how his terrier accompanies him by tram from his home in the suburbs of a large town to the university, in the centre of the town. It often elects to return home by itself, and always selects a tram in which to do so. If it finds the tram is going in the wrong direction, it jumps off, and either selects another, or continues its journey homewards on foot.

In connection with the training of dogs for messenger work, I have found two points in connection with the homing instinct, which rather seem to contradict each other. First of all, it is observable that they do take note of objects on the road, to assist them in their return homewards. One finds this by noting, that a young dog under training, will sometimes take a correct course homewards, and then at cross roads take the wrong turning. Showing, that it has noticed the fact of the break in the road, but has erred in the choice of the next move. I have seen such a dog, a little further advanced in his training, run down the wrong road some way, then stop, hesitate, and turn back, and regain the cross-roads, and carry on along the right road. In this case, the dog's sense of direction had been, first of all, guided, then misled, by the visible appearances of the route. Now the second point is interesting, because it practically excludes the theory that noticing the aspect of the country over which it has previously been taken, is the manner in which the dog returns. It is, that dogs work as well at night as in the day, and equally so in mist. In fact, I may say that observations seem to point to the fact that trained dogs, and even half-trained ones, work better under these conditions than in daylight. And this was also borne out in the field. The keepers have related to me that on certain nights, when the conditions were so bad, the night so dark and thick, the ground so water-logged and shell-marked, and on certain occasions quite new to the dogs, that they were fearful that these would prove too much even for their faithful followers. But the curious point was brought out, that the dogs seem to work much better than usual, at such times. As one man said : " It seemed as though ' Jock ' divined my fears, and put out an extra effort to show they were needless."

I remember one test I made at the school with forty dogs. They were taken in various directions simultaneously, for two miles outwards, and released at a given moment. The night was especially chosen, as being moonless, and with a dense fog as well. It was, in fact, pitch-dark, of such darkness as could be felt. The average time for the return was fifteen minutes, though a few did so in ten minutes. A few also took twenty minutes, and thirty-nine had returned within that time. Only one took over half an hour.

Of course, one reason for the more rapid return at night is the absence of temptation on the road, such as other dogs, vehicular traffic, and people. But this does not wholly account for the undoubted fact, that, although these temptations are absent, there are other difficulties intensified, and yet excellent results are obtained. It appears to me, therefore, that dogs do observe points on their outward journey, of which they make a note in the daytime, perhaps without any conscious intention. That the newly-trained dog does this especially, in order to help its sense of dircetion, but that, as the training proceeds, the dog finds this sense developing, and the safest thing to go by in the long run, and discards more and more the signs by the road as guide-marks, so that it soon prefers to take the bee-line, rather than trouble with the road, by which it was taken out. I am further of opinion that this is so, by the demeanour of the dogs on being led away for training. The young dog seems to keep a wary eye on its surroundings, as he goes along, as though registering the details in its memory. The old hands, on the contrary, trot off gaily enough, and I have noticed them, when passing through a village on their outward journey, amusing themselves with passing fancies, such as hurried inspections of dogs, cats, and other trivialities, which could not possibly help them on their return journey, and, when released, they would as likely as not ignore the route by which they had come, village and all, and take a nearer line across country.

At night-time, when there was no possibility of any help being received from the memory of the aspect of the outward route, the effort has to be concentrated on the sense of direction only, and that, as this is the real and legitimate source of the homing faculty, the results are at once more certain and rapid.

It would seem, therefore, that the causative guiding source of the homing faculty has its origin in the realm of metaphysics, rather than in external phenomena, and if any explanation is sought, it is here that investigation should be made.

First of all, we find an overwhelming desire in the dog's mind to get to a certain place. I, of course, discovered, as I have already explained elsewhere, that the surest foundation from which to arouse this desire, was the love of the dog to its master. Love, being an ever-primal, and, therefore, eternal quality, the effort involved in carrying out duties under this impulse, is such, that it is strong enough to sweep aside obstructions of every kind, and is the most dependable instinct available.

Starting with this all-guiding impulse, it is of interest to follow out the working of it in relation to the phenomena, which come to the dog, in its attempts to reach a certain spot. On consulting several learned minds, there are some interesting statements to be found by Mr. Romanes, amongst others, on the subject of reason in human beings and in animals, which suggest many possibilities to those who are cultivating the homing instinct in dogs. In his book on " Animal Intelligence " he says :

" Reason is a faculty, which is concerned in the intentional adaptation of means to ends. It therefore implies the conscious knowledge of the relation between means employed, and ends attained, and may be exercised in adaptation to circumstances, novel alike to the experience of the individual, and to that of the species. In other words, it implies the power of perceiving analogies, or ratios, and is in this sense equivalent to the term 'ratiocination,' or faculty of discerning inferences from a perceived equivalency of relations."

He then proceeds to follow this statement on Reason, with an interesting discussion on the co-operation of the mental quality of inference, in conjunction with that of perception. To illustrate how closely these two qualities are allied, Sir David Brewster is quoted as noticing the fact, that when looking through a window, on the pane of which there is a fly or gnat, if the eyes are adjusted for a considerable distance, so that the gnat is not clearly focussed, the mind at once infers, that it is a bird or some much larger object, seen at a greater distance. " Now this shows that in the case of all our visual perceptions, mental inference is perpetually at work, compensating for the effects of distance, in diminishing apparent size." We all know also, how the sense of hearing is deceived in the same manner, as when we hear a lesser sound near us, and infer that it is a loud sound a long way off, and *vice versâ.*

To quote Mr. Romanes again : " No less constant must be the work of mental inference, in compensating for the effects of the ' blind spot ' upon the retina. For if the vision be directed to a coloured surface, the part of the surface, which, on account of the blind spot, is not really seen, yet appears to be seen ; and not only so, but it appears to be coloured the same tint as the rest of the surface, whatever this may happen to be. Unconscious inference supplies the colour.

" The first or early stage of inference then is, that in which inference arises *in or together with* perception, as when we infer that a gnat is a bird, or that the portion of a surface, corresponding to the blind spot of the retina, is coloured like the surrounding portions of the surface. Inference may here be said to be a constituent part of perception. That this is the true explanation of the matter is rendered evident, not only from the deductive consideration first stated, but also from the inductive verification, which is received from the facts, which arise, when a man, who has been born blind, has been suddenly made to see. A good case of this kind is the celebrated one of the youth, (twelve years of age), whom Mr. Cheselden couched for removing congenital cataracts from both eyes."

Mr. Cheselden shows that although the boy saw, his judgment as to the things that " touched his eyes " (as he expressed it) was entirely guided by his sense of touch. Continuing, he says " he thought no objects so agreeable as those which were smooth and regular, though he could form no judgment of their shape, or guess what it was in any object that was pleasing to him. He knew not the shape of anything, nor any one thing from another, however different in shape or in magnitude ; but on being told what things were, whose form he before knew from feeling, he would

Messenger dogs clearing obstacle

[To face p. 191.

[To face p. 177.

Sending off a message

carefully observe that he might know them again, but having too many objects to learn at once, he forgot many of them. Having forgotten which was the cat, and which was the dog, he was ashamed to ask, but catching the cat, (which he knew by feeling), he was observed to look at her steadfastly, and then setting her down, said : ' So puss, I shall know you another time.' We thought he soon knew what pictures were, that were shown to him, but we found afterwards, that we were mistaken ; about two months after he was couched, he discovered they represented solid bodies, when to that time he considered them as only parti-coloured plains, or surfaces diversified, with a variety of paints ; but even then, he was no less surprised, expecting the pictures would feel like the things they represented, and was amazed when he found those parts, which by their light and shadow appeared round and uneven, felt only flat like the rest, and asked which was the lying sense,—the feeling or seeing."

In commenting on the above case, Mr. Romanes sums up the matter by adding ·

" Meanwhile it is enough to remember, that the case proves the utility of all our visual perceptions to depend upon the ingredient of mental inference, which is supplied by habitual association ; and, of course, we cannot doubt, that the same is true of perceptions vielded by other senses."

In pondering on the issues which such a statement involves, one is led into new paths of conjecture, and these, in their turn, point to many possibilities, which may in the future become realized facts.

For instance, it proves that all real education must start from within. That, on the education of the qualities of mind, depends the very appearance of the world in which we live. That things are not created as we see them, but they only appear to us as we *think* we see them. Following along this line of argument, does it not seem possible, that, as the quality of mere human intellect becomes merged in the divine aspirations of the soul, and the qualities of mind are thus purified and magnified, the results of this will be once more the perception of things as they really are, and have always been,—namely, perfect and indestructible? Now to come back to the mentality of the dog, and, indeed, to all animals which are using this impulse of way-finding, we observe that they are led to use it when under some sort of strong emotion. I have shown, that in the dog, I have found that of love, to be the motive power most successful in obtaining good results. In other animals, the idea of preservation of the species, causing individual animals, or whole colonies, to seek warmer climes, or safer rearing grounds. In fact, the same indomitable instinct, which makes the good soldier, namely, the preservation of his country, home, and family.

Once a child fell into the Serpentine. Someone rushed to the rescue, and a great crowd gathered round the bank. At that moment, a little, old, grey-haired woman, with fiercely set face, hurled herself through the crowd. Powerful men were dashed aside, as though they were nine-pins, and in a few seconds she had cleared a path for herself through the dense mass of people, impelled by strength she had been quite unconscious of, until called out under stress of this great emotion—love, for she was the child's grandmother.

It would therefore seem, that our animals, under stress of a definite necessity, become conscious of certain phenomena of which they make use. That we ourselves do not realize what these are, is no argument that they are not there, nor in our anxiety to explain the manner in which the animals accomplish the results, need we pin them down to our limited methods of understanding in any particular direction. Rather let us learn from the animals, and see if we cannot regain certain qualities of mind which we, no doubt, originally had, but have now lost, and which they retain.

I gather, therefore, that the intense desire to reach a given place impels the dog forward ; that as it yields to this impulse, that a certain guiding sense, which is in itself quite independent of any assistance from external pheno mena, comes to its aid, and the sense of direction is, *in* this very sense—that the dog desires to be there, and *follows this desire*, rather than troubling about the aspect of the surroundings in getting there. The more it becomes accustomed to throw all its effort into this intuitive prompting, the more it discards any temporary assistance it may be tempted to use, in the first place, such as noting turns in the road, and other external aids, and also the more it improves in its way-finding duties. The deduction, in fact, seems to be plain, that the desire itself brings its own lesson, and a world of intelligence is opened up to the dog, and to all animals, under stress of this governing force, of which we human beings are quite unconscious, because we have not yet exercised this particular mental effort along the same lines as the animals.

It will therefore be seen, that those promptings which have their origin in what we call instinct, are due to an intelligence quite apart from, and infinitely above, any guidance from the senses. While man accepts gratefully the many wonderful inventions which have come to him, as aids in his present manner of living, there is no doubt, that in his increasing dependence on material contrivances, he has sacrificed much wonderful knowledge, which would have come to him, had he trained himself to listen more attentively to the " still, small voice " within. That we will eventually be compelled, to depend wholly on this guidance, and wholly to discard the material props we rest on to-day is certain, and we can, even now, see evidences of the tendency in this direction, in the gradual dematerializing of so many original forces. Thus—telegraphy is no longer confined to wires, light is obtained from certain elements in combination, propulsion, from the evaporation of gas. Matter itself is disappearing under analysis, and appears as the " electron," which our chief authorities in the world of chemistry define as " energy," and frankly admit that from this point, they hand the whole question over to the metaphysician.

Thus it is apparent, that in some ways, we can still learn much from the animals, and that in their dependence upon the intuitive utterances, derived from voices long unheard by man, they are on the right road towards the solution of many things which at present remain a mystery to us.

Under this mental propulsion, the senses of sight, and hearing, and scenting become greatly intensified, and the great desire in the dog's mind to detect sounds in the far distance, in the performance of its work, is the great impetus, whereby the trainer can cultivate hearing and scenting in the sentry and guard dog.

And it would seem that these senses have their origin in mind.

There are many animals that have these senses accentuated in remarkable ways. During the Battle of Jutland, there were many people who observed the curious behaviour of the pheasants in various parts of the country, down the East Coast. They manifested every sign of excitement. Rooks also seem to hear or feel climatic disturbances from afar, and there is little doubt, that animals, as a whole, are sensitive to vibrations in the atmosphere to a very remarkable degree. There are instances of this sensitiveness, as we all know, amongst human beings, and generally it would be observed when they are in a state of high mental excitement and desire. Thus we can recall the well-known story of Jessie of Lucknow, who heard the pipes of General Havelock's relieving force, many hours before anyone in the besieged Residency could do so. She steadfastly asserted she heard the pipes approaching, when those around her deemed her demented, as they were quite unable to detect any such sound. I quote two verses of a poem by Grace Campbell, which commemorates this incident of the Mutiny ·

" Hark, surely I'm no' wildly dreamin'
  For I hear it plainly now. .
  Ye cannot, ye never heard it
  On the far-off mountain brow ;
  For in your southern childhood, ye were nourished saft and warm
  Nor watched upon the cauld hillside
  The rising of the storm.
  Aye ! Now the soldiers hear it, and answer with a cheer
  As, ' The Campbells are a-comin' ' falls on each anxious ear.
  The cannons roar their thunder, an' the sappers work in vain
  For high aboon the din o' war,
  Resounds the welcome strain.

" An' nearer still, an' nearer still,
  An' now again 'tis ' Auld Lang Syne,'
  Its kindly notes like life bluid rin,
  Rin through this puir sad heart o' mine ;
  Oh, leddy, dinna swoon awa' ; look up, the evil's past,
  They're comin' now to dee wi' us, or save us at the last.
  Then let us humbly, thankfully, down on our knees and pray,
  For those who come thro' bluid and fire, to rescue us this day.
  That He may o'er them spread His shield,
  Stretch forth His arm and save
  Bold Havelock an' his Highlanders,
  The bravest o' the brave."

That this way-finding will some day be understood, and, therefore, possible of execution for us all, is probable.

That our Great Master, as an example, had this understanding, we gather from His walking over the sea in the dark, to the ship in which were His disciples. In St. John the incident is described as follows :

> " And it was now dark, and Jesus was not come to them.
> And the sea arose by reason of a great wind that blew,
> So when they had rowed about five and twenty or thirty furlongs, they see Jesus walking on the sea, and drawing nigh unto the ship : and they were afraid.
> But he saith unto them, It is I ; be not afraid.
> Then they willingly received him into the ship : and immediately the ship was at the land whither they went.

The Master's absolute dependence on the All-pervading Guiding Principle, caused Him not only to find His way to the ship in the dark, storm-tossed lake, but also enabled Him to embrace in his care, His beloved disciples, and their ship as well, so that " immediately the ship was at the land whither they went." He desired to be there, and behold ! He was there.

CHAPTER VII

GUARD DOGS

" There watched before the Miser's gate,
   A very cur, whom all men seemed to hate,
   Gaunt, savage, shaggy with an eye that shone
   Like a live coal, and he possessed but one,
   . . . His master prized him much, his name was Fang."

CRABBE.

BEEORE enlarging on the work done in the war by dogs, in connection with the protection of property, etc., it may be of interest to remark on the extreme antiquity of this disposition in the dog to guard territory or property. In the historical chapter in this book, there is already reference to this, but it would appear that this quality of mind is possessed, even by carnivorous animals in their wild state. Professor Romanes states :

" Most carnivorous animals in their wild state have an idea of property, and the manner in which certain predaceous carnivora take possession of more or less definite areas, as their hunting grounds, implies an incipient notion of the same thing. From this germ, thus supplied by nature, the art of man has operated in the case of the dog, till now, the idea of defending his master's property has become in this animal truly instinctive."

Mr. Romanes gives an amusing instance of this instinctive habit of guarding, in the case of a young puppy which he reared :

183

" Because I was perfectly certain that, in this case, the idea of protecting property was innate or instinctive. I have seen this dog escort a donkey, which had baskets on its back filled with apples. Although the dog did not know he was being observed, he accompanied the donkey all the way up the long hill, for the express purpose of guarding the apples. For every time the donkey turned his head to take an apple out of the baskets, the terrier sprang up and snapped at his nose ; and such was the vigilance of the dog, that although his companion was keenly desirous of tasting the fruit, he never allowed him to get a single apple during the half-hour they were together."

The desire for speech in the dogs—that is as an audible mode of self-expression, is an instinct, on which we depend largely in connection with our watch dogs. It has been observed, that the faculty of expression itself through sound, is regulated largely by the environment in which the dog finds itself. Thus Mr. Romanes says, " Ulloa noticed, that in Juan Fernandez the dogs did not attempt to bark till taught to do so by the importation of some dogs from Europe, their first attempts, being strange and unnatural." Hancock says, that " European dogs, when conveyed to Guinea, in three or four generations ceased to bark, and only howled like the dogs, native of that coast. Lastly, it is now well known, that the dogs of Labrador are silent as to barking. So that the habit of barking, which is so general among domestic dogs, as to be of the nature of an instinct, is nevertheless seen to vary with geographical position."

In an interesting chapter on language in lower man, Dr. Lauder Lindsay says :

" There are many people, destitute of written and printed language, and not a few savage races, which can scarcely be said to possess a spoken language, or even distinctly articulate speech. In certain cases, their language, of whatever character, is very limited and rudimentary. Thus, certain aborigines of Borneo, have no language of their own, and only learn with great labour to pronounce a few Malay words. Savage peoples have frequently mnemonic signs ; the language of expression in them is much the same as it is in many animals. Thus, their mode of salutation or greeting is not more expressive, consisting as it does either of

1. Some simple gesture.
2. Touching noses, or
3. Rubbing other parts of the body against each other.

" All their language consists of mere inarticulate sounds of the nature of shrieks—i.e., in certain natives of the Philippine Islands, or among the South African Bushmen. Brazilian Boto Kudos speak little to one another, but rather mutually grunt and snuffle. The Apache Indian speaks little, rather in gesture than in sounds. The speech of the Fans of Western Africa, is a collection of gutturals, unintelligible to white races. It can scarcely be called a language in the human sense of that word. The talk of the savages of Borneo and Sumatra, is described as a sort of cackle or croak. Generally, savages are accustomed to talk more by gesture and looks, than by voice. Thus, the Veddas of Ceylon use only signs, grimaces and guttural sounds. Houzeau remarks on the paucity of letter sounds in savage languages."

In the chapter on Instinct, I have recorded my observations with regard to the influence, exercised on the dog, by the attitude of mind possessed by its master, and also by that of the majority of minds in its particular environment ; therefore, for the same reason would facility of expression forsake a dog, if it were removed to any land, where the inhabitants were less fluent of speech and of ideas. This would, of course, happen in connection with semi-civilized and uncivilized bodies of people. Naturally, their intellects are circumscribed, and as naturally, therefore, their speech is in a much narrower groove. Their dogs will at once reflect this lack, and while their sense of ownership will in nowise deteriorate, they will find other means of communicating their impressions, rather than by barking, which is the form of speech of the civilized dog.

As a dog becomes very closely in touch with its owner, that is to say, when a dog is fortunate enough to come into the possession of an owner who, while regarding it as a dog, also realizes in it the presence of qualities, such as reason, honesty, wit, affection, pluck,—in fact, the like qualities of the human mind—the desire to exhibit these manifestations of intelligence becomes very strong in the animal. It seeks for every means in its power to reach out to the invitation offered, to express these different characteristics, and develops the power of speech to an increasing degree. The bark is made use of in varying tones, to express contrasting emotions. There is the short, playful bark, when it is inducing one to accompany it for a walk. This is accompanied by broad smiles, and ingratiating little whines, and, finally, the episode is closed with a loud, triumphant bark, when the object has been attained, and the expedition has commenced.

There is the bark of welcome, noisy and boisterous, accompanied with much facial expression and bodily gesture. In both these modes of self-expression, the clarion note of warning, which is so noticeable in the watch-dog's bark, is absent, and how telling it is in contrast! There is no mistaking it, to one who knows his dog's mind. A dog, thoroughly and suddenly aroused to sudden danger, at once conceives the necessity for warning his master, and the force of his feeling is manifested in a supremely concentrated effort. With some dogs I have had, I have been able to judge exactly the degree of danger, and what is to be expected, by the quality of the warning bark. I have noticed, that when the dog judges, that what it sees or hears, is of a peculiarly alarming nature, the bark very often is combined with a prolonged howl, and I have often wondered, whether some remembrance does not return, of the time, when the canine ancestors guarded the camps of old on the lonely plains, infested by ravening animals, and the howl was then the only means of expressing the note of warning. A curious instance of a dog divining danger through sound, came under my notice. It was at the time of the terrific explosion of the munition works at Silvertown, Poplar. The sound of the explosion was heard at my house outside London, and in the room in which I was sitting with the dog. The windows also shook, but the impression I received, was as of a shot-gun, fired fairly close to the house,—a sound which the dog had frequently heard, and which he always resented and barked at, in an ordinary way. At the time of the explosion, however, it threw up its head, and let forth his most concentrated form of watch-dog bark, in which there was a large proportion of howl, and continued this for some time after the sound, which was practically instantaneous, had ceased. I then knew that something had happened, beyond what I myself had grasped. This habit of barking, to let its master know of approaching danger, is also due to the fact, that the guard dog has been usually placed in such a position, outside the camp or house, so that it has to exert its vocal powers to the fullest extent, in order to reach the ears of the owner. For the inverse reason, dogs that are trained for sentry work become more and more silent, as they become interested in their work, and accustomed to the conditions. They are always in close contact with the sentry, and feel more in touch with him, so that there is no necessity to bark loudly, but they give him warning by other means, such as low growling, and a very alert attitude. Picket the same dog, a couple of hundred yards outside the lines by itself, and it will let the guard know by barking, of enemy approach, because it will know that this is the only way it can communicate satisfactorily.

One could write lengthily on speech in dogs. It is a subject, which has not been much studied or experimented with, but which opens up immensely interesting possibilities. The most intelligent dogs exhibit the most comical and fascinating ways of communicating their fancies, desires and mandates. They smile like human beings, they talk,—expressing pleasure and annoyance,—they scold, they grumble, and are, in fact, never at a loss to clearly express themselves. In fact, the family dog, as everyone knows who is fortunate enough to be in possession of the right sort, rules with a rod of iron, has a very high standard as to punctuality, and other modes of behaviour for the members of the family, and leaves no stone unturned to keep them up to the mark. As this is a digression, however, I will hope at some other period to follow up the interesting question of speech in animals, particularly in dogs, both towards human beings, and to each other.

I would merely add, that it is extremely interesting to study the manner in which trained guard dogs communicate with each other. In the New Forest, I had an entire valley set aside for this class of dog. Their kennels and wires were placed on each side of the valley, on the top of the slopes, and the dogs were enabled to see the surrounding country to great advantage. Each dog would be from one hundred to two hundred yards apart. It was absolutely impossible to approach any part of the valley, undetected, by night or day. The best-trained dogs were placed at the most vulnerable points, and also at those posts which commanded the most extensive views. I have often observed the tests made with strangers or men disguised. The nearest outpost dogs would suddenly seem to be arrested, gazing with fixed attention at the far-off approach of the stranger, who would be using every endeavour to creep up under cover, and as unnoticed as possible. Then it would run hurriedly down its wire to its neighbour, and request his immediate presence and attention. Number Two would then rush out to the end of his wire, and both would consult together as to possibilities of danger. They would then agree that the matter wanted looking into, and would bark. At this sound, Number Three, who might be a fairly new arrival, and not quite alive to his duties, and had been reposing in comfort in his kennel, would run along his wire in a state of bewilderment, gazing wildly in all directions for the foe, until directed by his more highly-trained brother to the right quarter. Number Three now thinks he had better let off a bark, too, as the incident certainly looks suspicious. By this time all the other sentinels are thoroughly aroused, and on the qui vive, and are running up and down their wires, calling out to each other their views on the outrageous impudence of any stranger, daring to enter their valley, and adjuring each other to rouse up, and put the attempt down, with a strong hand immediately.

I have frequently found also, that the dogs trained like this, become very interested in their work, and that if they, by any chance, escape from their wires at night, they do not attempt to stray away, but remain close at hand.

Did people sufficiently realize the fact, it would be found that the guarding habit in dogs, which, as I have shown elsewhere, seems to have been instinctive since prehistoric times, is as valuable to humanity as is the power of traction in horses. This last-named attribute is admitted, and, therefore man derives great assistance and benefit from it ; but this much more inherently natural gift in the dog, which can be adapted so marvellously to the needs of man, is only recognized and employed in a desultory fashion. The very prevalent outbreak of burglary and crime, which has been apparent since the war ceased, has been made largely possible by the exclusion of dogs from the household life. This was due, first of all, to the shortage of food during the war, when many people, who preferred their own appetite to that of the faithful family friend, had their good dog destroyed, and also to the exaggerated panic that swept over the country, when one or two dogs exhibited signs of excitement, hurriedly attributed to rabies. I would here mention, that there are several kinds of dog madness or excitement, which the ignorant and mischievous attribute at once to rabies, but which are not so at all.

Anything more deplorable than the spectacle of the poor, homeless, harassed, starving dogs that fled about the country, when the panic was at its height, has seldom been seen in this country, which prides itself on its humanity, and the treacherous, faithless, and cowardly qualities in the human mind, which introduced and permitted this brutal persecution of a helpless animal, well deserves to receive punishment, which is even now seen, in increased undetected crime all over the country. Man's natural guardian has been destroyed in such numbers, that the assassin and burglar can approach and depart unmolested. The remark of an old writer, and quoted by Mr. Darwin, might well be remembered, when a course of injustice is meted out to the faithful associate of man. " A dog is the only thing on this earth that loves you more than he loves himself."

When the War Office decided that guard dogs were also to be trained at the school, the following breeds were appealed for, in addition to those mentioned in the chapter on Messenger Dogs : Great Danes, mastiffs, bull-mastiffs, bull-terriers, retrievers, bull-dogs, and crosses of these breeds.

The selection and training of these guard dogs was one of the chief duties of the War Dog School. As each dog arrived, it was first tested for dispatch-carrying, and if, after a time, it showed no aptitude for this, it was then tested for guard duty, and put on a special part of the ground set aside for this branch of the training. The dogs rested during the day, and were trained at night, and the men, who were especially selected for the training of these guard dogs, rested during the day like the dogs, and came on for duty on night shifts.

The dogs were attached by a running chain to long wires, fifty to one hundred yards long, fastened to stakes in the ground. Each dog had a kennel to retire to in case of inclement weather at night. The duty of the trainers was to advance at various distances and angles, and observe the growing acumen of the dogs, as their senses of sight, hearing, scent, and general alertness became trained.

I have already said that the demand for these dogs came at a time when the man-power question was becoming very serious. It was increasingly difficult for the stores, magazines and filling factories to be adequately guarded. The advent of the dogs seems to have saved the situation, wherever they were employed.

It was further arranged, that an N.C.O. from each protection company, was to visit the War Dog School for two or three days' instruction in the proper placing of the dogs, in relation to the needs of his particular station, and also to be taught the correct method of management. It may be mentioned here, that on the correct placing and management of the dogs, depends the whole success of the idea. A list of regulations was carefully drawn up, based on a careful study of the dogs' needs when on duty. A well-trained dog will give valuable results if these regulations are carried out, and not one of them can be relaxed if the highest efficiency is desired from the dog. For instance, the rule that the dog must be removed during the day to a quiet spot to rest is an extremely important one to observe. Many people imagine that dogs can be on guard during the whole of the twenty-four hours, but this is not so. They need sleep as much as human beings, and it is better that they should have it during the day, when the property can be supervised by the sentries without assistance. Then the necessity of a short walk is also important, as is also correct feeding and at the right time,—which is on coming off duty in the morning. The result of these rules, properly carried out, is, that the dog goes on duty very fresh, and quite comfortable in every way. Now the placing of the wires for the dogs round the areas to be guarded, requires the exercise of intelligence and common sense. On one occasion I found the dogs placed close up to a building inside of which there was a constant roar of machinery, whereby their sense of hearing was getting quite blunted. In another case, the dogs had their wires placed in such a way, that the only footsteps they could hear were those of the sentries. These positions being adjusted the dogs were able to carry out their duties properly.

When the whole scheme of guard dogs was first approached, I was asked if I did not think that poison would be one of the chief dangers to which the dogs would be subjected. I replied that I did not apprehend any great possibility of this, as no unauthorized person would be able to get near enough to the dogs to administer it before his presence would be notified by the dogs, and the sentries would interfere. As it has turned out, I have not had a single report of a casualty from this cause. The only difficulty which I anticipated might arise, was the possibility that the individual officers and men, who had charge of the dogs, might wish to save themselves this trouble, and send in bad or indifferent reports, so as to have the dogs removed. This fear was, I am glad to say, falsified, and, on the contrary, the reports testify to the greatly increased sense of security and assistance in their duties, which the sentries derived from the presence of the dogs.

On the return from duty to the War Dog School on the demobilization of the various defence corps, it was gratifying to find, that the dogs came in, in first-class condition, fat and well cared for and happy-looking, which is a further testimony to the fact that they were appreciated by officers and men.

The sense of guardianship, which is inherent in some dogs, and by judicious training can be intensified, is wonderfully shown forth in the following reports, chosen out of several hundreds of similar burden, which were sent in by the officials in charge of the dogs, at the various centres where the dogs were stationed. The great point to notice is the general consensus of opinion, as to the efficient manner in which the dogs did their work, also that in nearly every case, the presence of the dogs enabled the number of the sentries to be reduced, and giving to those remaining a greater sense of security.

In the first report, the dog is considered of greater value than a sentry :

VERWOOD MAGAZINE

I have the honour to furnish the following respecting the Magazine Guard Dog under my charge at this station. I have not the slightest hesitation in stating that this dog was by far a greater protection than a sentry, and the part patrolled by him was undoubtedly absolutely secure ; he was so generally feared by the people here, that they would not approach the precincts of the magazine, and have approached the county police with a view to getting the dog removed, a matter that met with no favour from me ; the chief reason of this complaint was, that the R.E. fencing was no boundary for him, as happened on two or three occasions.

The dog's work consisted of night patrol, resting through the day, approximately 120 yards' run, and by the state of the track he did it well, as it was beaten to a hard path ; the dog was secured to a lead, and this ran on a line extending the 120 yards, as it was not fixed near the fence, and a rather long lead ; the dog did practically one-half of the sentry work of the enclosure.

(Signed) C. MONK,

O.C. Det., Verwood Magazine.

The next report confirms this opinion :

THORNE

I beg to report that the dogs I had under my charge at Thorne rendered very valuable assistance to the sentries on duty, especially during the night.

They were attached to wires, which enabled them to traverse the full length of the stacking ground, and it was practically impossible for anyone to approach the stacks without the dogs warning the sentry ; in fact, in my opinion, they did their work quite as well as a flying sentry At the least sign of any person approaching, they were always on the alert.

I have the honour to be, Sir,

Your obedient Servant,

(Signed) H. DENTON, Cpl.

In the following report the scenting power of the dogs has been noted

NORTH WALSHAM

I have pleasure in informing you that the three guard dogs which have been used at Stalham, Martham, and North Walsham have, in each instance, carried out their duties in a very satisfactory manner.

By their use it was possible to mount only a single guard at night, instead of the double guard, as is usual in the case of guards for ammunition dumps.

It has been found that these dogs will scent a stranger approaching at night a very considerable time before their presence was known by the soldier on his post, and, in my opinion, these dogs have quite justified their employment in ammunition dumps as watch dogs.

(Signed) B. T. WARD, Major, R.F.A.,

O.C. 1206th Battery, R.F.A.

North Walsham, Norfolk,

I used generally to ask the officers to report to me any case of attempted aggression, but the fact of dogs being employed seems to have been sufficient in nearly every case in preventing anything of this sort. The next report illustrates this :

13*

WEST BECKHAM

The following report on the watch dog doing duty with this unit is forwarded for your information :

The dog was posted outside the entrance to the Main Ammunition Dump of the 223rd Mixed Brigade. The possession of this dog enabled the military authority to reduce the guard from fifteen men down to a patrol of seven men. The dog had wonderful intelligence,—he knew the footsteps of the patrol, and when hearing strange footsteps he created a tremendous disturbance, thereby warning the occupants of the hut a few yards away from the dog's post.

There was no instance of prevented aggression—it had become well known that the dog was on the spot, and I think that this fact prevented would-be intruders from attempting to gain admission to the dump. I had one man told off to care for the dog—the animal got used to him—but no other man dared go near him.

In my opinion, watch dogs are a great asset in the service, and I would like to see them fully utilized in the peace-time army.

(Signed) B. S. BALL, Capt. R.F.A.
416th Amm. Column.

West Beckham, Holt, Norfolk,

These reports all testify to the saving of man-power :

BANBURY

With reference to a report on the work of the dogs—I can only say that experience has proved that the factory has been adequately guarded, and I am satisfied that the dogs have been an important factor in the guarding of our stores. Of the four dogs, three were placed on duty at dusk, and taken off at daybreak—each dog having one day off in four. Long runs were provided at each of the three stores, which contained large quantities of explosives.

With the aid of the dogs, we were able to guard the whole of the stores area with six constables (two on each of five shifts of eight hours), whereas had it been necessary to place constables at each store, a matter I should have considered had we not had the dogs, this would have necessitated employing at least a further six constables. I am pleased to say that no instances of aggression have occurred at this factory.

Yours truly,
(Signed) H. D. SNOWBALL,
General Manager.

Banbury, Oxon.

HAYLE

In reply to yours, 25,000, dated February 12th, 1919, one of the two dogs was kept at Pinhoe, and the other at Monks Road, Exeter, to assist in guarding stores of cordite at those places. On arrival of the dogs, the guard of each place was reduced from two N.C.O.'s and twelve men to one N.C.O. and seven men. There was a barbed wire entanglement round each store (formerly brick works), and the dog was kept inside the entanglement. There is no recorded instance of aggression having been prevented. The dogs were very intelligent and well trained, and quite well suited for their work.

(Signed) WILLIAM THOMAS, Capt.,
O.C. No. 251 Protection Company, R.D.C.

Hayle.

GEORGETOWN, PAISLEY

I am pleased to inform you that the work of the war dogs on this station has been entirely satisfactory. To begin with, we had twenty-four dogs, three of which died, so that all through we have had twenty-one dogs, which were employed by night only on the loneliest and most dangerous posts to accompany the sentries, and relieve them of as much strain as possible. Each dog was attached to a long wire, which ran the length of the sentry's post.

Had there been no dogs, it would have been necessary on many of the posts to have employed double sentries, so that the saving in man-power has come to about twenty men per night. There has been no occasion on which aggression was prevented by the dogs, although on many occasions their own aggression was a source of great inconvenience to visiting rounds.

(Signed) P. FORREST, 2nd Lieut.,
For O.C. No. 202 Protection Coy., R.D.C.

Georgetown, Paisley,

COLCHESTER

The unit under my command finds the guards at three ammunition dumps, and I have had a war dog at each.

The dogs have been on a running chain, and have enabled one post at least, at each of the dumps, to be dispensed with. They have only been employed at night. The dogs have released for other duties at least nine men.

I have no knowledge of any instances of aggression at any dump.

(Signed) I. H. CROSS, Major,
Commanding 69th Protection Coy., R.D.C.

Colchester.

DORCHESTER

I beg to report that there have been two dogs attached to guards under my command : one a chow, with the detachment guarding the Hamworthy Magazine ; the other, a mastiff, with the detachment guarding the Verwood Magazine.

The Officer i/c of these guards reports that both these dogs have done excellent work ; by their use I have been able to release six men on each guard.

(Signed) J. WORTH, Major,

Commanding Prison Guard, R.D.C.

Dorchester.

BOURNE, LINCS.

Four of the dogs were utilized as sentries at the Holwell Magazine and proved most useful, particularly during the darkness of the winter months, and it was only necessary to have one post, employing three men by night and by day, the dogs doing the rest, thereby saving at least nine others.

At Dudley, where only one dog was utilized, the same thing applies, the saving of three men from sentry go.

Yours obediently,

(Signed) CAPT. ——

O.C. 165th Protection Coy., R.D.C.

Manor House, Bourne, Lincs.

NEWPORT, MON.

The number of men employed as sentries, on the police patrol system, was four for one post.

To effectively guard the magazine without the aid of the dogs would have necessitated twelve men for three posts, so that it may be taken that eight men were in ·th way released for other duties.

The dogs were employed to give warning to the sentry on duty of the approach after nightfall of any person to the vicinity of the barbed wire fence surrounding the magazine enclosure. They were placed one dog on each of the four sides of the enclosure inside the fence, and attached to a wire run of about twenty-five yards, parallel to, and about three yards from, the fence.

No instance of actual aggression has been reported to me, but I have no doubt that the dogs acted as an effective deterrent, and may be considered as effective for the class of work on which they were employed.

(Signed) M. BRUCE, Lieut.,

O.C. Det., 331st Protection Coy., R.D.C.

Athletic Grounds, Newport, Mon.

GLENFIELD

Five dogs were used here to guard the ammunition dump. They always gave warning of the approach of any strangers. The guard used to consist of eighteen men before the arrival of the dogs, and only nine after their arrival.

(Signed) PTE. ——,

For O.C. Det., 136th Protection Coy., R.D.C.

Heather Brickworks, Glenfield.

ST. THOMAS

I have to report that the dogs at this depot were used for guarding the premises, which at that time consisted of several scattered buildings and a large yard. Without these dogs it would have been necessary to have a standing guard of six men and one N.C.O. ; with these dogs it was only necessary to keep one man on night duty. This I consider was of great service, and proved a great saving to the public.

(Signed) S. BIRD, Lieut., R.A.S.C.,
Officer i/c Supplies, Exeter Sub-District.
R.A.S.C., Haven Road, St. Thomas, Exeter.

At certain centres the dogs were used by the sentries on patrol duty, when they were usually taken out on the leash. The following reports illustrate this method of working ·

SALTERFORTH

In reference to your order *re* dogs, the duty which the above were doing was magazine watch dogs ; each dog did about one mile patrol on a lead with a man. They proved satisfactory in every way, also whenever a civilian came near they would bark. The dogs were not on a loose wire, but always on a lead.

(Signed) T. A. ASTON, Sergt.,
For O.C. 153rd Protection Coy., R.D.C.
Salterforth.

NEWCASTLE-ON-TYNE

Two dogs which are being returned to 200th Coy., on the 12th inst., have been at Stockton Hay Storage, where they performed very useful work by giving assistance to the sentries under a very difficult patrol, on which there was a considerable amount of trespass. The dogs accompanied the sentries on their patrol, being on the leash, and almost invariably gave warning of an approach before the sentries heard it themselves.

The dogs were used alternately on the Stock Yard, which was a very large one, and on the chopping shed and loading wharves.

The latter was really a very difficult patrol, as the shed had, as well as the chopping machinery and supplies of forage in it, a lot of disused iron-rolling machinery, and covered a large area.

(Signed) JAMES BRAND, Capt.,

151st Protection Coy., R.D.C.

Handysides Buildings, Percy Street,

Newcastle-on-Tyne.

ABERDEEN

I have the honour to report that the work of the dogs with outlying detachments of this company has been satisfactory.

It was estimated that these dogs were equal to one sentry, and a reduction in personnel of ten men was attributable to their presence.

These dogs are doing patrol work along with sentries on night duty, and were also employed inside barbed wire entanglements to prevent approach of unauthorized persons to certain Government property.

No active aggression has been attempted, but notice was always given by the dogs barking freely at any strangers approaching, and also of people loitering in the vicinity.

I have the honour to be, Sir,

Your obedient servant,

(Signed) M. TAYLOR, Major,

Commanding No. 214 Protection Coy., R.D.C.

Fonthill Barracks, Aberdeen.

BINFIELD

The watch dog at Binfield Magazine was worked as follows :

Acted as sentry from 5 p.m. until 5 a.m. He used to patrol the magazine with sentries at the time of clocking up the tell-tale clock every hour. No strangers dare come near—he always gave warning. Owing to his work, the guard was reduced from one sergeant and twenty-eight men to one corporal and six men. He did his work most satisfactorily, and we are sorry to lose him.

For O.C.,
6th Battn. City of London Regt.

The report of the dogs used at the Chislehurst Caves shows how useful they can be for searching this enclosed sort of ground :

REPORT ON TWO DOGS USED AT CHISLEHURST CAVES

These two dogs were used on patrol, and did the work in searching out the dene holes, undergrowth of the woods, and throughout the woods. On the word " Search," the dogs searched the undergrowth to look for suspicious persons, and I consider the work of the dogs was excellent. They were used for guarding ammunition stores in the caves.

At night, without the dogs, it would have been impossible to patrol the woods. In these holes any persons could easily be concealed.

(Signed) CORPL. SPARK,
For O.C. 103rd Protection Coy., R.D.C.

CHISLEHURST

I have the honour to report that war dogs which were under my command at Chislehurst were invaluable in the work they were used for.

They were taken on patrol work, and used to search undergrowth and dene holes where it was impossible for a man to obtain a foothold.

In this case they did not release any men, the guard having been reduced before the dogs arrived.

(Signed) E. H. RINSEY, Lieut.,
For O.C. No. 103 Protection Coy., R.D.C.
Chislehurst.

It was found that these dogs very quickly distinguish between soldiers and civilians.

REPORT ON WATCH DOG AT VERWOOD

This dog was on duty from dark to daylight, working on a steel wire 140 yards in length ; he took the place of one sentry by night. He was a very valuable dog in his services, being very dangerous to civilians and not allowing anyone in or near the magazine.

(Signed) PTE. GOW,
For O.C. 254th Protection Coy., R.D.C.
Verwood.

RATBY, LEICESTER

Three dogs were used for guarding the munition dump ; they were on wires during the night, but taken off during the day and fed once in the morning. If any civilians came near, they always gave the alarm, and would have attacked. Two sentries patrolled alongside the dogs at night.

(Signed) PTE. ——,
For O.C. 156th Protection Coy., R.D.C.
Ratby, near Leicester.

REPORT ON WATCH DOG AT DARTFORD, KENT

This dog has been on an attached post at Fort Halsted ; he was used with the sentry on a lead from 10 p.m. to 6 a.m. He distinguished well between civilians and men in khaki, and he even knew the steps of the relieving sentry at night, but did not take any notice, while he always barked at the footsteps of civilians.

(Signed) ROGERS, Corpl.,

For O.C. 118th Protection Coy., R.D.C.

Dartford, Kent.

DRINGHOUSES

The following four dogs, which were sent to Middleton Colliery, I found to be fierce when approached by a civilian. They were all capable of the duties for which they were intended

Black smooth-haired retriever, black curly-haired retriever, black and tan Airedale terrier, black and white cross-bred Pom and English terrier.

(Signed) A. HUMPHRIES, Corpl., N.C.O. i/c Guard,

For O.C. 200th Protection Coy., R.D.C.

Dringhouses, York.

The moral effect of the presence of the dogs in most neighbourhoods seemed to be strong, as is shown in the following report :

OLDBURY

The establishment of this detachment guarding Tanks and Tank testing ground, was, previous to June 3rd, 1918, three N.C.O.'s and twenty-eight men, providing four posts, the men doing ordinary sentry go, two on and four off.

With the advent of the dogs we were able to release

eight of these men, the remaining twenty doing patrol work, four hours on and twelve off, mounting the dogs with them at dusk and relieving them soon after daylight.

There were no particular instances where aggression was actually prevented, but the moral effect was great, as the general impression prevailed in the neighbourhood that it would be preferable to encounter an armed sentry than one of the dogs.

(Signed) O. STAFFORD LAMBERT, Lieut.,
O.C. Det., 261st Protection Coy., R.D.C.
Site " C," H.M. Factory, Oldbury.

There is strong evidence to show the greater sense of security which was felt by the sentries as the result of the presence of the dogs :

LOUGHBOROUGH

I was in charge of six watch dogs at 156th Protection Company, Normanton Hills, Loughborough. I had six dogs on four posts ; they were posted just before dusk. The dogs were on wire runs about twenty yards in length, guarding a T.N.T. compound. They were satisfactory, and gave warning of any approaching strangers. The sentries felt more secure with the dogs than without them.

(Signed) BRING, Corpl.,
For O.C. 156th Protection Coy., R.D.C.
Loughborough.

REPORT ON WAR DOGS' SERVICES WITH 154TH PROTECTION COMPANY, R.D.C.

(1) Barnbow.	10 runs.	6 sentries dispensed with.
(2) Middleton.	4 runs.	2 sentries dispensed with.
(3) Loisterdyke.	5 posts.	1 sentry dispensed with.
(4) Coldre Vale.	2 runs.	1 sentry dispensed with.

Work Done :

Guarding.	(1) Munitions factories.
	(2) Explosives magazine.
	(3) Forage store.
	(4) Picric acid store dump.
How placed.	1, 2 and 4, on wire runs adjoining sentry posts.
	(3) Fixed posts.
Value placed on dogs' services.	Useful work done, particularly by night, as additional ears and eyes for the sentries.

Ipswich

I am pleased to report that the dogs have been very serviceable on their duties as watch dogs over ammunition dumps. In all cases where they have been in use, I have been enabled to reduce the guard by half; they have always given due notice of anyone approaching the post, besides being a source of security to the guards and patrols. Posts and wire have been in use in different positions, and the dog put on different wires at different times ; this has worked well.

(Signed) E. H. Coombe, Major and O.C.
Ipswich.

Ringwood

I beg to report that the dog which is in use at this store as watch dog is certainly a success, as the animal does not only give confidence in the night watchman in discharging his duties, but I should say also releases three men for such duty. The dog is comfortably housed, but up to the present there have been no aggressors.

For your information, please.

Yours obediently,
(Signed) Harry Bailey, Corpl.
Storekeeper, Hay Store, Ringwood.

LEIGHTON BUZZARD

I beg to report that the work of the dogs on the Woburn Sands Magazine has been very effective.

They are very keen on their work, and their continued use reduces the strength of the guard required there to a minimum.

(Signed) J. W. GREGORY, Lieut.,
O.C. Det., 70th Protection Coy., R.D.C.

To :
    O.C. 70th Protection Coy., R.D.C.,
        Leighton Buzzard.

A reduction in the hours of duty of the sentries is here noted :

With reference to the work of the War Dog, attached to a detachment of this battalion, stationed at Binfield, the following is a statement made by men of the guard :

With the aid of this dog, it was possible for each sentry to do six hours on duty instead of two hours on and four hours off. This probably means the release of three or four men.

The duty engaged on was guarding a magazine at Binfield.

The dog was with the sentry while at his post, preventing anyone approaching, and going the rounds with the guard, preventing anyone loitering near the magazine.

The men state that the dog was extremely useful, and a very valuable sentry.

(Signed) C. CLAY, Capt. and Adjutant,
For Officer Commanding,
6th (R.) Battn. City of London Rifles.

Bramley.

Guard dog guarding a magazine.

Morning parade of guard dogs.

[To face p. 208.

A group of trained guard dogs.

Morning parade of war dogs

[*To face p*. 209.

Some very fine Airedales were sent also to the Base Headquarters in Italy. The officer in whose charge they were wrote to me ·

" I am satisfied that the dogs have been a complete success. They have taken the place of four N.C.O.'s and twelve men daily."

The following report deals with the last work of the guard dogs before they were demobilized ·

With reference to your visit with the O.C. Troops and your queries as to the usefulness of Watch Dogs, I have to report that I find these dogs of the greatest assistance in closed stores.

When I took over the supply depot two months ago, I was having stores broken into nightly ; but since the advent of the dogs, there has been no case of a store being broken open.

On two occasions stores had been tampered with, and it is evident the persons attempting the entry of the stores had thought better of it, on discovering the canine occupants.

LIEUT.-COLONEL SYKES,
O.C., R.A.S.C., Bulford Sub-District.

Bulford.

The following were the official regulations issued to each centre where Guard Dogs were employed

REGULATIONS FOR THE CARE AND MANAGEMENT OF GUARD DOGS EMPLOYED AT VULNERABLE POINTS

The employment of Guard Dogs enables an enclosure to be adequately guarded with the minimum of sentries or watchmen, and owing to the dogs' keen sense of hearing and smell, gives greater security than can be obtained by men alone.

The presence of dogs becomes a well-known deterrent.

(1) *Selection of Dogs.*

The selection and training of dogs is undertaken by the Commandant, War Dog School, Shoeburyness, who will dispatch them on demand to complete an authorized establishment.

(2) *Dogs on Wires.*

The best method of using dogs is to attach them to running wires placed along or around zones or buildings it is desired should be protected.

The wire can, if need be, be placed so that there is a continuous ring of wire, with one dog just able to meet the next dog at each end of its wire. This is the most invulnerable method.

There should be a clear space between adjacent runs.

The run wire may be of light steel rope ; it should be tightly strained between stout pickets about one foot from the ground, and of suitable length, not exceeding one hundred yards.

(3) *Sentry Duty.*

The approach of an intruder will be heard by at least one of the dogs, which will at once give the alarm to the others ; it is then the sentry's duty to at once investigate the cause.

(4) *Dogs required.*

The number of dogs required will depend on the amount of ground which requires protecting.

(5) *Kennels.*

The dogs should be provided with kennels of some sort,

when on duty, placed beside the running wire, where they can retire in the event of very inclement weather.

(6) *Patrol Dogs.*

A dog on a slip lead may accompany a sentry or watch-man on beats (which cannot well be protected by a running wire) in guarding railway sidings and trucks on them.

(7) *Prevention of Poisoning.*

In the event of dogs being required to guard a building surrounded by a fence or wall, their running wires should be placed away from the fence and near the building, so that " Poison " cannot easily be thrown to them.

While the danger of poison cannot be wholly eliminated, it will be difficult for this to be administered if the sentry does his duty, by investigating the first alarm given by the dog. And so far, experience goes to prove that this danger can practically be discounted.

(8) *Dogs off Duty (Daytime).*

The dogs are to be taken away during the daytime, and put to rest in a closed shed or stable. They should be fed on coming off duty once in twenty-four hours, and then chained to a bed of straw, to induce them to lie down and sleep. They should be kept isolated from people except their own keeper.

(9) *Dogs on Duty (Night).*

On going on duty at night they should be exercised for a short time before being chained to the wires; they will then be alert and fresh after their rest, and ready for duty.

(10) *Selection of Keepers for Dogs.*

A man excellent for his knowledge of dogs should be detailed to attend to them. He should keep the sleeping and running places clean, and prepare the dogs' food. He also should exercise them, and take them to and from duty at stated hours. He should also keep them nicely groomed and see that the bowls of water for each dog, at both day and night positions, are kept filled with clean water.

The selection of keepers in charge of guard dogs is of high importance. They should be chosen from men who have been gamekeepers, shepherds, or Hunts' servants.

(11) *Attention to Dogs' Comfort.*

(i.) The day and night quarters should be thoroughly cleansed once a day and occasionally cleaned out with disinfectant.

(ii.) The dog should be brushed with a hard brush and combed once daily.

Should the dog get wet on duty, he should be rubbed dry.

(12) *Feeding.*

(i.) The feeding of each dog is according to the Government ration, i.e., one pound of biscuits per diem, plus $\frac{1}{2}$ pound of cooked horse-flesh.

(If horse-flesh is not obtainable, an equal amount of meat refuse from the men's dinners can be substituted.)

(ii.) The dog must have the above ration per diem.

(13) *Cooking.*

These should be cooked together. If it is difficult to provide the biscuits and horse-flesh, the meal may consist of $1\frac{1}{2}$ lbs. of cookhouse offal, which should be composed of soup, bread scraps, meat, etc., etc.

(iii.) A bowl of clean water should always be in reach of the dog.

(iv.) A dog on duty by day should be fed by night.

(v.) Dogs used for duty at night should be fed immediately on coming off in the morning, but on no account must be fed before going on duty.

(14) *Ailments.*

(i) It should be borne in mind that the less medicine given to the dog, the better he is.

(ii.) In case of wounds, broken limbs, etc., apply to the Army Veterinary Corps.

(15) *Supervision.*

The dogs are under the supervision of the Officer Commanding the area vulnerable points.

He will be responsible that officers of the R.D.C. see that all men in charge of guard dogs are provided with a copy of these instructions, and see that the same are carried out.

(17) *Bedding.*

It has been decided that bedding shall be provided for War Dogs during winter months and during sickness.

Wood shavings and bracken should be used if available, but, if not, straw may be demanded from Supply, at the scale of five lbs. per week.

CHAPTER VIII

SENTRY DOGS

" The unwearied watch their list'ning leaders keep,
  And couching close repel invading sleep,
  So faithful dogs their . . . charge maintain
  They start, they gaze around, watch every side, and turn to every
    sound."   HOMER'S *Iliad.*

THERE should be a great future for the Sentry Dog, which must be understood as quite apart from the Guard or Defence Dog. The duties of the two dogs differ, in that the guard dog is required to defend a certain area, while the sentry dog has to take up its duties with any soldier and at any spot. This is more difficult work, and calls for increased intelligence, hearing and scent on the part of the dog.

During the first few months of the war, before any official action had been taken in the direction of training military dogs, I had supplied a good many to the armies on the Western Front, and also to the expeditionary forces in Egypt and Mesopotamia.

An Airedale I supplied to an officer of the Berkshire Regiment was taken on patrol one night. It suddenly stopped and began to growl. The party heard and saw nothing suspicious, but the officer ordered the men to lie flat. Immediately afterwards, an enemy patrol passed by, close to them, without noticing. Our patrols then rose noiselessly, and captured them all.

Some dogs that were sent out to an infantry regiment in Egypt, averted what might have been a serious disaster. It was on the same day as the Yeomanry were so severely attacked, and when there was a dense mist. The infantry were also attacked, but the dogs were too quick, and so clearly indicated the approach of the enemy, that an order was given to fire into the mist. This had an immediate effect, and the attack was checked. When the mist cleared away, large numbers of enemy dead were found.

I also sent some good Airedale sentries to the flooded areas of the Belgian front, and they were much appreciated, and there were eighteen Airedales with the South-West African Force. General Botha was very pleased with these, especially on one occasion, when they were the means of warning of a large enemy ambush, and whereby a considerable capture of the enemy was effected.

Sentry dogs are particularly suitable, where the conditions are those of open warfare. For this reason, there was not so much interest taken in them for the Western Front as time went on, and the position of our army became more entrenched. On certain parts of the front, however, which were not so consolidated, and especially towards the end, they would have been useful.

I have mentioned already that some sentry dogs were trained at the War Dog School, and were sent out to Salonica. Airedales had been especially asked for, so they were all of this breed ; but, as I will point out further on, it would be a mistake to limit the choice of dog to this kind. They formed a very handsome contingent, and went out in charge of some specially trained men. Very good work was done after arrival, and no doubt very large use would have been made of this sort of sentry aid on this front, as it was found that on forward posts in the mountains, the dogs were of great service in detecting enemy movement at night. About this time, however, the fighting began to subside. There is not the slightest doubt, that these dogs would always be of inestimable service at all isolated posts, open to enemy attack at night.

On the North-West Frontier of India, for instance, there should be an organized permanent sentry-dog service. It would be extremely difficult for a sentry to be approached at night, even by the most subtle rifle thief, without the dog giving him sufficient warning to put him on his guard, and the fact that he had such an ally by his side would give him greatly enhanced confidence.

Among Army officers I have found many objectors to the idea of using dogs with sentries, and the arguments they advance are always the same ; I should say, however, that the objections come in every case from those who have not tried the dogs. I have not found any of the objections proven in actual practice. I will admit at the same time, that this work in the Army must always be administered by an expert. The dogs must be properly trained at the training-school, and the whole service supervised and controlled by an officer, who thoroughly understands the necessities of the work from the dog point of view.

I will here mention the arguments of the objectors :

1. That there is danger in the fact, that a sentry, having a dog to depend on, will be tempted to be careless in his work.

2. That the dog's barking would reveal the position, and draw the enemy fire.

My answer to the first objection is, that under those conditions, where there is no particular danger to life from enemy attack, and where the sentry might, therefore, not feel the same necessity for alertness, the work is likely to be better done, if a dog is posted with him. If the sentry is naturally lazy, or open to bribes, there is no remedy, if he is by himself ; whereas the dog cannot be bribed, and does not sleep, so that, at all events, the situation is rendered more difficult for the intruder, as he can never count on the dog, even if he thinks he might undermine the sentry's alertness or fidelity.

In the case of active warfare, the sentry, in his own interests, is less likely to sleep, and the danger of a man doing so, owing to undue fatigue, or any other cause, is greatly lessened if he has a dog with him.

The sentry dog does not sleep at night, and will either keep his sentry awake, or wake him up, and, in fact, represents the second string to the bow.

The whole matter may be summed up by emphasizing the obvious fact, that where it might be difficult to approach a sentry post with only a man on duty, it would be a hundred times more so, if there is also a trained sentry dog to reckon with.

In dispensing with these dogs, it may be said, that a very effective means of defence against unwarned attack is neglected.

In the case of the second objection, that the dog would give warning and draw the enemy fire, it may certainly be admitted that there are occasions when absolute silence is essential. At these times it would be safer not to post the dog, although even here, by the use of a strap muzzle, any noise which the dog would make could be controlled to a great extent, while by its alert attitude, it would give the sentry warning long before he himself was aware of enemy movement. Apart from this, there are scores of occasions, when no risk whatever is incurred by the dog growling, or even barking.

The Saving of Man-Power

Sentry dogs can also be the means of greatly reducing the sentries, and are thus a valuable asset for the reduction of man-power.

The Type of Dog

The qualities required in these dogs are, acute hearing and scent, sagacity, fidelity, and a strong sense of duty. Any dog showing these attributes can be developed into a good sentry dog, provided it is the right size, which must be that of a collie or Airedale, or large Irish terrier—in fact, middle size. Anything smaller is not so able to stand long marches, nor would be sufficiently powerful in other respects.

White dogs should be avoided, and, as a whole, dogs are better than bitches. There are exceptions to every rule, but I find that dogs are rather more aggressive, and less self-centred than bitches, which are of a milder and less alert disposition.

It seems to be supposed that Airedales are essentially the best for this work, but this is not necessarily the case, as many other breeds of this size are equally good. The Airedale standard is certainly a good one, as the hardiness and fondness for the master exhibited by this breed are excellent qualities on which to start work. But many collies and retrievers, of the rugged sort, are first-rate, as well as crosses of all these breeds. A good weather-resisting coat is necessary, even if the dogs are for service in a hot climate, as during the hot weather it is easy to clip them, and the hair can be allowed to grow again as the cold weather approaches.

The Training

The training of these dogs must be carried on at the official training school, and must be under expert management. It is useless to imagine that any dogs, picked up here and there, can be utilized by a unit for its sentries. The dogs, to understand the work properly, must be carefully trained, and this must be done at night at the school. The training commences at dusk, when the dogs are led from their kennels by soldier keepers to various posts in isolated spots. Persons representing the enemy are instructed to approach from various directions. Accurate note is taken of the time and the distance at which the dog first takes notice, and how much ahead he is of the sentry, in detecting the approach of the enemy. After a course of this training, the dog becomes well aware that he is expected to be on the look-out, and his senses, already naturally acute, are developed in a remarkable way. The training is somewhat slow, as it is not possible to do more than two or three attacks each night, and a good deal of patience and understanding is required in the trainer, and in those in charge. Day training is not necessary, as it is essential that the dog should rest during the day, so that it may be thoroughly alert at night. In any case, in the daylight, the sentry can easily detect the enemy himself from afar, so that he has no need for the dog at this time.

Feeding and Kennelling

Sentry dogs, both when under training, and after they are drafted from the training school to the various units, must be kept, during the day, in a quiet and isolated spot, and unvisited by anyone except the men told off as keepers to attend to them. These men should be selected on account of a previous knowledge of dogs, and when posted to a unit, supervision over both men and dogs should be carried out by a specially detailed officer. The isolation of the dogs is a most important point, as if they become accustomed to see strangers constantly, they lose their alertness and sharpness. A good way is to place their kennels, which should be the ordinary box variety, in a stable, or compound, which can be locked up. They should be made very comfortable with straw in their kennels, so that they rest well.

Their meal should be given, on coming off duty, in the very early morning, and should be ample. They must on no account be fed at night.

CORRECT POSTING AND MANAGEMENT

When sentry dogs are first drafted from the training school to any unit, a little consideration must be shown them in the first instance on arrival. They must be allowed time to settle, and the first tests must not be too severe. After a few days, the dogs will have developed the possessive sense for their new environment, and the sentries will also understand the method of handling them. It will be understood, that these dogs will have already gone through a considerable period of training, and all that is necessary now, is, that those who have the handling of them, should be themselves sufficiently educated in the methods of communication employed by the dog, to be able to interpret those signs. Therefore, the training of the sentries should also include definite instruction on the rules to observe when sentry dogs are employed. It should be pointed out, that the effect of employing dogs, and of carefully observing the rules of management, will. be to greatly safeguard the sentry himself, and to enable him to carry out his duty with increased efficiency.

Rules

1. The dog should be posted at dusk or after dark, and must go off duty in the early hours. It is highly important that they must never be on duty at an hour or spot where there is much traffic, as they thereby deteriorate.

2. The dog must be handed over to the sentry by the keeper, who will have attached a leather lead to the dog's collar, and the sentry, who should have been previously instructed on his procedure in connection with the dog, will lead it away, and will keep the dog beside him on the lead all the time. It has been suggested that it would be a good plan to picket the dog a hundred yards or so beyond the sentry, so that it can give warning ahead, but this is a mistake. The dog should be close to the sentry, so that the latter can study and feel its movements, as it will be found that the dog will begin to give warning by its attitude alone, long before it actually makes any sound. The sentry will find that the dog at this hour of nightfall is in a high state of tension and suspicion. All its senses are doubly acute, and even if it is quite dark, he will feel the sudden cessation of movement, the muscular tension, and the rising hair on the part of his companion. These signs will indicate that some suspicious sound has been heard. It is his duty then to give his full attention to this warning, and to listen intently himself. If the dog gradually assumes a normal attitude, the exciting cause, whatever it was, has passed away ; if it commences to give low growls, the sentry can be quite certain that there is cause for extreme watchfulness, and must be prepared for immediate action. It should be clearly emphasized, how greatly the sentry's own safety is enhanced by this observance of the dog's move-

ments, as the latter will give signs of uneasiness when the enemy is yet a long way off, and thus give plenty of time to prepare. It will not bark outright, as a rule, until the foe is much closer.

By having the dog close at hand also, the sentry can control it easily, and can, if necessary, adjust the muzzle.

PATROLLING

The instructions in Rules 1 and 2 apply equally when a dog is attached for duty to a patrol. It should be led at the head of the patrol, and, except under exceptional circumstances, should not be allowed off the lead. The exception would be, when it can be put in charge of someone with whom it is well acquainted, and when the party is passing through enclosed country. The dog should only be allowed to beat a few yards ahead.

3. Where there are permanent outposts, it is easier for the dogs, if each one is taken nightly to the same post. They thus get to know the lie of the ground well.

4. *Equipment:* The sentry dog, when on duty, should be equipped with a good strong collar with a brass plate, on which is the dog's official number, and also the number of the unit to which it is attached. A strap muzzle with adjustable straps, and a leather lead are also required.

I have already stated that on such frontiers as the North-West Provinces of India, where a more or less permanent state of war exists, sentry dogs would be invaluable at all times, and our investing troops in Mesopotamia would find them very useful. In all countries under our control, where there are uncivilized, or semi-civilized, populations, there should be permanent services of dogs. In war, they are particularly useful in jungle, and savage warfare, when the troops are advancing through enclosed country, and are liable to be ambushed.

I here give a statement, written by a non-commissioned officer, who saw service in German East Africa in the war. He afterwards came for instruction at the War Dog School, and the article was written after his course, and when he thoroughly understood the possibilities and limitations of this sort of dog service ·

USES OF DOGS IN SAVAGE WARFARE

PATROL

In savage warfare, where patrols have to penetrate dense bush, and are liable to be ambushed any time, two dogs accompanying the advance guard, and allowed to go freely ahead—say, 150 to 200 yards—and also permitted to wander into the bush, would practically eliminate any risk of the main patrol party being cut up. (Patrol parties usually are about fifty strong in dense bush country.)

One instance I may quote was at a post named Bura, East Africa, on the military railway from Voi to Maktau. A large body had to patrol the roadway, which ran parallel to the railway, and on the return journey came back along the railway track. In November, 1915, a patrol were on the above-mentioned duty, and everything went all right, until a very dense part of the forest was reached, where two trails crossed. The advance party were allowed to pass unmolested, but immediately the main body of the patrol arrived, a large force of Germans opened fire, and practically annihilated our patrol. If the advance guard had been accompanied by two dogs, (not on leash), the possibility would have been that the enemy would have been detected, and the patrol saved.

With Mounted Infantry

Dogs running loose, accompanying a mounted patrol, would be of great assistance, as the dogs would be able to detect any enemy waiting in ambush, or enemy scouts seeking intelligence, as it is a most difficult problem to solve, how to deal with the Intelligence Department of an enemy in a dense tropical bush, where so much cover is afforded a scout.

Two good reliable dogs with a mounted patrol, entering dense bush, would no doubt betray the presence of anyone in hiding, and would also be of great assistance in tracking the enemy when stealing away.

Guarding Railways

At the construction of the military railway from Voi to Maktau, in East Africa, there was great difficulty experienced in checking raiding parties of the enemy, who penetrated our guards and blew the line up. If there had been dogs used, at various intervals along the line, during the night patrol, I am sure the Germans would not have been able to have accomplished their dynamiting operations. Paul J. Rainy, Esq., the American sportsman, was at Voi with a few Airedales, and used them to track the raiding parties after the damage was done, and, as far as I know, he was quite successful.

Blockhouses

A dog, posted at night with a sentry, at the blockhouse, would enable the sentry to detect the advance of an enemy with greater sharpness, and at a much longer distance than any sentry could possibly do.

Sentry dog on duty.

'ront

Sentry dog   This dog went out with the Expeditionary Force in 1914
and was killed on the Aisne

Sentry dog on Western Front, sent to Belgian Army in 1914.

Outposts

A dog with an outpost, or outlying picket, would be of great assistance in savage warfare, as the bush being so thick it is next to impossible to detect an enemy creeping up to give a surprise attack, and, of course, the picket would, unless great vigilance is exercised, be taken by surprise, and possibly the result would be disastrous for the encampment, as once a picket is done away with without much noise, the camp could easily be susceptible to a surprise attack in force. So with the assistance of a good alert dog with each picket, the danger would greatly be eliminated.

Guarding a Camp

A camp pitched in the midst of a dense bush is always liable to surprise attack, unless a very strong cordon of pickets is posted. Dogs, placed a distance of half a mile from camp, at intervals of thirty yards apart, would, on the advance of an enemy, give the alarm to the out-line or in-line pickets, as the case may be, and, therefore, the camp would not be taken by surprise. Furthermore, dogs picketed as mentioned above would certainly save life, and do away with a large number of sentries, especially if the force was depleted in strength by sickness, as is often the case in the tropics.

The colonel of a British infantry regiment made the following statement to me :

Dogs for Mesopotamia

" I think that as watch dogs to replace sentries, they would be invaluable.

" The Arab, especially south of Kut, is a born looter, and no one, who has not had practical experience out there, can realize the ease, with which an Arab can outwit the very best sentry, be he Indian or British.

" Dogs, with their keener powers of smelling and hearing, would be most useful in the guarding of dumps and magazines.

" I would suggest that they be trained to kill noiselessly, if possible."

(Signed) WHITTALL, Lieut.-Colonel
i/c Oxfordshire Light Infantry.

I think the following argument of a correspondent to the *Glasgow Herald*, in favour of sentry and scout dogs, is clearly put :

" It has always been my opinion—with all deference to those who will dismiss the theory without discussion, but with the comment of ' Rubbish ! '—that, had our troops, when marching to the fatal Magersfontein, had the assistance of a few reliable sentinel or scouting dogs, that engagement, instead of being the cause of much humiliation and sorrow to our country, would have been another added to the list of glorious victories inscribed on the colours of our Highland regiments. If anyone would say there is no food for thought in this statement, let me ask him, in the first place, if he knows anything about dogs ? Then he may consider how near to the enemy's rifles our men had come when they were first fired on, and, as a matter of fact, ambushed and trapped. How much farther away would a trained sentinel dog have warned them that they were coming nearer to the enemy than they thought, and, finally, had our troops been warned of the Boers' whereabouts, five minutes before they were, what the chances of the battle would have been then! What our gallant fellows did, even though surprised in unreadiness by a cunning enemy, is common knowledge to the world. An outcast cur marching with our force that night, might have been the cause of the frustration of the enemy's well-laid plans. And a great many of us can remember the fearful times for our regiments during the Zulu and Sudanese wars.

" The awful nerve tension of our sentries during dark nights, the straining of the feeble human senses of hearing and seeing to prevent a savage and fiendish foe from surprising and butchering the main body of our army, while snatching a few hours' rest on the veldt, or in the zareba, would have been much lessened, and the sense of security of the resting warriors more real, had a few dogs with their marvellous sight, scent and hearing, been assisting the British arms. A careful scout, assisted by a trained dog he knew, and which knew him, could scarcely fall into ambush."

While speaking of the American Army later on in this volume, I mention the fact, that I had laid before the American War Office, at their request, a scheme for the employment of trained military dogs. This was before the Great War. My recommendations were not adopted, and the result was, that when their army arrived in Europe, they had no dogs whatever, and had to borrow from the French and English armies, who could ill spare them.

It appears that another officer had already made recommendations on the subject, and I give his statement :

" An American officer, Captain M. F. Steele, of the 6th Cavalry, after varied experience of the conditions of warfare in the Philippines, strongly urges that dogs should be attached to the army. He says that 'Dogs are the only scouts that can secure a small detachment against ambush on the trails through these tropical jungles. The bush is so dense, that flankers are out of the question, and the trails are so crooked, and over such rough territory, that the leading man, at one or two hundred yards, is out of sight of the main party. The insurgents, lying in ambush, usually or often let the leading man pass, and open with a volley upon the waggons, and main party of the escort. They open from apparently impenetrable jungle, and at a range of from thirty to two hundred yards. They fire one or two volleys, then usually run away. Sometimes, never a man of them can be seen, and our men have simply to fire into the jungle, and trust to luck.

" ' The orders at present from the superiors are, that the insurrectors shall not attack in parties less than fifty, and they shall attack none but very small parties of Americans, and that they shall always make use of ambuscades.' This officer possessed a dog named ' Don,' and he asserts that, up to date, no detachment, with which it has been out, has fallen into ambuscade. ' He went with us last winter on General Schaen's long southern campaign and lived for more than a month on scraps of hard bread and bacon. He covered six times as much ground every day as any man of the column.' "

The following is an interesting result obtained by a dog in quite a different part of the world, and is written by a gentleman in Java. The dog was a black Newfoundland :

" One evening, returning from a party, the dog attacked a Dutch soldier on guard duty, with the result that the Dutch officials gave me twenty-four hours' notice to remove the dog from their territory.

" At this time the Dutch were at war with the Atchinese, and, fortunately for me, a few companies of regulars were leaving for the front, and one of the officers offered to buy the dog, to save me further trouble.

" The dog accompanied the regiment, and was the means of saving three officers, and about forty men, from a surprise, which the Dutch Government promptly recognized, by decorating the dog with a silver collar and medal."

I have mentioned elsewhere, that sentry dogs were sent out to our troops from my own kennels for use in the Abor Expedition in North India.

It may, therefore, be of interest to include the report on the work of these animals, which appeared in the London Press at the time. This class of warfare is always with us, in connection with the preservation of our extended Empire.

" Before the encounter of November 7th, one of the dogs accompanying the advance guard, gave timely warning of the presence of Abors. The dogs are also employed at night-time, being used by the Gurkha sentries, who keep them on a chain to supplement their own vigilance."

On another occasion the dispatch sent was as follows :

" The expedition has now reached Rotung, a gathering place of the Abors, which was found to have been burned. After marching unopposed to the limit of the made road, the striking force began the ascent of the rising ground beyond the Lelek river, through a thick bamboo forest.

" Information had been received to the effect that a stockade might be met with, and the Gurkha scouts, who were accompanied by Major Richardson's war dogs, were accordingly ordered to keep a sharp look-out.

" The dogs again proved their efficiency, as they gave

warning to the outposts, of the presence of the enemy's scouts, before they were seen by the Naga coolies."

Another report also brings out the point of view I am advocating, namely, that sentry dogs should be considered the natural accompaniment of the sentry

I beg to forward a report called for, on the value of the dog presented to my company by Major Richardson. The dog—an Airedale terrier—arrived just before brigade training. Major Richardson forwarded full instructions as to its care, feeding and training. On three occasions I had the opportunity of using the dog on outpost duties at night. Each time I found the presence of the dog to be of the greatest value. He either remained beside the sentry, or went with a patrol. His value consists in the fact, that he can, and does, detect the approach of human beings some considerable time before the eye or ear of the average man can distinguish anything. The result is, that the sentry or patrol is fully on the alert, and it is impossible for them to be either ambushed or rushed.

The dog is no expense, as he feeds on the remains of the men's dinner. He is never allowed to run loose in camp or barracks, and no one is allowed to feed him except the man in charge of him. I am of opinion that it would be a very valuable asset to have four of these dogs attached to every infantry battalion for service in the field. I hope, at next company training to make more extensive trials of his usefulness. I should add, that his method of indicating the approach of anyone at night is nearly silent. It consists of a low growl, and a stiffening of his body, almost like a pointer.

(Signed) A. C. TEMPERLEY, Captain,

Commanding No. 4 Coy., Norfolk Regiment.

September 23rd, 1912.

In another part of this book, I describe the system of dogs' service in the German Army during the war, and draw attention to the fact, that the chief testing ground which led to such a greatly increased interest in the whole subject by the German higher command, was that of the Herrero Campaign in South-West Africa, in which such remarkable results were obtained, that the whole of the trained dogs in Germany were placed on a war register, ready for the stupendous conflict, which had been planned for years.

The country of the Herreros is covered, to a great extent, with dense scrub, and the sentry dogs were of the greatest service, in preventing the troops falling into ambuscades.

It will be noted, in the following testimony, related by a German soldier, in that campaign, and which appeared in a German magazine, that both he and his dog, had previous training and experience with the police. It can, therefore, be conceived, how enormously valuable were the police dogs of Germany, which existed in large quantities, on the outbreak of the Great War. They actually constituted part of the German armament, and had been taken into account seriously as such, in preparation for hostilities ·

" At the outbreak of the disturbances in South-West Africa, I was serving as sergeant of police at Eisleben. I was called up as a reservist, and posted to the 1st Regiment of Field Force. By order of the War Office, I took two dogs, one of which I had for police duty, and another the present of the German Sheepdog Society. After landing at Swakopmund, I was sent with the dogs immediately to the interior.

" In spite of the long journey, want of exercise, change

of climate, long periods of want of water, the stony ground and sharp grass, my dogs were, with the exception of a few days, always fresh and ready for work, and always on the alert. My dogs showed their excellence as sentry dogs. I handed over one to First Lieutenant Bahr, of the 10th Dragoons, whose duty it was to clear the country of straggling Herreros. This dog accompanied him in all his expeditions, and proved himself entirely reliable and useful, and was always in good health.

" The sentries were only posted a very short distance in front of the pickets, and there was no use for messenger work. As sentries the dogs did excellent work, in occupied posts, at wells and cattle posts, and such-like, and prevented many surprises and stealing of cattle.

" It must be absolutely laid down that dogs' feet are absolutely hard, and that they are accustomed to work all day, or they are useless.

" Captain Hinsh, Headquarters Staff, reports his dogs are a great protection to the column to which he was attached. Lieutenant V. Doring, 2nd Field Regiment, 19th Dragoons, stated his dogs have given excellent results on patrol, in action and in camp and on the march."

I remember the Kaiser, in one of his characteristically flamboyant speeches, just about the time of the outbreak of the Great War, stating that, in the event of the enemies of Germany attempting to dictate to that State, " every dog and cat in the country would march for the defence of the Fatherland."

This was naturally taken as a mere figure of speech, in this country, and *Punch* gave an amusing description of probable eventualities in such a case, in which it was suggested that care need be taken, that the regiments of cats, should not precede the regiment of dogs, or the result would be disastrous to the former!

While recognizing that anyone would naturally be amused at this joke, there are two lessons, nevertheless, that can be learned from it, namely, the average attitude of levity in this country towards the serious assistance that can be obtained by using dogs with the troops, and also the fact that, at that very moment, several hundred highly-trained dogs were being hurriedly mobilized from the German police and other bodies, and sent up with the army in the field, where they would, without doubt, be of the greatest service. With regard to the dogs, certainly the Kaiser, while no doubt intending that his speech should be taken merely to emphasize the national attitude of his country, knew perfectly well, that this was no empty boast, but an actual fact. The cats also, as a matter of fact, were carefully organized later on, and no doubt many of them did duty as serviceable waistcoats for chilly Boches!

In studying a clever handbook on scouting recently, I read with interest the difficulties to be encountered by the scout, when carrying out his duties on active service, and the excellent advice offered as to the best method for overcoming them. In one sentence the author mentions: "There will usually be a dog in the background of a farm-house."

Glancing further with interest to see what proposals were offered, in view of such a serious obstacle, I find, however, that none whatever are forthcoming. If anyone, on reading this, should remark: "Let them poison the dog," my answer to that would be: Let them try to get near enough to do it!

CHAPTER IX

THE FRENCH ARMY

" With eye upraised his master's look to scan
    The joy, the solace, and the aid of man,
    The rich man's guardian, and the poor man's friend,
    The only being faithful to the end."

                                                    CRABBE.

AS I have already mentioned, the French had been experimenting in a semi-official manner for several years before the war. In 1914, the enormous amount of affairs of extreme urgency which confronted the French War Office, submerged the question of the employment of dogs for the army, and those patriotic Frenchmen, who had been working so hard to bring the matter to official notice for years, had very disheartening experiences to go through, before the actual urgency of their efforts were appreciated. One of the dog clubs sent a number of dogs to the front, but so badly managed was the working, through lack of facilities and official backing, that the whole scheme came near to breaking down altogether.

In December, 1914, the French newspaper *Le Temps*, drew attention to the fact that the Germans were using large numbers of trained dogs with their troops, and the question was asked why the same aid was not organized for the benefit of the French soldiers. This announcement drew forth quantities of letters from officers and men in the army, explaining how extremely useful in many positions dogs would be to them, and asking urgently that trained specimens should be supplied.

Again another effort was made, and General Castelnau accorded facilities for the employment of dogs with his army. Great difficulties were again met with, by those responsible for this new effort, chiefly owing to contrary and confusing directions, and also to the difficulty of obtaining authority to demand suitable men to act as keepers for the dogs. The scheme was for the second time, within measurable distance of failure. There is food for reflection in this, as showing the extreme importance of correct organization, if dogs are to be employed at all. The reason is plain. Owing to the highly sensitive temperament of the dog, the question of his use in war, must be approached in the same manner, as when proposing to utilize a highly delicate and scientific instrument. If done so in this spirit, the very sensitiveness of the means employed will be found to be an advantageous asset. If careful rules are formed, all of which tend to protect and encourage this delicate instinct of the dog, the results will be found to justify all efforts in this direction.

In the meantime the fact remained that the Germans were using successfully large numbers of dogs in the field, and the question was again asked in France, if the French Army was to be behindhand in this matter?

At this point Monsieur Megnin, of Paris, intervened. He had been for some years interested in the training of dogs, and had used his influence to encourage the use of police and army dogs. Having, therefore, a good deal of practical experience, when he obtained permission from General de Maudhuy to form a kennel of trained dogs for the French Army, he was sufficiently instructed, and by this time officially supported to initiate and administer a scheme, whereby four principal training kennels were formed. At these kennels, dogs were trained as sentries, as messengers, and also as porters. This last form of dog service was never utilized for the British Army. It would most certainly have been much more difficult for us to have instructed the soldiers in the management of such dogs, than for the French instructors, the reason being, that in France, dogs are so extensively used in civilian life in this connection, while in England it is actually against the law to use dogs for draught purposes, and the working man has, therefore, no understanding of this exceedingly useful method of traction. I would here mention, that I do not consider the use of dogs for this purpose entails at this period any question of cruelty to the dog. Having studied the subject carefully abroad, I find it certainly the case, that the draught dog takes the liveliest interest in its duties, and thoroughly enjoys the arduous work involved. It must be remembered that dogs are very fond of exercise for one thing, and, further, that a dog with an object in life is very much happier than an " habitual loafer." These dogs not only draw their master's goods from place to place, but also guard them as well, and it is most interesting to watch the behaviour of a dog, when it is left in charge during the absence of the owner. Taking up a position of supervision, either on top of the cart or underneath it, it maintains an absolutely unassailable attitude towards any attempts at approach on the part of strangers. When the master reappears, the dog, delighted at the prospect of movement, leaps to its feet, and on the word of command throws all its strength into the collar, sometimes rounding a corner at express speed, and yet with wonderful calculation as to avoiding collision with the kerb. Whatever may have been the treatment accorded to their dogs by the French in the past, it is certain, that at this time, they look upon their draught dogs as very valuable assets in connection with their work, and they treat them well.

These four kennels were the embryo of the entire messenger dog service in the French Army. From them arose the large training establishment at Satory, which corresponded to that started for our own army at Shoeburyness about the same time. The Commandant of the French School was Captain Malric, an officer who had before the war devoted a considerable time to the study of trained dogs, and had experimented with them as sentries while on service in Madagascar. The method of recruiting the dogs in France was rather different from that employed for our own army. The dog clubs of France were asked to co-operate for this purpose, and each club took over a certain section of the country, from which they drew the suitable and available dogs. Many of these were gifts and others were strays. There is not the same choice of suitable material in France as in England, as there are not so many varieties of breeds, but the different types of shepherd dogs —(de Brie, de Beauce, and Alsatian and Belgian)—were excellent for the purpose, and as many English Airedales and Scotch collies were obtained as possible. These were all sorted out, according to their capabilities, and trained as messengers, as sentries and patrols, or as draught and pack dogs. The proportion of dogs cast altogether was smaller than in the British training school, owing to the fact, that so many dogs, which were incapable of learning the first two duties, could quite easily be trained for draught work. Two dogs easily drew two hundred kilos., and they were harnessed to little carts. The pack dogs were able to carry twelve to fifteen kilos., and they were used for carrying dixies of soup, etc., and also ammunition to the front line. These were considered of the greatest service to the troops, and gradually, as in England, the whole organization of the dogs of war began to reflect the import- ance with which the authorities regarded it. There was this difference between the two countries, however. The French gave the whole subject great publicity, being thor- oughly aware, that by doing so, they would enlist the sym- pathy of the public, and obtain thereby a steady supply of suitable dogs for the work. Every opportunity was, there- fore, taken, both by illustration and account, of bringing the progress of the organization to the notice of the Press. This was a very good thing from the point of view of the recruiting of the dogs. In England, on the contrary, strict secrecy was for a long time maintained on the subject by the authorities, and while our own papers gladly accepted the very excellent photographs, etc., which came across the Channel, they had no information whatever, until near the end of the war, as to the dogs of our own army. In this way, an erroneous impression was prevalent, that the French effort in connection with Army dogs was much greater, and on a much larger scale, than was that of the British authorities. Such was, however, not the case.

At the Armistice, every army of the French forces had its kennel of trained dogs.

In an article commenting on the work of the French dogs in an illustrated paper called *Larousse Mensuel*, Monsieur Megnin quotes a statement made by a colonel commanding in the field as follows :

" The Lieut.-Colonel commanding the 52nd Regiment of Infantry desires to record the fact to all, of the death of Sentry Dog ' Lion,' number 147, and of Messenger Dog ' Lion,' Number 164, both killed at Hill 304.

" These two faithful comrades of the soldier had rendered on numerous occasions the most precious services to the regiment."

I herewith give a statement on the employment of dogs with the French Army, which is signed by General Gouraud, who is a firm believer in military dogs. The endorsement from such an eminent leader in the field gives great encouragement to those who have been struggling with indifference, if not with actual opposition, in many directions :

> Headquarters, Fourth Army,
> Third School, No. 3133,
> September 8th, 1917.

On the Employment of Dogs of War (French Army)

" The Minister of War places at the disposition of the army, sentry dogs, dogs for patrol and for attack, dogs for draught and pack purposes, ambulance dogs and ratting dogs, and also messenger dogs.

The sentry and patrol dogs can only render useful service when the distance between the opposing trenches is sufficient to ensure that the sounds of the enemy do not come to them too continually. This condition was only realized occasionally on the front, as, for instance, on those sectors on the Aisne.

After experience it has been found that ambulance dogs can only render service to the wounded in a war of movement.

The messenger dog, on the contrary, appears to be a valuable auxiliary.

MESSENGER DOGS

The dog, more rapid and a much lesser mark than a man, can on many occasions replace the runner.

There is no reason to fear that the messenger dog will run to the enemy. As a matter of fact, animals very soon acquire a sense of danger. Horses, donkeys, mules, which become loose, hurry to the rear. The dog, owing to its aversion of a human race with which it is not familiar, and which it distinguishes by a totally different scent, does not hesitate, if it does not succeed in finding its starting post, but proceeds to the rest-kennel, far from the explosions and noises of battle, rather than cross the dangerous zone of the battlefield as a deserter.

THE TRAINING OF MESSENGER DOGS AT THE ARMY
KENNEL

All the training of messenger dogs depends on the utilization and development of the most important quality of this animal—namely, its fidelity and its attachment to its master. This highly-developed instinct, its strong sense of scent, its sure sense of locality, its rapidity of movement, render it possible for the dog to find him in very difficult circumstances.

THE EMPLOYMENT OF THE DOG CORPS

The position for the services of the messenger dogs cannot be decided too definitely. Certain units use them regimentally, and at other times with the divisions. The result of this experience enables a great economy of couriers to take place."

I here interrupt the report to comment on this subject of the proper placing of the messenger dogs in the field.

In the British Army, the whole messenger dog service had been concentrated under the signal service (Royal Engineers). This was quite a good method, as far as it went, and in the urgent necessity of the hour, was perhaps the best that could be devised, in order to ensure rapidity of organization · but there is no doubt, that while it was highly important that the signal service should receive its full complement of dogs, it would also have been of great value, if each division of our army had also had corps of dogs independently of the signal service. I know several divisional generals were strongly of this opinion, and had the war continued much longer, additional organization, along these lines, would, no doubt, have been instituted. The dogs would then have been available for different corps in the divisions, such as the Machine-Gun Corps, with which they would have been exceedingly useful. I had many applications from officers of this corps for messenger dogs. They stated, that when a machine-gun party was sent out with the attacking troops, they had very often no means of knowing if it had reached its objective safely, and they would have been very glad of a dog to send up with the party to be slipped with the necessary information. In any future organization I should certainly recommend a wider concentration of the Dog Corps.

To return to General Gouraud's report

" It is to the interest of all to assist in the period of stabilizing during the dog's training. The training thus accomplished, the dog is capable of fulfilling its mission during the attacks, or during the war of movement.

On all occasions it is necessary to follow these directions : The dog which it is desired to use as a messenger must be conducted to the point of departure by a stranger · · ·

there no one troubles about him, no caresses, no feeding. He is at once installed in a dug-out during the shelling. When he is required, someone who is a stranger to the dog approaches, and places the dispatch in the metal box, which is attached to the collar. The dog is then loosed, and the direction he is to follow is indicated by a wave of the hand. The dog departs at once, and despite all obstacles, rejoins his master. On arrival, the dog is rewarded, caressed, petted. He also finds nourishment awaiting him, and his desired friend.

This method of procedure is always attended with the best results.

The allocation to the infantry regiments is fixed at six dogs per battalion—these numbers can be augmented if the results are satisfactory.

The division has fifty dogs to dispose of. They are to be considered as being attached to the corps, and not to the sector. They are established at a well-chosen rest-kennel, well isolated. Here all newly-issued dogs are delivered, and also those dogs held in reserve, or which require rest.

PERSONNEL

The direction of the rest-kennel is entrusted to a non-commissioned officer. He is charged to superintend the training and exercising, and to watch the satisfactory working of the messenger-dog service in the division. He pays frequent visits to the trenches to inspect the work.

All the personnel requires selection with discernment. Men who have been in the habit of using dogs, and living with them should be recruited from the corps, such as huntsmen, shepherds and trainers. Two men per company suffice or four or six men per regiment, under the orders of a corporal. These men are then sent to the kennel of the army, to take over their dogs, and to get to know them and to receive instruction in their management. They will stay for a period of eight days.

FEEDING OF THE DOGS

The corps do not receive any payment for the feeding of the dogs. Their nourishment is derived from the ordinary regimental refuse. The soup is to be made from the refuse, and served to them tepid.

A receptacle containing clean water is placed in the vicinity of each animal.

EQUIPMENT OF DOGS

Each dog, on leaving the Army kennel, carries a collar, a chain, a metal cylinder to hold the dispatches, and a muzzle if he is noisy. Each dog has a register, which is sent with him to his corps, and is returned to the army kennel if he dies, or is lost.

THE DEMANDS FOR DOGS

The divisions should make their applications for dogs to the Army Headquarters. They should be received before the fifteenth of each month.

All dogs incapacitated from illness, wounds, or other causes, are to be restored to the Army kennel.

Beside messenger dogs, the Army kennel will also provide a certain number of sentry dogs, also some ratting dogs, and, under certain conditions, dogs for attack, and draught and pack dogs.

Each month a report will be made to Army Headquarters, as to the work done by the dogs.

Discipline

Commanding officers will not arrive at satisfactory results with messenger dogs, unless the personnel is very judiciously chosen, and also that the strictest observance of the regulations connected with the dogs is maintained. All officers and men should be made to understand, that they only serve to impede the work, and prevent the dog succeeding in its object, if they call it, caress it, or give it to eat. The dog belongs to one sole master, and everyone else should treat it with indifference.

All commanding officers are asked to collect from their sectors all stray dogs, and send them to the Army kennel. They will thus assist in the recruiting of the dogs, which is often difficult."

(Signed) Gouraud.

Headquarters.

I have quoted this report pretty fully, as it gives a fair idea of the weight and importance attached to the war dog service for the French Army, and the care and attention bestowed on the details by those of the highest commands.

I here give some reports sent to Headquarters by French commanding officers ·

Sentry Dogs

First Cavalry Corps.—Very useful. The sentry dogs in this unit rendered very valuable services.

Ninth Regiment of Cuirassiers.—During the night of June 25th the two dogs growled forty minutes before the garrison was aware of the approach of two strong patrols of the enemy, which intended a raid on our lines.

417th Regiment of Infantry.—The dogs have rendered

service on reconnaissance duty, notably on the nights 24th and 25th March, in front of Vendeuille, when they revealed the presence of the enemy.

236th Regiment of Infantry.—On May 29th, 1917, the dog " Rusée " gave notice of the presence of the enemy, which had managed to slip behind our rear, and had attempted to seize a sentry.

One dog is notified as having rendered valuable services on the Somme, in a listening post, by giving warning of the approach of enemy patrols. Another dog, employed by 1st Regiment Zouaves, rendered good services as a watch dog. The dogs were especially useful during the attacks on Mont Haut, when the troops were exceedingly fatigued. They averted a surprise from an enemy attack.

On the night of February 21st-22nd, 1916, the sentry dog " Lutu " prevented a raid on the Post Saint Joseph, sector de Celles.

On the 26th April, 1916, at dawn, the sentry dog " Polol," 8th Company, 115th Regiment of Infantry, prevented an enemy attack on our lines.

With the 348th Regiment of Infantry, the dog " Titi " averted a strong enemy attack, which tried to penetrate our lines on the Fecht, before the sector Mattle Sud. By its growling and by its disturbed attitude, the dog enabled the outpost to divine the approach of the enemy. (Night of 31st August, 1916.)

165th Regiment of Infantry.—In the sector Tête de Faux, the dog " Dick," belonging to the 10th Company, notified three times by his growlings, the presence of the enemy in front of our lines.

On the 16th April, 1917, during the reconnaissance of a patrol, " Dick " detected the presence of an enemy patrol, thus preventing our own from falling into an ambuscade.

With the 8th Army, during the month of May, five enemy patrols were detected at a good distance ; also a group of signallers working at their wires.

During the month of June, in spite of the fact that the number of dogs in the line had been much reduced by the removal of a number of units, a dog with the 315th Regiment of Infantry, which was on patrol, detected the presence of the enemy, and immediately attacked him.

The 147th Regiment notifies that a dog detected the presence of an enemy patrol directed against one of our working parties. (Sector Grande Carrière, Berry-au-Bac, May, 1917.)

The dog " Souck," of the 328th Regiment, perfectly indicated the approach of the enemy in their direction, at the end of April, 1917.

With the 20th Division, during the attacks in Champagne, on the 2nd and 3rd of May, 1917, the dogs prevented many surprise attacks on the part of the enemy.

With the 31st Corps of the Army, a sentry dog, with the 329th Regiment, in March, 1916, at the Etang de Vargevaux, detected an enemy patrol and prevented a surprise.

Patrol Dogs

A dog for attack was placed at the disposal of Lieutenant-Commander of the Prisoners' Workshops, on account of the thefts that had taken place by the prisoners. The results obtained were excellent, and this practice will be extended.

Messenger Dogs

On the attack on the Moullin de Laffaux a messenger dog carried two very useful messages between the reserve battalion and the colonel, crossing through the barrage.

9th Regiment of Cuirassiers.—In the same affair, a dog

made the journey four times between the front line and the officer commanding the battalion, and during a violent barrage. The messages were brought by the dog, in about forty minutes, while a runner took one hour and ten minutes.

The 24th D. I. organized a service of sentry and messenger dogs, in the sector Neuville St. Vaast, at the end of 1916, under difficult circumstances. It was at Maison de Champagne that the dogs were the most distinguished. Four dogs covered a distance of fifteen hundred metres in eight minutes several times during the day, under a bombardment of gas and high-explosive shells. At Auberrive, the dogs of several companies very usefully doubled the telephone and runner methods of communication. The dogs followed their masters in the conquered trenches, in the new sector at Auberrive.

With the 8th Army, during the month of February, 1916, the messenger dog, " Pacht," conducted by two soldiers to an observation post at the Fort Regnault, carried messages over a ravine bombarded by artillery and machine-gun fire.

On the night of 19th April, 1917, at the Camp de Colardeble, with a reconnoitring party, before a contemplated attack, communication was established by the dog " Dagon," who carried the first communication from the patrol, who had no other messenger.

During the night of 16th April, 1917, communication was established by this dog, " Dagon," under a very violent bombardment. The dog arrived at Headquarters with a request for reinforcements long before the message was received by telephone.

With the 13th Army Corps.—Good results were obtained with messenger dogs, particularly in front of St. Quentin.

From a letter from Colonel Gaube.—I interest myself particularly in the messenger dogs, which went backwards and forwards innumerable times, and gave very good results at Bezonvaux. (Signed) GAUBE.

THE BELGIAN ARMY

Before the war, the Belgian Army had considered, to a certain extent, the employment of dogs in war. As the tendency in that country is to employ so many dogs for draught purposes in civilian life, it was natural that the attention of the military authorities should be directed to the adaptation of this form of service to army needs. Therefore, one of the chief forms of military service the Belgian dogs rendered, was in drawing small carriages containing machine guns. Two dogs were harnessed to each carriage, and during the first months of the war in the retreat from Liège, this proved a very valuable service, when every form of traction was of immense value to the retreating army. After this, it was difficult to maintain this form of dog service, owing to the fact that the harness and formation of the carts was only adapted for dogs of a certain size, and these dogs had also to be of equal size and of considerable stature. Belgium being almost completely overrun by the enemy, recruiting of this particular type of dog, of which a speciality is made in that country, was impossible, and soon afterwards the requirements of the French Army pretty well absorbed all dogs of this type. A kennel was, however, started in France, and placed in charge of an officer expert at the work, to cater for the needs of the Belgian Army. Here a certain number of sentry dogs were trained, also some messenger dogs, but, again reverting to the national form of dog service, mostly dogs for draught purposes.

The principal objection to the vehicle-drawing dogs is the fact, that good roads are needed to enable them to get their loads along, and pack dogs are, therefore, in most circumstances on the battlefield, the more useful.

THE ITALIAN ARMY

The warfare of the Italian Army having been mostly confined to the mountains, it was found that the quickest way of organizing a service of dogs, was to utilize those dogs already accustomed to these regions. These were the large sheep dogs used at all times by the inhabitants of those parts for protecting their flocks, and also their premises. Some of these are very savage, and can be adapted as excellent sentry and guard dogs. Except for these, of which full use was made by the Italian Army, both as sentries and as draught dogs, no other form of training seems to have been initiated.

THE AMERICAN ARMY

The American Army had no official organization whatever for the training of military dogs when it entered the war. On arrival in France, the troops were thankful to avail themselves of the services of the British and French war dogs, whenever they could do so. I may say also, that as far as our own army dogs were concerned, the keepers found the American officers and men very pleasant to work with. That is to say, they recognized that the work was decidedly technical, and, therefore, if success was to be obtained, all must unite in observing the regulations concerning the dogs. In this way matters proceeded harmoniously, and much good work was done with the American troops by the dogs.

It might be as well, however, if the American Army

in my neighbourhood, sent over by the American Government to inspect some new form of searchlight, I took the liberty of seeking him out, and laid before him certain suggestions, which I was certain would be of great use to the American Army for the war in Mexico. He asked me to make a full report, which I did, with maps and illustrations. I, however, never heard anything more of the matter. It would have been well, had the American War Office taken up the subject seriously then, and they would have been prepared to supply their troops with trained dogs, when the great testing time of the nations came.

THE GERMAN ARMY

There is no branch of the German war machine that reveals the thoroughness of enemy organization down to the smallest details in preparation for this great war that was expected to place Germany on the pinnacle of success, than the method in which the dog-power of the country was organized as an auxiliary to the army. For some years the Government had encouraged the institutions for training military dogs, and these were open for all the world to see. But there was much more behind this, which did not appear to outsiders. For one thing, the large organization of police dogs, was a camouflaged system of service, always available in the event of war. Besides this, there was a very elaborate association of dog clubs. These were at one time separate institutions, each one standing for a particular breed of dog, and they were much on the same basis, as are the dog clubs in this country at the present time, which do not pretend to do more than improve the breeds from a show point of view, and to arrange dog shows. The Germans have, however, always made a feature of training dogs in connection with their clubs. In our own country, we have our gun dog and sheep dog trials, but this particular aspect of the education of dogs is carried on in Germany on a much larger scale. During the Herrero War—the German West African Colony—sixty trained dogs were sent out with the troops from Germany, and many experiments were made with them. These tests must have been considered to be of a promising nature, as after that time, the whole question of dog training in Germany was taken up much more seriously, and under Royal and official patronage.

All these aforementioned dog clubs were now amalgamated, and formed one huge Association, which called itself " Der Verein für Deutsche Schäferhunde." The Crown Prince was president, and the affairs of the organization were directed by military officers. Branches were inaugurated all over Germany, and in Austria as well, and shows were constantly held to display the training standards attained. The association kept and issued annually a list of dogs under training, and against each entry was inscribed notes relating to that particular animal's capabilities. This book was open for all to purchase, who wished to do so, but the fact was that the whole association was a war organization, and each of the branches was ordered to keep a secret register of those dogs considered especially suitable for war purposes.

When war broke out, those dogs which were already with the army, went with their regiments straight to the front, while the owners of those dogs which had received approval at the exhibitions of training skill, and whose names appeared in the association lists, were ordered to mobilize immediately. This represented the reserve army of dogs. In the meantime, vigorous recruiting work for dogs went on all over Germany and Austria, and as these were collected, they were sent to training establishments, which were opened at various principal towns in Germany. Here they were trained by especially qualified men, under expert military officers. When trained, the dogs were drafted to the Army kennels. Each army had its kennel, and from these centres, the dogs were issued to the troops in the line. In the first advance into Belgium, and France, the enemy lost no opportunity of seizing all suitable dogs, and sending them into Germany to be trained. Not only this, but they even offered to purchase dogs for the work from owners in Germany, and gave up to fifty marks per dog. Also, in Germany, as in France, the greatest publicity was given to the subject of the war dogs, and both by illustration and account of the exploits performed by the dogs in the field, the public were encouraged to interest themselves in the matter, and to help on the work, much in the same way that the propaganda in aid of the Red Cross in this country was carried on. This publicity given to the subject must have made the work of the dogs in the field much easier, both for the dogs themselves, and for those who were training and handling them, as the full object of their utilization would be understood by all ranks, and all would unite together to assist the good work. There is no doubt that the work in the British Army was considerably hampered for some time by the policy of secrecy pursued, and I should certainly recommend that this should not be adopted on a future occasion. Owing to this clever method of encouragement and registration pursued before the war, it has been stated, that at the commencement of hostilities, Germany was able to put into the field almost immediately about six thousand dogs, which were utilized on both fronts. Ludendorff gave his signed order for this concentration and utilization, and, furthermore, detailed an officer on the Headquarters Staff, to direct the whole movement. It will be seen from this, the very great importance which was attached to this work.

For many years before the war I had been aware of the fact that German agents were constantly at work in this country, studying our various British breeds, and importing certain of them in large numbers into Germany, for use with their military and police establishments, those with the police being convertible at short notice into military dogs. Scotch collies and Airedales were much sought after, and at one time a man—a German—carried on a steady export trade of these dogs to his country. It is with a certain measure of satisfaction, that I recall the fact, that it was the sense of exasperation which I felt at the exploitation of our dogs for their own purposes, that spurred me on to persist, in spite of every discouragement, in the furtherance of the work of police dog and military dog training for our own country. This, and the absolute conviction that some day the wonderful qualities of the dog, as an aid to man under every condition in which man might be placed, would be recognized and utilized.

I here give a translation of a document dealing with the work of the war dogs in the field, which was captured from a German Headquarters :

THE EMPLOYMENT OF MESSENGER DOGS

DIRECTIONS FOR TRAINING MESSENGER DOGS

I.—Object

" Economy in labour and human life by the use of dogs for rapid transmission of written information (or sketches)

II.—Organization

Messenger dogs are constituent parts of the organization of infantry signalling detachments. An infantry regiment may have a maximum of 12 dogs allotted to it, and an independent battalion, 6. The allotment is made by the Messenger Dog Sections (*Meldehundstaffeln*) at Army Headquarters.

Every Army Headquarters on the Western Front has at its disposal a Messenger Dog Section (consisting of one officer, staff trainers and dogs). It undertakes the training of dogs sent from Germany, serves as depot for first equipment and subsequent drafts, instructs the messenger dog attendants appointed by the infantry, and carries out the additional training of the dogs whose work at the front has been unsatisfactory. On the East and South-East Fronts, groups of armies only are provided with Messenger Dog Sections.

The men required are detailed by the troops, an attendant and an assistant attendant (attendant file) to each dog, and also, if possible, a supernumerary attendant to be instructed as messenger dog attendant with the Army Headquarters concerned. The period of instruction lasts from three to five weeks. *Those men only are to be accepted who have a genuine love of dogs. On this essentially the animals' performances depend.*

Should divisions be transferred from the army concerned during the men's period of instruction, the men will remain until the end of their instruction and then be returned to their division.

Messenger Dog Sections are collecting centres for all information relating to messenger dogs within their own army area. All reports of successes, failures, suggestions, etc., are to be communicated to them. The closest co-operation is requisite between commanders of Messenger Dog Sections and Signal Commanders.

The War Dog School (*Kriegs-Hunde-Schule*) in the zone of Army Detachment A is directly under the officer commanding the Director of Signals.

Its duties are :

(1) The supply of all drafts of dogs.

(2) The distribution of drafts of dogs (untrained) among the various Messenger Dog Sections, as directed by the C.O. of the Signal Service.

(3) Training of officers to command Messenger Dog Sections.

(4) Instruction of men as staff-trainers.

(5) Formation of a reserve of trained dogs (directions will be issued from time to time).

The War Dog School further performs the duties of Messenger Dog Section to Army Detachment A. In this capacity it is placed under the orders of the Headquarters of this Detachment.

Headquarters of Army Groups decide which divisions or independent units are to be provided with messenger dogs.

Regiments are required to keep the register of dogs handed over to them by Messenger Dog Sections, and it is their duty to report, when required, on the dogs' performances and present stations to the Messenger Dog Section from which the dogs allotted to them are drawn. Dogs in replacement of those lost are delivered by the Messenger Dog Section to that army to which the unit in question belongs at the time. All losses of messenger dogs are to be notified in writing to this Messenger Dog Section, the register of dogs, and, if possible, the equipment being forwarded.

III.—BREEDS

The following are the breeds chiefly employed as messenger dogs : German sheep dogs, Dobermannpinschers, Airedale terriers and Rottweilers.

IV.—THE TRANSMISSION OF MESSAGES

The dog runs backwards and forwards between two attendants (attendant file, consisting of attendant and assistant attendant). Both attendants must be well known to the dog. In order to make the dog familiar with the stretch of country over which messages are to be carried, the assistant goes with the dog from the end where the attendant is waiting to the other end. From there he sends back the dog, which finds its way again to the starting point by its sense of locality. The dog is now ready for use, and may be sent backwards and forwards between the two men of the file. Each end of the route may be occupied by a dog. The information to be sent is placed in a tin case, or dispatch bag, on the dog's collar. Dispatches brought by the dog may only be taken from it by its attendants.

A change of route inside the same sector is to be avoided, as the dog is otherwise inclined to run off on the earlier route.

ter Richardson and -- -- het paip

Training war dogs   In the trenches at the school (part of the ground).

[*To face p. 278.*]

The attendant and his assistant must remain at opposite ends of the route. Where this is not the case, and one of the attendants is forced to leave his post, owing to patrols, for example, it is still possible to use the messenger dog ; but its work in such cases is essentially unreliable, as it is obliged to pick up and follow the man's trail by smell. This, as a rule, is rendered very difficult owing to many external influences. In such a case, moreover, the dog would have to be specially trained in tracking."

I here interrupt the report to point out that the system of training here advocated, is that of the liaison, or the two-keeper method. I have elsewhere discussed the advantages and the disadvantages of this system, as against the one-way-return-to-keeper method. Of course, much depends on the rapidity of output demanded. Germany had such large quantities of dogs, fully trained and ready to put into the field, at the outbreak of war, that there was not the same urgency placed on the training staff, and they could pursue the slower form of training ; but, as I have already said, there are, apart from rapidity of output, several other distinct advantages to be obtained by specializing, certainly for the greater number of messenger dogs, in the one route method.

V.—TACTICAL EMPLOYMENT

" No special preparations for carrying out communication by messenger dog are necessary.

Communication by messenger dog should be attempted in all cases where the transmission of written information (or sketches) of value and relief for other means of communication or runners are desired, especially

In difficult country (marshes, mountains, snow).

In exposed sectors under enemy observation.

When technical means of communication fail.

When the telephone is not to be used from danger of tapping.

Its employment is suitable as a permanent communication between two fixed points, e.g., the Commander of front-line troops and battle headquarters of a regiment, regimental battle headquarters and telephone exchange, an O.P. of an important formation and telephone exchange, or between a fixed and moving point, e.g., the leader of a raid and an advancing patrol.

Messenger dogs may also be used in cable-laying, and in sending forward carrier-pigeons, ammunition and rations.

A dog must be accustomed at practice to all disturbances that are likely to arise under service conditions, e.g., difficulties of the ground, battle noises, etc. Unusual disturbances, e.g., the smell of a bitch on heat, painful wounds and drum-fire, may, nevertheless, cause the animal to refuse to work.

A dog must run its message route two or three times a day. This must be done for practice, even when there is no occasion for sending information. Too frequent running without a rest exhausts a dog and makes its work untrustworthy. Even when a dog has finished its training, it must continually have further practice. Therefore, when the unit is at rest, attendant files should be given opportunities of exercising the dogs as part of their duty (general training and practice journeys).

The efficiency of a dog mainly depends on the choice of its attendants and their special instruction. Faulty treatment very speedily lessens the efficiency of the animals.

VI.—Administration of the Messenger Dog Service in a Regiment

The number of dogs not kept for service purposes should be strictly limited. Stray dogs (especially bitches on heat) easily lead messenger dogs to refuse to work. Officers and men should have this explained to them, and also the object and use of messenger dogs.

Only those principles of training and working messenger dogs taught at Messenger Dog Sections are authoritative. Officers and men should be forbidden to have any dealings with the dogs, or to interfere in the execution of their training. Intentional troubling of dogs by the troops should be strictly punished.

In the case of a dog giving up, the attendant himself should be used as a runner. In any case, the attendants should be employed solely in the Signal Service, e.g., as pigeon attendants, at pigeon stations.

In no case may messenger dogs be used for other purposes than transmission of information.

The men composing an attendant file should not be changed.

A dog will only work in a trustworthy manner between men of a file who are instructed and known to it. On emergency, the trained supernumerary attendant takes his place in the file."

It will be observed from the last paragraph the seriousness with which any interference with the dogs at work by the troops was viewed, and that it was to be regarded as a strictly punishable offence. The regulation also, that if the dog failed in bringing in a message, the keeper was to be used as the runner to replace it would certainly

17*

have the effect of " gingering " up things all round, and is another instance of the way Germans make war !

" Immediately the dog reaches the attendant, or his assistant, its dispatch collar should be taken off and not put on again until the moment that the animal is sent back. The putting on of the collar will thus be a sign to the dog that its journey is beginning. Should the attendant have to take the message brought by the dog a little further (e.g., from the telephone exchange to battle headquarters), the dog should not be taken with him, but tied up and left behind at the terminal point of the route, in order that this point may be retained by the dog as a fixed datum for its return.

Should a dog not be sent back immediately on its arrival, attention must be given to its kennelling, and, if necessary, its cleaning and drying.

The attendant and his assistants must, if possible, compare their watches daily.

Dogs which have repeatedly failed, bitches on heat, as well as animals which cannot be worked on account of illness, wounds, and so on, must be sent for exchange to the Messenger Dog Section of the Army Headquarters concerned, accompanied by the dog-registers, equipment and attendant file.

Bitches should not be crossed, nor dogs used for breeding.

VII.—Protection from Gas

As a protection from gas, it will generally suffice to keep the messenger dogs in dug-outs which are protected by gas-proof roofing from the penetration of poison gases.

Experiments are being conducted with a view to the provision of a gas-mask for dogs.

VIII.—CARE AND FEEDING

Care should be taken that the dogs are well housed. The animal must, as far as possible, have a dry kennel, free from draughts and bomb-proof. It is advisable to make a small excavation for the dog in the dug-out. It must always be kept on the chain and only taken out for exercise. In order to maintain the efficiency of the dogs, careful attention and feeding are very important. Dogs should be brushed and combed daily, and fed only by their attendants. In winter they may only be washed when heated rooms are available. After being washed, they should be rubbed dry and thoroughly brushed. Dogs must be taken to a veterinary surgeon regularly—the most convenient time being in connection with horse-inspection—so that infectious diseases may be discovered in time, or prevented.

Regulations for feeding are laid down in Army Order 45 of September 15th, 1917, as follows:

Daily food ration for service dogs·

1. The Deputy Intendance of the IV. Army Corps will serve out dog biscuits to the Field Army through the Supply Depot. This food having been served out, the daily ration comprises: 750 gr. of dog biscuit and 1 litre of men's warm rations (the vegetable portion, taken from field-kitchens, etc., if possible, containing 100 gr. of pearl barley, groats, or similar substance).

2. Failing dog biscuit, there will be served out·
   (a) 500 gr. of offal, or, if this be not obtainable, 500 gr. of meat, with 300 gr. of pearl barley, groats, or similar substance, added, or, where necessary, 1,000 gr. of mashed potatoes.

(b) When offal, or meat, is absent, 600 gr. of dried horse meat (or sinewy offal), with 250 gr. of pearl barley, groats, or the like, added, or, if need be, 1,000 gr. of mashed potatoes.

(c) When there is absolutely no offal, or meat, 50 gr. of fatty matter, with the addition of 400 gr. of pearl barley, groats, or the like, or, if need be, 1,500 gr. of mashed potatoes and 500 gr. of crushed pulse foods.

The weight is reckoned in the uncooked state, with potatoes unpeeled.

The portions of offal to be used are : embryos, vaginæ, walls of stomach, *Bruhlungen* of slaughtered animals, condemned meat, and other butcher's offal not affected in a way injurious to health, but out of the question for human food (navels, buttocks, testicles, ovaries).

If it be necessary for bread to take the place of vegetable food, it is to be served out in quantities of, for (a) and (b), 250 gr., and for (c), 500 gr.

Food is to be cooked and served lukewarm. Attention should be paid to variety in vegetable food where possible.

Bones are to be given as a special addition.

If necessary, the dogs receive their food from the field kitchen (men's daily ration).

IX.—Veterinary Service

The chief veterinary surgeon has issued the following regulations for the veterinary service of Messenger Dog formations in Order No. 3015 of the 17th September, 1917 ·

The regulations for the veterinary service in Messenger Dog Sections are laid down by the Army veterinary surgeons, for the messenger dogs of infantry regiments by divisional veterinary surgeons. Any veterinary surgeon may be called in for urgent assistance, or the advanced collecting stations of veterinary hospitals may be used For more serious surgical action, veterinary hospital surgeons will-give their services.

In Messenger Dog Sections it is advisable to erect a kennel for sick dogs with an infectious kennel separated therefrom, and also that too large detachments of dogs be not housed together, in order that the spread of any infectious disease may be limited.

The most usual dressings for wounds are in charge of the shoeing smiths, or veterinary assistants, attached to the first-line transport. All other drugs required will be demanded by the veterinary surgeon concerned, and will be obtainable, in cases where they are not to be procured from the veterinary supply waggons, or bearer companies, from the advanced depot of medical stores.

At the suggestion of the competent veterinary surgeon, a small store of the most necessary drugs and dressings may be kept at Messenger Dog Sections in a small medicine chest made for the purpose. The storage of a small quantity of " Kamala " (for curing worms) at advanced depots of medical stores will be arranged for.

Distemper serum, as well as all other drugs, is to be applied for by the competent veterinary surgeon through the divisional veterinary surgeon, or the army veterinary surgeon, as the case may be, from the advanced depot of medical stores, which will obtain the serum from the Berlin Army Veterinary School."

It is apparent from the carefully-thought-out details of this report that very great importance was attached to the messenger dogs by the German Higher Command.

CHAPTER X

" Be thou diligent to know the state of thy flocks, and look well to thy herds."—PROVERBS.

IN considering the question of the general management and policy of the War Dog School, it has to be remembered that as a nation we have not hitherto placed military preparation in the forefront of our national policy. It seems unlikely that this attitude will be altered to any extent in the future, therefore, in the event of this organization of War Dogs being again required on a large scale, much the same conditions and problems will again be encountered, by those officers, whose duty it may be to work the scheme up again. A few remarks and suggestions might, therefore, be of assistance in the light of future requirements. Were a definite organization kept running permanently in peace-time, even though on a quite small scale, it would always be a great assistance in national emergency, as it would keep a nucleus of officers and men in training, and, of course, a certain number of dogs. I mention the personnel of the school first, as being in every way the most important part of the whole work. The question of the supply of dogs takes quite a secondary place. The great difficulty that arises at the outset, to those chiefly responsible for the success of the whole work, is the risk of success being endangered, by the obstruction or control of those, who are uninitiated in, and, therefore, unable to appreciate the necessary conditions for obtaining that very success. In giving an account of the work in the French Army I mention the fact, that twice over, the scheme was practically closed down, owing to this lack of understanding, and duality of control. If this happened in France, where there has always been a greater tendency to consider subsidiary schemes in the Army, it must always be recognized as a possible danger at any time in this country. The fact is, that very few people indeed really understand and appreciate the capabilities of the dog sufficiently, to be in any way qualified to adjudicate on the management of the Dog School of Instruction, or on the management in the field, without advice of those technically instructed from this point of view. It would, therefore, be as well, that this should be thoroughly recognized, and that those responsible for the training of the dogs, should also be made responsible for the entire working in the field, and for the necessary regulations governing them up to that point. In this way, much valuable time will be saved. Dogs are not machines. They are extremely sensitive, and, in fact, in some directions are much more so than man himself. Those who undertake to train and handle this delicate instrument, know that certain essentials must stand in the forefront of all regulations governing its actions, right down to the actual work in the field. Duality of control is, therefore, to be avoided.

There is always one point that would, in the future, be of great assistance in taking up this work again. That is, that the fact, which has been reiterated again and again for so many years, namely, the usefulness of the dog to the soldier, *has been proved*. There can be no further question on this score, and, therefore, the many struggles in the first months of the War Dog School, against distrust as to the possibilities of the work, would not be met with, in the same degree, ever again. But there is one point that needs to be emphasized, and that is, the importance of propaganda work on behalf of the dogs. This is necessary for two reasons. Firstly, with a view to interesting the public in the work, and of obtaining from this source gifts of suitable dogs for training, and also so that the soldiers should understand this means of aid, and of the methods necessary for the successful working. Co-operation on the part of the soldiers is very essential, and they are very quick to respond, when once they understand the fact, that something is being done to help them. When once the French authorities understood that their dogs were to be a success, the Censorship's restrictions were relaxed at once, and Press reporters and photographers were allowed to acquire what information they required. This wise discernment on the part of the French War Office, was of the greatest assistance to those training the dogs, and also to the dogs themselves when in the field, as very soon every *poilu* came to recognize the War Dogs, and to respect them as working comrades. This propaganda policy was carried on also in every way that would touch the imagination of the public, and every now and then various animals, which had particularly distinguished themselves in the field, were decorated in public.

The Germans also made a great point of publicity in connection with their War Dogs, and accounts of their prowess, and the necessity for procuring large quantities from the public as gifts, was emphasized. As a matter of fact, as I have explained this propaganda work had been going on in Germany for some few years before the war, under another name. The fact of the usefulness of the dog to the soldier, and of the importance of the subject, had never been lost sight of in that country in peace-time, and the machinery of the organization was in working order when the war commenced. Publicity was part of the machinery.

The policy of restraint and secrecy which was deemed advisable, at first, by our authorities, made the work very difficult, and although the restrictions were relaxed to a certain extent, as time went on, even up to the Armistice there was always a tendency to keep things dark, and the necessity for active propaganda was never fully recognized. From first to last, the policy of secrecy was a mistake, and the working of the dogs was only hampered thereby. While a good measure of publicity will ensure a knowledge of the work the dogs do percolating through all ranks in the Army, it is also advisable that there should be a certain number of officers and non-commissioned officers, under instruction at the school, whose duty it would be to superintend the work of the dogs and the keepers, when with the various units to which the latter might be drafted. The instruction given to these would be, of course, of a different nature, to that given to those men who were to be drafted into the actual dog service, which, of course, would be more technical, and therefore longer. The period of instruction for the visiting officers and N.C.O.'s would be for seven days, and during that time, they would watch the training of the dogs, and be instructed in the reasons for the regulations governing the service in the field. In the case of the messenger dogs, this would apply to officers and N.C.O.'s of the Signal Service, and if further organization of messenger dogs is inaugurated in connection with each army corps, then representatives from the various units should be sent to the school. Lectures should be given, both at the school, and also to the troops at the front.   This instructional work is also highly important, in connection with the sentry dogs, and guard dogs.   Those, whose duties bring them in contact with this class of dog, should also be instructed in management.   In this case, apart from the mere fact of learning the reasons for, and the necessity of observing, the regulations concerning the feeding, exercising, and training, etc., they would also be taught laws which govern sound, wind and scent, and by means of plans, would be shown the various methods of posting the dogs in the trenches, and also in relation to buildings, etc. All this is highly technical, and needs expert understanding, in order to bring out the full measure of successful working. Therefore, the importance of the instructional branch of the War Dog School, to those who manage the dogs in the various units, should in nowise be neglected.

Kennelling and Feeding

There are one or two points as to the kennelling and feeding which I would like to emphasize.   As the War Dog has to do his work out of doors, and under every sort of weather-stress, it is no use taking any methods of kennelling into consideration, that will not contribute to hardening him up, to meet the conditions.   Therefore, no form of elaborate indoor or built kennels should be utilized.   As a matter of fact, after a very close study, and long experience of the subject, I find the average built kennel, which is supposed to spell the last word in luxury, is really a very unsatisfactory arrangement.   First of all, it cannot be moved.   Secondly, the actual kennel is always too high in proportion to the size of the dog.   The result is, that one cannot change the ground, and also that the dog is not sufficiently warm inside the kennel in winter time. Artificial heat is, of course, out of the question, and would not be practical, even if available ; therefore the heat emanating from the dog itself should be utilized, and conserved, for its own advantage. As the greater portion of our climate is either wet or cold, the provision for this aspect is more important than for conditions of heat. I have found, that a good strong, box kennel is, from every point of view, the most inexpensive, and also the most comfortable for the dog, and I find it preferable to the most expensive and seemingly luxurious pattern. The size of the kennel should be such, that the dog is able to stand up, and turn round easily, but should be no bigger, for the reason that the warmth of the dog's body will establish a comfortable temperature for it, in this amount of cubic space. All the air that is necessary, will come from the ventilation holes, or from the doorway. Any extra space is unnecessary, and only takes away from the warmth. I may say here that I believe warmth at night, good food and cleanliness, to be the most important factors in keeping all animals in health and strength. The roof, which should be sloping, must be made to open for cleaning purposes, and a door to open and shut is important. Besides this, there should also be, for each kennel, a platform shelter. This must not be attached to the kennel itself, but must be movable, and the position for it is against the front of the kennel. The shelter is a great protection to the animal, both in rain, and sun, and wind. In summer time, the door can be permanently left open, but in winter time this should be shut the last thing at night, and plenty of straw supplied. It is advantageous, especially in winter, to have a surplus number of kennels, so that the dogs can be shifted frequently to fresh kennels, which have been previously thoroughly scrubbed and lime-washed and aired. This process of changing kennels should be carried out every fortnight, in winter time, if possible, provided there are sufficient spare kennels, and in summer time once a month. An important point also is, that the entire ground must be changed frequently, certainly once a month. The advantage of the portable kennel is quickly seen, as it is easy to shift a hundred of these in a day, by turning on men to that duty, and the comfort of the dogs is greatly increased. Another thing that may seem of small account, but makes for very greatly increased happiness and well-being, is to turn the kennels round according to which way the wind is blowing. The front should always be turned away from the wind. This question of shifting the kennels round must also be remembered in summer, in relation to the sun, when it is very hot, and the front should always be turned away from the sun. Dogs dislike extremes of heat or cold, and while they are undergoing training and hardening, I have found it much the most effectual way to mitigate these conditions for them in a practical manner. If this is done at that period, they will later be much better able to endure any rigours they might be temporarily asked to undergo. Even in the field, however, the instructions are, that every means must be taken to keep the dogs warm and out of the cold wind, when they are in the front line, and when they are at the rest kennels, careful regulations are in force, to this end.

The best position for the lines of kennels at the War Dog School is, if possible, under trees. When the school was in the New Forest, the shade of the beech trees was a great advantage in summer, and the pine trees afforded excellent protection from the rain, snow and wind in winter. The method of attaching the dogs to the kennels, depends on the duty each has to perform. The messenger dog should be chained with an eight-foot chain. It gets so much exercise during the twenty-four hours, that it is unnecessary, and, in fact, undesirable, that it should have any further liberty than this chain affords, as it is really brought to the kennel to rest. The guard and sentry dog, while under training, should have its kennel placed beside a wire fifty yards in length, and the dog should be attached to this by an eight-foot chain, and a running ring, so that it can run up and down. When drafted out for duty, provision must also be made for exercising each dog, apart from the exercise it gets on the wire, with which each will be provided.

FEEDING

A good nourishing diet is of great importance for the dog under training, and the best staple food for the daily menu is cooked horse-flesh and biscuits. The man responsible for the cooking of the food must be a very responsible character, as there is a good deal of judgment and care required in this duty, so as to make the fare tempting. The meat must be fresh, and must be very thoroughly boiled in large boilers. The soup resulting from this, should be very strong and good, and the biscuits should be put in a large receptacle, and the boiling soup should be poured over them. The meat should then be cut up in small pieces and mixed with the soup and biscuits, and the whole stirred well together by a spade. The mixture can then be left to cool. The amount of food accorded to each dog is one pound of dog biscuit and half a pound of horse-flesh, and when this is cooked together it will be found, with the soup, to fill a dog's feeding bowl to the brim. For the average dog, this is quite enough, but for those of the smaller size, less will be sufficient, and the surplus amount will be available for the dogs of the very large varieties, on the guard dogs section, which require at least a bowl and a half. There are always a certain number of dogs which arrive at the school in an underfed, poor condition, and these will require extra feeding. Therefore, a second service of food must always be available daily. The great test as to whether the head cook is doing his work satisfactorily, is to be found in observing if there is any food left in the bowls as a whole, apart from those apportioned to dogs which may be temporarily, off their food. If the food has been properly cooked and mixed, the bowls will be found to be quite empty, but if there is any left over, inquiry should at once be made into the capabilities of the head cook. The dogs that require extra feeding, should, in most cases, be placed under his particular care as to their food, and he should carry on this treatment in conjunction with the head nurse kennelman, who will also be watching the general health of these animals which require this extra attention, while not actually needing removal to the hospital. During the war, it was, of course, impossible to obtain milk, or fish, for extra feeding purposes, or for sick dogs ; but it was found, that by utilizing the best portions of the meat, and making strong soups, wonderfully successful results were obtained with weakly dogs. Much of this success, however, depends on the intelligence and capacity of the head cook, and he is a very important person indeed in the War Dog School, as the welfare of the entire kennel is, to a great extent, in his keeping. A meal of raw meat makes a change, which the dogs enjoy very much, and Sunday is a good day to select for this, as it involves less labour. A feed of plain, uncooked biscuits can sometimes

Part of the training ground at the War Dog School:

Off to the training ground.

Training war dogs to cross obstacles

[*To face p.* 273.

be given, as the hard food is good for the dogs' teeth ; but this should not be given often, as most dogs do not relish it, and do not eat enough.

It is highly necessary that all the dogs, especially the running dogs, should be well nourished. At the end of their training, under proper conditions, and when the work is not too much hurried, each dog should be fairly stout, but not fat, and with well-developed muscles. It will be understood that when once the fact of the necessity of the dogs was established, great pressure was brought that dogs should be turned out as rapidly as possible, and therefore the question of getting them quickly into fit, hard condition, under which they could profit by their training, was a very anxious and difficult one. I certainly found, that the most rapid and successful results were obtained by keeping the food and warmth question to the forefront, in dealing with the young recruits, and keeping a strong control over all methods of dosing and doctoring. In training the permanent staff of the War Dog School, most of whom were selected from among gamekeepers and hunt servants, I had, in every case, to impress this form of treatment very firmly, as it is a curious fact, that the usual method of treating a new acquirement in the dog line, is to immediately begin to doctor it in some form or other. Every expert has an infallible nostrum of his own. This tendency must be severely repressed, on behalf of the victim —the dog. It may be said, that the kennel, where there is a large, and very complete, much-used medicine chest, is badly managed, and the expert who can show empty medicine shelves, is much more likely to have healthy, happy dogs. I may say, also, that those men who turned out the best keepers in the school, very soon came to see, that the results obtained, by not treating the dog as a sort of sieve for tonics, purges, etc., but by adopting a simple, practical process of management, were much more satisfactory, rapid and wholesome.

The only building, where it is satisfactory to have artificial heat, is in the hospital, for severe cases of illness. A hut, warmed by stoves, will be found useful. The floor should be concrete, with easily flushed drains, and the movable kennels should be carried in here, as required. They can be placed as near to the stoves as may be necessary, according to the condition and temperature of the animal. The dog may be left to rest quietly in its kennel in this pleasant warmth, and with a soft, comfortable bed of straw, will be likely to throw off its complaint. It is also advisable that it should wear a coat. This warmed house will, however, only be needed in winter. In summer time, the open-air treatment is far the best, and the hospital should then take the form of a section of movable kennels, well removed from the rest of the school, and placed in a grass field. The worst cases can be chained to their kennels in the ordinary way, but those which are convalescent can be placed on the running wires, of which there should be a number. There should be more wires than dogs, so that the latter can be shifted about, and the ground should not be allowed to get too much used.

A few words as to the best position to choose for the Training School might be of service. There are many considerations to be taken into account, and certain unforeseen difficulties may arise, small in themselves, but which may upset all the other advantageous conditions. First of all, the surface of the ground must be of such a variable character, that it presents every sort of feature, which a battle-field possesses. Thus, broken ground, with ditches, water-courses, bogland, etc., is very suitable. The ground at Shoeburyness, where the War Dog School was first started, was extremely satisfactory from this point of view, as all these features were represented in the marshes by the sea. It was unfortunate that the area was too confined when, later on, a greatly increased establishment was ordered by the War Office. The change, however, to the New Forest was in no way disadvantageous in this respect, as the trackless woods, deep heather, bogs and streams, all added to the difficulties of the messenger dogs' homeward journey. The wide extent of country available here was useful, as it was possible to send out large quantities of dogs in a complete circle for several miles round, and in this way relays of pupils in different stages of training, could all be sent out at one time. There were sometimes as many as seventy or eighty dogs running at the same time. There is nothing so strengthening and hardening for the new dogs, as gradually increasing daily journeys over rough, difficult ground. Where an animal may have intensely disliked getting even its feet wet, (which many dogs do), it will come in time to plunge into a canal or river, and come home to its kennel to rest, without taking any harm, having been hardened up to this point, by being first trained through wet grass or heather, and across shallow streams. A paragraph from an official report which bears on this point, when referring to the working of the messenger dogs, may be quoted :

" The average distance from battalions to brigades, was about three and a half kilometres, and the time taken averaged twenty minutes. The best time was twelve minutes for three and a half kilometres There were one or two obstacles to be surmounted, viz. : in some cases two lines of wire, and in others, a canal to be crossed. Most of the dogs swam across."

When under training, the newly-arrived dog, however, should be hand-dried, if it comes in with its coat thoroughly wet, as just at first they are apt to get chilled, from this unusual condition. In winter time, also, all the dogs under training must have good warm beds of straw to dry themselves in. Those of more hardened condition, can be allowed to dry themselves in the straw, but it is a good plan, if it is very cold weather and they are very wet, and have been long journeys, to shut the doors of their kennels for a couple of hours, as they dry much more quickly in this way, and warm themselves up better. This advice applies also to wet days, as well as wet ground. If the weather is very wet, it is better to defer the training until it has cleared. When the dog is thoroughly broken and hardened, it will be able to stand any sort of weather condition without harm, but with several hundred dogs in varying degrees of training and health, the Commandant will be wise to defer the work for a few hours, even at the risk of losing this valuable time, (and in war-time every half-hour is of importance), if he wishes to avoid a crop of chills and complaints in a certain proportion of the dogs. During heavy rain, in fact, they should have the doors of their kennels closed. This may seem unduly pampering, but it is my experience that if care is exercised at this period of training to keep the dogs warm and dry when at rest, they harden much more quickly than if they are asked to face too severe conditions at first. In summer time, of course, this question of chill and damp does not so much arise, and usually the sun is hot enough to dry the coats after April ; but even in the summer the dogs under training, messenger dogs especially, should not be allowed to stand outside their kennels in heavy rain.

Another extremely important point, in regard to the

training ground is, that it should be within reach of villages, and of roads along which heavy traffic may be expected, as the messenger dog has to meet all these conditions at the Front. The villages present the greatest temptation to the dogs on account of the ash-heaps, food-shops and also the allurement of pleasant chats with local canine busybodies, who thoroughly delight in holding up a messenger dog, which may be conscientiously endeavouring to do its duty. The difficulty of the village dog at the front was one, which had to be taken seriously into consideration, and it would be better in future to face this situation in a more practical manner. In France, there were such large numbers of stray dogs in the devastated areas, that their presence was sometimes a serious menace to the successful working of the messenger dogs. In order to remedy this state of affairs, large numbers of these dogs were ordered to be destroyed by the G.O.C. in the various districts. This order was, from many points of view, considered a stern necessity at the time, but was a pity, as if it had been realized at first, how valuable the services of dogs would become to the Army, and how unequal would be the available supply to the demand, every one of these dogs would have been of use in some form or other, either to the British or the French Army. It should, therefore, be remembered in future, that while all dogs should be cleared from the war area, so as to leave the neighbourhood free for the military dogs, they should not be destroyed, but should be sent to the training centre, there to be adapted to the needs of the Army.

While under training, the messenger dogs must be run as much as possible through the villages, and it is a good plan to station a man in the village street, to see the dogs pass through, and to note the behaviour of each one under temptation, and to make a report on the matter to the instructor. I found it convenient, also, to have a good, trustworthy member of the training staff detailed to follow the working of the dogs on a bicycle. On this he was able to make a rapid survey of a large number of dogs, when on their homeward journey, and also to notice if the men themselves, who were sent to the school for training, and whose duty it was to take the dogs outward, were reliable. This man should be a non-commissioned officer, and should be especially chosen, as one likely to do his duty in this respect honourably, and fearlessly. It is for him to report any irregularity whatever, as to the conduct of the men on the road, either by dishonesty on their part in not going to the outward posts as ordered, or loitering on the way, or as to any rough treatment towards the dogs. It is advisable also that one of the officers of the training establishment, should also make unexpected rounds, either on a bicycle, or in a motor, as it is only by ceaseless vigilance, that a true estimate of the character of the men who are to handle the dogs in the field, can be obtained, and I have several times spoken of the extreme importance of allowing none but the very best characters, to pass into the Messenger Service. The natural tendency of the men to shield each other, has always to be taken into account, but it is fortunate that, in war-time especially, the sense of obligation to King and country will, with an ordinary upright soldier, override any personal temptation to screen a dishonest keeper.

There are some dogs which, while they are very plucky in every other direction, have a strain of timidity in their natures in relation to strange people, and these dogs often avoid villages if they can, and put themselves to great trouble to go round them instead. This disposition in the messenger dog is of great value, as it is, therefore, saved much temptation.

There should certainly be some high roads within reach of the school, along which lorry traffic travels. These noisy, lumbering vehicles are apt to scare a young dog, especially on a narrow road or street, and they have to learn to go past them under all circumstances. Dogs, when running by themselves, are much more careful, than when they are accustomed to walk abroad, accompanied by a careful master, and it is wonderful, taking into consideration the large number of dogs out on the roads, when under training, or at the Front, and also remembering the enormous amount of lorry and motor traffic, that so few dogs were run down.

There is no doubt, that the firing of the big guns at Shoeburyness was a great assistance in training the dogs to loud explosions, and the more or less steady reverberations of these guns during the war, accustomed them to the sound of artillery. If it had been possible to have expanded the available training ground, it would have been unwise to have moved from this area, but the sea on the east made one impassable barrier, and a river on the north, over which the men could not cross, made another. If at any time ground could be found combining suitability as to surface, and in conjunction with the presence of heavy artillery, it should certainly be chosen.

Rapidity of output, however, in time of war, completely overrides every consideration, and this can only be attained by the availability of a large portion of territory on which quantities of dogs can be trained simultaneously. It is possible, however, to obtain sufficient training in explosive sounds by using bombs, so that this difficulty can be met in places where there are no guns.

I have frequently emphasized the importance of propaganda work amongst the troops, on behalf of the dogs, and I would also mention the extreme urgency, that the G.O.C. of corps should take an interest in them. That he should personally inspect them occasionally, and call for reports on their work. The official report of the officer in charge of messenger dogs in the field says :

" Wherever the G.O.C. of a corps took interest in the kennels, allotted to his corps, good work was obtained from the dogs. This was especially noticeable with VIII., XIX., XXXII. Corps."

Another excellent recommendation is as follows :

" Commanders lack confidence in this means of communication until actually proved, and, therefore, every opportunity must be utilized of employing dogs during quiet periods between battles."

This process of education of public opinion on behalf of the dogs would be part of the propaganda I have already recommended elsewhere. Seeing, however, that it is now stated that dogs should be used as a means of communication, this will always help greatly in the future in impressing the fact, that they are considered one of the necessities of modern warfare, and officers who have never had their attention directed in this direction before, will now be compelled to inquire into the subject. That they will be repaid by its interesting nature, I can well assure them.

There is little doubt, but that dogs as an auxiliary to the soldier, have come to stay in our army, at all events, in the case of operations on a large scale, but that their use should be greatly extended in various directions in time of war, and that they should also remain on the permanent establishment of the peace-time army, so that the training work can be experimented upon and perfected and that there may not again be that difficulty, and strain of collecting and training hundreds of dogs in a very short period, is an argument I would very strongly urge as being worthy of consideration by our authorities. The heavy weight of indifference and prejudice, that had to be overcome, in the first years of the war, in the mind of the average British officer, and the fact, that when the subject was actually endorsed by the War Office, all form of propaganda was practically forbidden, resulted, that even up to the signing of the Armistice, there was an enormous proportion of our officers and men, who took no interest whatever, in the matter, chiefly because they were quite ignorant as to the results obtained. It must, therefore, be taken into consideration, in the future, that there is at present, a large section of public opinion, which might be inclined to express an opinion on the subject, which is really not qualified to do so, because insufficiently instructed. The fact must also always be remembered, which I have several times pointed out, that whenever anything new is being considered in this country, the national attitude of mind is generally that of inquiring as to whether it has ever been done before, and if they cannot find any evidence on this point, to condemn the whole thing out of hand. There is a tendency to regard with suspicion things that are new, simply because they are so. As a matter of fact, the employment of dogs in warfare is not new, but the average person is not aware of that.

I well remember meeting a distinguished General, some years before the war, who had a good deal of power to bring progressive measures to the notice of the highest military authorities of the time. I ventured to suggest that it might be worth while to devote some study to the question of Army dogs. He replied, that he was not only not interested in the subject, but strongly disapproved of such measures.

" My own action as a commanding officer would be to prohibit, under all circumstances, the use of dogs, in any connection, with a regiment in the field."

It is with the deepest regret that I remember this conversation, in view of the fact, that later this officer's cherished only son was killed in the war, under circum stances, that could probably have been reversed, had the regiment, to which the poor lad belonged, been provided with a few messenger dogs.

An important question arises when selecting a suitable training site, in connection with live stock. No time must be wasted by breaking the dogs to sheep, cattle, etc., for the obvious reason, that they do not have temptations of this sort on the battlefield, all herds and flocks having been cleared by the fleeing inhabitants or by the enemy. Therefore, the immediate vicinity of the training ground must not be too much of a pasturage ; thus the young dog, when it commences its training, is not distracted by any temptation to chase. Later on, when the idea of its work is fairly firmly established, and it is beginning to make journeys from the surrounding country further afield, it will not be so likely to interfere with any animals, as it will, by this time, have one definite idea implanted in its mind, to the exclusion of others. It will thus be seen, how similar is the dog to man in the fact, that when doing useful work, its thought does not stray to evil, and the well known verse of the friend of our childhood—Mr. Watts—applies to the canine race as well as to our own :

" And Satan finds some mischief still,
For idle hands to do."

During all the months of training, when hundreds of dogs had been running for miles round the training ground, there were only about four or five complaints of animals being molested, and I have seen the dogs pass through chicken yards, flocks of sheep, and herds of cattle without noticing them. But in order to attain this state of rectitude, they must not be tempted too early in the training, and all flocks should be ordered off the immediate neighbourhood of the kennels, and also for this reason downland, where the sheep can be seen for miles, would not be suitable territory to select.

CHAPTER XI

" The poor dog, in life the firmest friend,
  The first to welcome, foremost to defend,
  Whose honest heart is still his master's own,
  Who labours, fights, lives, breathes for him alone."

BYRON.

A T the present time the energies of our statesmen are directed to the conservation of the nation's finances, and rightly so. Hereby is necessitated the wholesale closing down of the countless departments that owe their being and growth to the exigencies of war. I would, therefore, like to point out, that there may be danger in this policy, in that certain branches, which in themselves make for economy, may be swept out of existence. In the case of the army dogs, it may be said, that it would be difficult to find a department from which such a standard of money-saving output, could be procured at such a low cost.

On a peace footing, the Training School could be run on a very economical scale, and a steady supply of guard, messenger, and sentry dogs could be sent out at small cost as required. I think I have shown, by what is previously stated in this book, that one of the chief advantages obtained from the employment of dogs, has been the great saving of man-power. Now this advantage would always be maintained relatively, no matter how much the army may be reduced.

It would, therefore, be advisable that a certain nucleus of the school should be maintained at one of the military training grounds. Here, under expert supervision, a certain number of dogs would be kept in training ready for drafting to any unit at home or abroad. All expeditionary forces to any part of the world should be supplied with a certain number of dogs of the three classes mentioned, and all our home stations, where there are vulnerable points of any sort, and which need guarding, should requisition dogs from the school. It would be found that large economies would be effected, by the safeguarding of valuable material, as the guard work would be very much more efficiently done with the aid of dogs, and also that the numbers of sentries could everywhere be reduced.

I would, however, again emphasize the very important fact, that this work can only be effective if carried on under expert management, as has been done during the war. Supervision requires to be kept up over those dogs drafted out, and this the O.C. at the Training School does by inspection or reports. The dogs need changing at times for the purposes of rest, or are not properly managed or posted, and this is soon rectified under correct control.

I may say that I had experience before the war, which confirms the above remarks. A certain official depart‑ ment bought some dogs from my kennels for guarding work at certain vulnerable areas. These dogs gave great satis‑ faction, and it was proposed to extend the idea. I was anxious to help, and offered them dogs at a price which was then under their actual value to me. The department officials, however, undertook to carry out the work on their own understanding, and procured a number of dogs. These were not properly trained or managed, and I heard com‑

plaints were expressed afterwards. Without expert super-vision the work need not be attempted.

The War Dog School might also be affiliated with the police force of the country, whereby trained patrol dogs could be served out for use in disturbed areas, in the suburbs and all lonely beats. The dogs thus trained could always be quickly mobilized for the army in time of war and would be of the highest service at all times.

In utilizing dogs for war purposes, there are sometimes protests expressed by those who think that this dear friend of man should not be drawn into the conflicts of man's making.

There is a story told that soon after the Creation, a great chasm began to open up in the ground, and man found himself on one side of it while all the animal creation was on the other. All the animals remained indifferent and acquiescent to the separation. The dog alone betrayed despair. With pitiful whining and imploring gestures, it strove to attract the man's attention across the widening chasm. The man gazed at the dog's wistful eyes and said : " Come ! " The dog jumped, and just reached the other side with his front paws. " You shall be my comrade," said the man, and reached out his arm and drew the dog up to safety beside him.

One may smile at this legendary story, but, nevertheless, the gulf which separates the intelligence of the dog from that of any other animal is very marked, and one notices this more than ever when one commences to train animals. The first and most striking difference is the joy of service. One may train other animals, such as horses, donkeys, cats, etc., and they will attain high standards of obedience and usefulness, but their work is all done more or less under compulsion, and with a sense of toil. The dog, on the other hand, leaps to his master's side when there is a prospect of working with him or for him. Here is no toil but joy and fervent co-operation, and a great sense of honourable calling. The moral sense is very highly deve. loped in the dog, and is very much appealed to when dog is asked to work for man. Willingness to serve, and a strong sense of right and wrong, are characteristics mani. fested from which many human beings might draw inspiration for their own actions. The good trainer will work on these two qualities, in the first place, and to these will soon be added unlimited love from the pupil. It is on this basis that all training work should be done. Coercion never accomplishes any reliable results. This statement is obvious, when it is recognized that those qualities which should be appealed to in the dog are immortal and actual, and are not subject to variableness, but rest on their own foundations. As these are cultivated there is definite reliability to depend on, which exists of itself as apart from any will power on the part of the trainer. No whips should exist in the training school and are never necessary; gentle, steady routine work is the right method of impressing the dog's intelligence, and kindly encouragement and caresses, will meet its desire to understand, better than coercive measures or rebukes.

It should clearly be understood, therefore, that the trained dog considers himself highly honoured by his position as a servant of His Majesty, and renders no reluctant service. From my observation along this line I have, in fact, come to the conclusion that a dog trained to some definite work, is happier than the average loafing dog, no matter how kindly the latter may be treated. I certainly found this to be the case with the army dogs. Their intelligence very much increases as the training work proceeds, and their demeanour of alert happiness equally so, while the working hours are eagerly looked forward to. Where the average person may not be in a position to observe the truth of this statement with regard to military dogs, he can always verify it to the extent of watching a shepherd's dog at work with the sheep. How seriously it takes its duties, how ardently it devotes its whole intelligence and attention to the sheep! One can imagine how heart-broken it would be at being prevented from doing this work! Could many human beings surpass it in sincerity and determination of faithful purpose? Could many even equal it?

Recognizing this wonderful living tie between man and dog, the question may be asked: Is it not right and just that in this great War for Principle, when everyone who is brave and good in the Empire, has given of his best, that the dog—man's faithful, loving " pal,"—should also be allowed to take part in the great Cause? The British Army will never fight except in a righteous cause, and the dog can safely be allowed the great honour of assisting.

THE END

Printed at The Chapel River Press, Kingston, Surrey.

**RETURN TO: CIRCULATION DEPARTMENT
198 Main Stacks**

LOAN PERIOD 1 Home Use	2	3
4	5	6

ALL BOOKS MAY BE RECALLED AFTER 7 DAYS.
Renewals and Recharges may be made 4 days prior to the due date.
Books may be renewed by calling 642-3405.

DUE AS STAMPED BELOW.

MAY 0 3 2004		
SEP 2 8 2004		
SENT ON ILL		
DEC 0 1 2004		
U. C. BERKELEY		

FORM NO. DD6
50M 5-03

UNIVERSITY OF CALIFORNIA, BERKELEY
Berkeley, California 94720–6000

Printed in Great Britain
by Amazon